YOUNG TENNESSEE BROWN

John Frederick von Hurst

PAGE PUBLISHING
Conneaut Lake, PA

First originally published by Page Publishing 2023

ISBN 979-8-88960-615-4 (pbk)
ISBN 979-8-88960-622-2 (digital)

Printed in the United States of America

For my grandfather, as he wished this
story be told and the family

Contents

Foreword

THIS IS A NOVEL based on the life of my grandfather, Fred Lloyd Whalen.

Except for the time spent in school and asleep, I spent the majority of my early life in his company and that of his son, my uncle Jack. They were my "rabbit hole," a place where few children growing up would ever see less participate in. It was a world of characters that were relatives, true and false friends, and life was an adventure. I learned the sense of family, what it was and wasn't.

My grandfather was a "hustler" in every sense of the word. Some considered him a "con man," and in certain ways, he was. I never met a person that didn't like him, and I knew even more who loved him. He was generous to all he knew and some whom he only met in the moment. I never really had a father. He knew it and more than made up for him. He was my best friend. Unlike my father, he never missed an event in my life. For all he gave me, showed me, and taught me, I will always be grateful. I am most grateful for the stories that he and my uncles, aunts, and others told and retold at every family get together and for the patience they exhibited as my cousins and I begged them to tell us again and again. It is these family stories that gave us the sense of our history and why we were the people we became. In most families, there is one person or event that sweeps up an entire generation, everyone within their sphere, and leaves an imprint that marks their lives. My grandfather was that person.

Prelude

EVEN NOW, IT'S HARD to remember a time when he wasn't there. I try to think back as far as I can, you know, the moment you first recall being alive, the first memory of light, and the recognition of another person. For me, it was an afternoon in 1948. My parents were having a large sofa delivered, and like everything else in the family's world, it was huge. It was coming through a window that had to be taken out because it was larger than the front door. I was looking through that hole in the wall when he came running down the walk with his arms out and pulled me outside. I was only eighteen months old, and my mother, who was herself huge with my little sister, was still perplexed about my memory of this event.

He called to me, "Palley, don't you move, I'll come get you!"

He pulled me through the window opening, threw me up into the air, and I wet my pants. He passed me back through the opening to my mother to be redressed. He called me "Palley" until he died. I was Johnny when we were in company and was his first male grandchild. This was the beginning of great adventure. Some will say that they would never want to relive their first twenty years, I am not one of those. The cast of characters that blessed and cursed this family play out in the story that follows.

Someone said, "Life is not a race to the grave!"

PART 1

Beginnings

Alton, Illinois

AND SO HIS ADVENTURE began, a journey into and through a life, days of light, gray, and dark that were strung together with no particular plan. As with most of us, we would be hard-pressed to put an exact time upon our beginning, but he could give it a day and almost an hour when life started for him. He was nearly three when the century turned. The guns firing, the church bells tolling, and the steam whistles blasting into the still of night did not stir this child's sleep. The everyday events in a young life were of no consequence to him. He did the same chores, played the popular games, and survived the illnesses of that time that punctuated a boy's world.

School was not his best subject. In fact, he never went beyond grade eight. He learned most things fast and usually the hard way. He had a head for figures and an early ability for reading. Later, he would say that it was all he really needed and that baseball was his best school subject, especially catcher. The Ursuline Sisters at St. Peter and Paul Catholic School were relieved to see him go, a good boy with a prankish sense of humor.

His early years were spent in the small Midwestern town of Alton, Illinois, on the Mississippi River, north of St. Louis. Alton was a community with a slow, easy nature. Most of the young people moved on early to Chicago or down river to St. Louis. The greater portion of the population was older folks who were worried about constipation, a condition that seemed to hang heavy in the air. The only two things that moved with regularity were the big river and the trains. Alton in those days was a safe way to grow older if one's ambitions were shallower than a mud flat. The place had more than its share of drowning and amputations and made most young people look forward to old age with skepticism. Life was closer to dull than most knives last to be, if that wasn't enough. Fred overheard an old-timer once say, "If heaven is for the good and hell is for the bad, then Alton is the Limbo for those that didn't have the sense to be either."

He was reared in a semireligious home by parents who made ends meet by working in the local economy. Fred's father worked for the railroad, and his mother was a seamstress. He was the last of three children and, therefore, his mother's darling. She'd often say that Edgar, the oldest, was a starter child and Beulah was for practice. Fred was full of mischief and considered a devil of sorts because as he grew, so did his tendency to tease and play pranks. His parents were a couple that seemed stark to some. His father was a tall well-built man of six feet blessed with inherent strength of body and character. His mother in turn was slight in stature and thus a contrast to his father. Edgar took after their father's frame, whereas Beulah was her mother. Fred was a combination of both, tall but lean.

Summer 1909

IT WAS JUNE OF 1909, and the river was running its course, warm and humid. School had ended a week earlier and the waters of the Mississippi in and around Alton were returning to normal after riding high through the spring. The days were getting longer, and the temperature was breaking later in the evening around eight o'clock. The days seemed slow in leaving and without relief. Horse wagons lined the streets and were punctuated with the black forms of the latest fad, the motorcar. Children had given up the sandlots to the men who had time to squeeze in a ball game before heading home for supper. Work began early and ended late for most, and gaslights were lighted at dust.

When most boys were home, he was still out. He carried a canvas bag with a sling. In its bottom rested his catcher's mitt covered by the evening paper, the *Alton Evening Telegraph*, which he delivered along the main streets of town. It was the most coveted of the routes, and he had fought to have it. The night was on its way, and the long shadows of buildings were filling the last bright cracks of a setting sun. Many people lived above the stores and shops, other businesses were just getting started, and the evening news was waiting to be consumed. His biggest stops were the hotels, saloons, and pool halls. He always carried extra papers because he knew he could sell them to the passerby. He saved his last paper for his father.

He knew how many papers were likely to be needed at every stop. His route was cash on delivery and no exceptions. He had learned the hard facts of credit early. He bought his papers from the

5

printer, and on Fridays, he carried two bags as more people were always in town. His second to last stop was Casey's Pool Hall. It was the biggest and the best, sixteen tables of green felt with pockets of hanging woven leather. There were two straight billiard tables with seating along one wall and a bar that lined the other. It was a dark and exciting place. It was a corner of the world where the odors of spilt beer and tobacco mixed in a haze of smoke. The striking of ivory balls, the dull thump of cushioned rails, and the click of the balls as they dropped onto others in the pockets began a rhythm that joined the colors that collided and ricocheted on a green field. It somehow suited the mathematics of his mind.

The doors into Casey's were smoked, etched glass with an arched transom proclaiming Casey's Saloon with the words Pool and Hall on the paired doors below. Each time he entered it seemed new and more exciting. Men moaned and cheered, swore, and stomped with every stroke. The creaking floorboards matched the squeaking of chalk on the leather cue tips. It was a world of shadows with pools of light spaced over stadiums of felt. Small points of light flared and dulled with every breath and bobbed up and down with conversation. The players were ghosts who became visible only in the cones of light that shown on the tables. They were just a hand, arm, shoulder, and head of a phantom that popped in and out of the smoked light.

He dropped the papers on the bar. He could see the reflections of the entire space caught in the beveled mirrors behind the bar. As he looked along its expanse, he saw Casey himself walking up behind him. He was as Irish as they made them. He had sandy red hair with a heavy mustached lip and a red-tipped nose. He was not the biggest of men, but he was fair and honest with a temper that matched his father's. He was quick to smile and was always pleasant to his paperboy. He reached into his pocket with one hand and brought out a clip of greenbacks. The other hand reached out for the boy's shoulder.

"Here you go, lad," he said, turning the boy around. "You best be getting along. It's a ways to the yards and the whistle be a blowin' soon. You know I promised your father, Fred."

The boy turned and nodded his head. He stuck the money in his britches, and he headed for the doors. He looked back as he reached to let himself out. A shout in the back turned every head toward the back, including Casey. Fred let the door go and slipped over to a dark corner where an empty table resided and dragged his fingers along the edge of its rail. He felt the cloth with his fingers the way a blind person examines another's face. He let his bags slip from his shoulders. He touched the cool ivory balls and rolled them into each other, watching them carom off the rails and into pockets. Casey had let him play in the past, showing him how to hold the cue, position of fingers and hands along with the basics of a number of games. It had all but ended when his father found him there one night. Fred had not heard the train whistle.

*****

The train moved slowly through the yard, its great pistons and drivers slowly turning the wheels to a stop. Steam released, and pressure valves were closed. The throttle was all-forward, and the heaving engine and its string of cars was now idle. The yard crew made its way along the track as John Whalen, engineer, swung out from the cab and climbed down from the engine. He was a solid man, a bit over six feet, with large hands and broad shoulders. He had worked on the road gang as a youngster and had eventually worked his way onto the trains and finally into the cab. He was thirty-five but looked much older. He removed his cap, and his long, black hair tumbled in wet strands along his forehead. He was a handsome man with rugged good looks. He was Black Irish with a temper to match. His friends called him Stormy.

"Hey, Charlie!" he yelled over the noise that filled the yard. "The main pressure gauge is cracked, and the needle is sticking. It scares the hell out you once in a while!"

Charlie looked up and smiled. "I'll get the steamfitter on it, and before you ask, I haven't seen your boy."

John grabbed Charlie's shoulder in his usual gesture of thanks and noticed the grimace on his friend's face. He often forgot that his friendly grips were painful to most people. He apologized and smiled, but as he turned away, darkness came to his face. His eyes looked down the yard. Fred was nowhere in sight. It had been a year since he agreed to let him hawk papers after school, and during that time, his youngest had met him every night, walking back home together.

The Whalen home was a few streets from the yards. He would go there first on the chance they'd meet on the way. John knew Winifred would expect him. Being late under any circumstance caused her worry. Trains were notorious for breaking down or worse. With her, it was always the latter. Even though he was only gone to Chicago and back each day, she never got used to waking alone in the mornings. He called her "Nan" and would lean over and kiss her goodbye the mornings he left early. She would sit by the window or on the porch mending something and wait for the two of them to come laughing up the street. They had three children. Edgar, the oldest, was so serious and slow to warm to those around him. Nan knew he would leave soon and find his own way. Beulah, the middle child, was not unpleasant but suffered from a cocked eye that gave her a quizzical look. Although John loved all his children, Fred was his favorite, the one he was hardest on. The father saw in this son the boy he was and the man he could have been.

Today, she sat with apples in her lap, peeling and coring to make a pie for supper the next night. It was the only day that John had off. The only morning she could reach over and find him there. This was to be their evening, and tomorrow night was their only early dinner of the week. The wall clock struck seven, and she looked up from her chair. It was John. He was alone. She could see the dark disappointment in his way. The way he walked, the way he looked was that of a man struggling with his emotions. It was the cough that concerned her most. A sound she heard most nights over the last few years. It was the only thing other than the train that worried her days.

John looked up from his mumbling thoughts and saw his dark reflection in her face. Nan always had a smile and open arms for her boys when they come home, especially bright when he was in this state. He would try to change the feeling and rage, a look they both feared, that Irish thing. He knew if it wasn't his face, it was the coughing. It had started before he left his load tally at the yard house and gotten progressively worse as he neared home. Beads of sweat began to run down his forehead and temples. Even the heat of the engine's boiler and firebox door couldn't bring out this much perspiration. The doctor believed the coal dust from years as a fireman and now an engineer was the underlying cause. He was told to give up railroading work and move to dryer climes. It was all he knew, all he had, all he could provide his family.

He smiled half-heartedly as he climbed the steps to the porch. He reached for Nan and kissed her cheek and almost hugging her breath away. He asked, "Is Fred here?"

"No, I expected to see him with you," she gasped. "You know he could have just had more papers than usual to sell. You shouldn't get yourself all worked up like this. It's not good for you."

"I should have not let him get that job. It got him involved downtown, and a twelve-year-old boy can see just too much! It gets him money before he knows what its worth," he said, stepping back. "And what does he spend it on?"

"Well, I can show you what he spent it on today." She turned and pointed to the flowers still wrapped in paper on the table. "He left them an hour or so ago, and he still had a full bag of papers with him."

John turned to leave. Nan reached for his big hand and gave him the towel she had covering her apples.

"Here, wipe off your face before you go down there," she offered.

He took the towel, fresh with apple scent, and wiped his head, face, and neck. He tossed the towel with his hat onto the swing at the end of the porch. Nan reached for the oil rag in his overalls back pocket and pulled it out, replacing it with her handkerchief from her apron.

"There, I don't want you wiping your face while you're gone with that greasy rag!" she smiled, hoping to lighten his humor.

He reached for her handkerchief and sniffed it slowly, smiled, and turned away, heading toward town. He looked back and saw her there, standing and watching him. He knew she would not go back to her chair until he disappeared around the corner. When he was out of sight, he reached in his shirt pocket and removed a matching

9

handkerchief and exchanged it for the fresh one. It was the part of her he kept close every day. He looked ahead, and his face returned with the same measure of darkness.

*****

Fred had not heard his father's distinctive whistle pattern when the engine crossed at the Alton station boundary. John had done that for years to let Nan know he was home. He did it for Fred too. He knew his boy. Fred would be caught up in a moment and not note the time. He had to be startled or cued in some way or other to break the hold of whatever caught his fancy. His father had told him that it was rude and inconsiderate to his mother not to be home washed and ready for supper. Before the paper job, it was baseball that was his downfall. Now, it was Casey's that lured him into deafness to all that his family held important. It was true this day. He was held beyond his control, mesmerized by the motion of balls bouncing in a field of green felt.

Just before he gotten his paper job, he had followed an older friend into Casey's to help him square up the boy's father who was known to drink too much and play pool too long. Fred had never seen a pool table or been in a saloon. He was tall for his age but thinner than his height would suggest. His frame was from his mother, but his strength came just as honestly. Bigger boys and older boys soon discovered that messing with Fred was not healthy. It would take both boys to get his friend's father out and home, but not before Fred was bitten. He at once saw the geometry of the game even if he had no idea what geometry was or that it applied to the angles balls were stroked into each other and or the rails. It filled his head with linear thoughts. Objects were moving in all directions. It was better than baseball.

Retrieving his friend's father did one other thing to Fred. He learned that alcohol was not attractive. The drunken state left you stupid, incapacitated, and vulnerable to others. The boys got the man home but not before Fred had promised himself to learn the game.

Fred was not a shy boy. He walked into Casey's and auditioned for a job. He saw during his initial visit that the floors were covered with extraneous material, one of which was sawdust used to cover other things. He grabbed a broom and began sweeping. In a short time, Casey himself stopped him. Taking hold of the broom, he turned the boy around.

"What the hell you think you're doing, lad?" Casey said, putting his face almost nose to nose with Fred and looking hard at the boy.

"I'm working here, thank you!" Fred responded as if in a huff.

"That's so?" Casey returned, trying to free the broom from the boy's hand. "And who hired you?"

"Mr. Casey hired me!" he shouted so no one could miss it. "And who are you, sir?"

"Well, lad, I'm Mr. O'Sullivan," Casey replied. Casey saw no change in the boy's determined manner or appearance. "Mr. Casey O'Sullivan," he added. "I own this place, thank you now!"

Without missing a beat, Fred changed broom hands and offered his hand to the big Irishman.

"And, Mr. O'Sullivan, how do you like my work so far?" He smiled.

Casey's mouth dropped, and before he knew it, a smile washed over him and he laughed. "And just how much am I paying you, lad?" he inquired, hoping to catch the boy off guard.

"Four bits I believe is fair for two hours picking up here," said Fred. "And you know, I'll be here every day except when my father's home. You can depend on it."

"And just who did I hire, young sir?" Casey asked.

"I'm Fred Whalen, sir," he said. "And I'm much obliged."

Fred did not miss a day. His mother thought only that he was playing ball, and he met his father each night at the yards. The secret job was safe. The problem became the money. He could spend it only for candy; his parents would question anything else. So he buried it in a jar out behind the house. The jar got bigger, and Fred learned to play pool. In fact, he became a good player. He watched men gamble on games and saw sums of money change hands every afternoon. The whistle sounded, and he would hurry to the yards.

11

Winter 1912

FRED'S FATHER WAS A railroad legend of sorts. He had started in the yards in Alton and had moved up to conductor putting freights together. During his conductor days, he had been involved in a fight with two disgruntled railroad employees who were fired for cause. They chose to get even one early morning by setting a string of boxcars on fire. They had doused them in kerosene and lighted them up.

John noticed them running from the string of burning cars with the kerosene can and gave chase. A northbound freight was slowing, moving out of the yard, and the men had jumped on two cars in front of the caboose. Fred's father got to the caboose just as the train gained speed onto the main line. The men saw John make the train and began moving forward across the top of the cars. John climbed to the caboose roof and started jumping cars in the pursuit heading toward the engine. Car jumping on an accelerating train is considered foolhardy and deathly dangerous. The black engine smoke trailed along the car tops, partially blinding all involved. The pursuit was thrilling for those witnesses in Alton watching from the streets as the train rushed through crossings on its way north.

As the arsonists reached the tender, they realized it was too late to jump. The train was now at full speed and running over the river wet lands that was traversed via the trestle that keeps the rails safe from flooding. The two men turned to fight. John Whalen met them three cars from the engine. The men where no match for the well-built Irishman, and they quickly gave up. The brakeman stopped the train when they cleared the wet lands and helped Fred's father tie them to the handrails in the caboose. The story was front page of *The Alton Evening Telegraph* the very next night. Nan nearly beat John to death with the paper that same night. Fred glowed in his father's fame, but it also exposed his secret job.

*****

John Whalen was not happy about his son's jobs. Nan had convinced him it was harmless and a good lesson learned, that work was a living. He had a parent's fear that the life on display in the pool hall would give Fred the wrong impression about the world and what was important. He liked Casey and checked on his son one afternoon on his way to the yards. Walking into the hall, he looked around for Fred but did not see him. He caught Casey's eye and motioned to him. The Irishman nodded and walked up to the big engineer.

"Casey, where's my boy?" he asked still looking around.

"He's out back dumping trash, John," was the reply. "You know he's a good worker. He keeps this place picked up and minds his work."

"I want you to promise me you won't let him get started playing on these tables. This is not something his mother and I want him caught up in."

Casey smiled and assured him he'd not let Fred do any more than work. He promised to keep an eye on him. The two men shook hands, and John left the hall heading to the trains. He trusted Casey but still worried on the pastimes of young boys. He knew of the type of man that frequented pool halls, and his son would not become one if he had his way. At the yard, he and the conductor made up the early freight to Chicago. John Whalen released the brake and began the slow easing of the throttle. The drive wheels spun and grabbed as the long set of cars jolted forward one after the other. He sounded the whistle as he moved through the switching blocks and headed north out of the Alton yards. He'd be back that afternoon.

Fred had established a thriving route around the center of Alton. Brown's Hotel was a virtual gold mine of nickels and tips. Mr. Brown made it a point of having the latest news available to his guests, including the Chicago papers that came down with the daily trains. Fred had made a deal with Brown to pick them up and deliver them to the front desk along with the *Alton Evening Telegraph*. The clerk had instructions to give Fred fifty cents for the service. While in the lobby, the boy would hawk his papers to the patrons and visitors in the lobby. On one occasion, a gentleman bought a paper and gave Fred a whole dime. As Fred attempted to make change, the man waved his hand and nodded to the boy that no change was required.

"Thank you kindly, sir," Fred quipped.

"You are very welcome!" the man returned, looking at the boy more closely.

The man realized that this boy was mostly wearing homespun and that work was something the lad needed to do. He looked over his shoulder to the men's parlor, a room off the lobby whose doors were always closed. He put his hand on the boy's shoulder and looked down at him.

"How would you like to sell the rest of those papers before you leave the hotel?" he asked, smiling.

"That would be swell, sir!" the boy chirped.

"Well, follow me, son, and we'll just go over here to the parlor." He motioned with his paper. "I think the gentlemen inside will take all you have."

Fred followed the gentleman across the lobby, and as the man opened one of the paired, etched glass doors, Fred stepped into a new world. A world of red velvet and paneled wood where smoke curled above seated men locked in serious conversation. They sipped on chilled drinks and chewed on cigars, rolling them from side to side from one corner of their mouth to the other. The air was thick with smoke and voices. Men jested, laughed, and patted each other with slaps on the back. Arms waved and fingers pointed. The room was alive with sound and motion. A long oak bar ran the length of the room with mirrors and oil paintings of bare-bosomed women. This was a place like no other with sights he had never imagined, not at all like Casey's.

Through all the noise, only one sound stood out with any familiarity to him, a click and then another. His head turned, his ears and eyes trying to locate the sound. In a room off the parlor, through another pair of oak and glass doors, he caught a glimpse of a table as men moved around it. He sold his papers haphazardly, slowly moving toward the other room. When he got to the doorway, he saw it. The most beautiful billiard table he'd ever seen. It seemed the tables at Casey's were second-class imitations. As he moved closer, he noticed a second table beyond the first. It was a straight pocket billiards table.

Men were moving around the second table at a respectable distance watching two men. One sat in a leather and oak stool at one end with a cue in his hand. The other was Mr. Brown, and he was moving methodically around the felt-playing surface holding his cue lightly in his hand. His attention was focused on the position of the balls in relation to the ivory cue ball. It was apparent his opponent had just broken the rack, and Brown was looking for his best first shot. Brown looked up and noticed Fred's riveted gaze on the table. He looked to his opponent and hesitated.

"Fourteen off the rail into the side," he said while tapping the pocket in front of him.

He reached for the chalk and efficiently turned it on the tip of his cue and in one continuous motion placed it on the rail as his stick drew back and his left hand and fingers lighted gracefully around the business end of his cue. Brown bowed to the table and with one quick pump stroked the ball. The cue ball firmly collided with the fourteen, sending it to the opposite rail, rebounding it into the designated side pocket while the ivory ball ran slowly down the length of the table, sending the two balls into the corner pocket and coming to rest a few inches away from the main body of balls near the break end of the table.

Without hesitation, Brown called the nine. It was frozen in the pack. He pointed to the closest corner. He quickly re-chalked and moved into position. His stroke split the nine from the cluster, sending it into the called pocket while the clustered balls broke in all directions. He quickly made six more shots and turned to his seated opponent.

"I believe that's a hundred balls."

He slid the ring markers over and picked up the two $50 lying on the rail. Turning to the seated man, he asked him if he would like to wager the double.

"I only shot once on the initial break. I've learned an expensive lesson," he said, getting off the stool.

"Your much too good for my money!"

Brown thanked the man and turned to Fred. "How about you, young sir? Would you care to wager your paper money this afternoon?" He smiled as he re-chalked his cue.

The boy reached into his pockets and emptied them on to a nearby table. Before he could start counting out the money, Brown came over and slapped a $10 gold piece down. The boy looked up in disbelief.

"That looks like the equal to all that change!" the gentleman quipped. "You bring that over here and put it on the rail. Grab yourself a stick and let's see what you've got."

Brown reached into his vest pocket and pulled out another double eagle and laid it beside the other. He watched the boy look at the available cues on the rack. Fred twisted them each in turn and looked around for other walls racks nearby. Not seeing any that were close, he walked back to Brown.

"I don't see any that are up to the task. How about I use yours this time?"

The man laughed and put his hand on Fred's shoulder. He handed him the stick and told him to rack the balls and break. The boy moved quickly around the table, gathering the balls from the leather pockets. He set the rack and carefully removed it. Taking the cue ball in hand, he moved to the opposite end. He chalked the stick and started to place the ball.

"Let's decide what game we are playing here, young man, before you go bust these up. How about straight pool, continuous rack, and the first to make twenty-five is the winner?"

Fred nodded and placed the ball just off center. He bridged his left hand and struck the ball. The rack received the hit, sending only one ball to the cushion and barely disturbing the set. The cue ball came off the rail and stopped frozen to a ball in the pack. Brown could not believe the boy's luck. This left him with only a safety shot at best. He tapped the ivory ball, sending another ball to the rail but in doing so opened up the pack. Fred made two balls quickly and paused. He had run thirty balls at Casey's once or twice, but this meant money. For an instant, he wished he hadn't jumped into this, but there was no turning back now.

Fred's heart raced. He knew Mr. Brown could hear it pounding in his chest. He took his time lining up shot after shot until one ball remained. He put down the stick and gathered the pocketed balls, putting them in the rack. He again removed the rack as not to disturbed the remaining object ball and the white ball near it and the rack. The count was fourteen to nil. He was eleven balls from winning more money than he had ever hoped to see. He chalked and bridged. Again taking his time, he struck the ball. The cue ball sent the object ball to the called corner and broke the new rack across the felt sea. As he moved around the table to take the next shot, Brown watched him intently. The boy moved like a cat, and he had a natural stroke. He knew the boy was playing on spunk alone and that he had already done the near impossible for a boy his age and experience.

Fred bent to make the shot. He had called the pocket as Brown approached the table. Fred pulled back slowly and single-pumped the stick. He heard the engine whistle as the tip met the ball; it headed for the six. As the cue ball left the tip, he knew. His stroke had been slightly off. It was over. He knew Brown would run the table. Brown reached for the cue ball, snatching it up from the table.

"You win, young man!" he called so that everyone could hear. "I was beat the minute you broke the second rack."

"But…" Fred stammered.

Brown put up his hand and told the boy to take the coins. "I hope you will give me the opportunity to get even one day," he said. "Now I have dinner plans, and your work here is over. Will I see you tomorrow?"

Fred grabbed the two gold coins, nodded, and rushed to the street. He would have to run all the way. He had promised his father.

Pooling Assets

THE BOY AT FOURTEEN years old had a number of moneymaking schemes. He would mow neighbors' lawns and do odd jobs. He would buy apples and other fresh fruit from Cowsley Grocery Store on Sunday and meet the special train car that brought the Western Military Academy cadets to church in Alton. Sometimes, he would cover other boys' paper routes for them and venture into the better neighborhoods of Alton.

Alton had its wealthy residential areas. Blocks of large Victorian homes lined many streets. The town was a major river port as well as a train hub. Granaries lined the limestone banks in the dock area, and commerce of all sorts had at one time sent Alton rocketing ahead in growth compared to its close southern neighbor, St. Louis. It was the gathering point for all of Madison County. It was during a stint covering for a friend's paper route that Fred met Dick Lynn, the son of a wealthy businessman.

Fred had stopped in the store when an older boy saw him pull out his money to buy a soda. The boy was older and in the company of another lad. He poked his friend, and they followed Fred from the store. Catching up to Fred, they turned him around.

Fred had finished dropping his papers when two boys caught up to him.

"Hey, how would you like to come over to my house with Chet and me?" he asked, turning to smile at Chet. "I have a pool table, and we could play. What do you say?"

It was Saturday, and he didn't have to be home yet. He had wondered what the inside of these homes looked like, and besides, he loved to play pool.

"Sure!" he responded. "Are you sure your folks won't mind? I mean do they let you play pocket billiards?" He was more worried about the difference in their attire. Fred's mother was a seamstress and was training his older sister. These boys had store bought, and their clothes were better than the Whalens could afford.

"Not to worry," Dick said. "My folks aren't home."

He followed the boys into the house. His eyes took in everything in an inventory of furnishing and items he had only seen in catalogs or store shop windows. They wandered through the rooms that changed size and decor until Dick opened the door to a room of brown wood and silk wall coverings. It was most elegant. Dick instructed both boys to look around, and he left the room.

He returned with a small metal box that he put on a side table. He lifted the lid and extracted a number of coins and paper bills. He counted out $2 and waved them in Fred's face.

"We play for money here!" he chided. "Can you stand the action?"

Fred knew what "action" meant. He had heard the term often in the pool hall. Without hesitation, he checked his change and had just a little over two dollars himself. He placed it on the table next to Dick's bills and waited for further instructions. Being a mannered boy, he would let his host choose the game.

"You know how to play eight ball, don't you?" he asked.

Fred nodded and asked, "What are the house rules?"

Having gotten that out of the way, he walked to the rack of sticks and chose one. He rolled it on the table and realized these were better than most at Casey's. Dick took his cue down, and Chet racked the balls. This table was a five by ten whereas the tables he'd played on were four by eights. There were some four and a half by nine, but this was a fancy one.

He knew Dick considered him inferior in more than just ability, yet this only made this game more important. He let Dick break. No balls dropped, so Fred began shooting. In a short time, Fred adjusted for table size and narrowly beat his host. Dick felt the loss was a lucky break for Fred and challenged him to another, double or nothing. The results were the same until Fred owned the metal box.

Fred was exploding inside as he left the house. He had beaten an older boy on the boy's table and got all his money to boot. This boosted his confidence to the next level, and he headed home to bury this along with his other stash. It wasn't long before his parents became suspicious about some things that started appearing among their son's belongings. This led to his father following him from the house to the yard behind the shed. He watched as Fred dug up the treasure trove and confronted him. Fred heard his father's knee joints crack as he bent down behind him. Fred, on hands and knees, having exposed the tops of the jar and the metal box, looked reluctantly over his shoulder.

"What have we here?" his father asked in a rather curious but stern tone.

The boy was obviously startled and began to stammer. "This is my money from work and other things!"

"What other things?" his father asked.

"Winnings?" he choked, with hopes it would be left there.

"You are gambling now?" His father's face was beginning to darken.

Fred's mind flew through every possible excuse to change the fact that he indeed had gambled, but what about the two gold pieces from Mr. Brown? They were not with this loot. He chose his reply quickly.

"Yes, but just once!" he offered, hoping against the odds that it would suffice and that further inquiry would not follow. He was wrong.

"Whom were you gambling with? The men at Casey's?"

"No, sir, not there. At a boy's house."

"Bring all that inside. Now!"

Fred finished uncovering the jar and tin as his father stood and watched. John waited for his son to step in front, and they walked to the back porch door. Nan had heard the commotion and was the opening the screen door for both to enter.

"What in heaven's name in going on with you two?" she asked, wiping her hands on her apron.

"Show your mother what you had buried in the backyard." His father motioned, stepping to one side.

The boy offered up the cache. Nan's eyes widened, and her mouth dropped as she reached out for the glass jar. She set it on a shelf inside the door.

"And what is in the tin box?" she asked softly.

"More money," Fred replied, handing it to her.

"So this is what you have been using to buy those extra things I've noticed around?" she half queried, already knowing the answer. "This seems to be much more than newspaper money. I suspect that we need not count it."

"Twenty-six dollars and thirty-two cents," he said with some pride.

"Nan, it's not the amount of money but how he came by it!"

"You surely don't think he stole it. Not Fred!" She looked to Fred and then her husband.

"Tell us how you came by such money," John asked.

Without hesitation, the boy told them he had won it from Dick Lynn, an uptown boy. John Whalen's face was growing darker when Nan stepped between the boy and his father.

"I'm sure we can straighten this out if you just go to the Lynn house and ask the boy or his father." She interjected to forestall her husband's growing anger. "I know this is my old candy jar filled with change, but I don't recognize this tin. I'll keep the jar, and you two take the tin with you to the Lynns."

John Whalen's face and neck were glowing red as he took the tin and handed it to Fred. The man began to cough, and sweat rose on his forehead. Nan gave him a nearby towel and put her arm around his waist.

"Now don't you get all worked up. This is not what you think it is, but go do as I ask and with a calm heart," she counseled.

The father and son left the porch and walked to the street. Fred quietly walked with his father, his head down, wondering what would come of all this. His father's breathing was not regular as it seemed he was holding the urge to cough back. The doctor had said the symptoms John exhibited were very much those associated with what was known then as lung fever. He had asked if John had ever coughed any blood up. John had said not, but then it would be something he hid from the family.

As they came closer to the Lynn house, Fred's father asked him to point it out. Upon determining the home, he told his son not to speak and that he alone would deal with this matter. The father and son walked to the edge of the front steps. The house was massive and ringed with a porch of turned posts and balustrades. Large French doors opened up the interior to the porch. It was a fine example of period architecture.

Not knowing what to expect, Fred held back a bit as they stood before a large splendid door. John reached back, catching Fred's shoulder and brought him forward just in front of him.

"Pull the bell handle," he said.

Fred reached and pulled, not knowing what to expect. He heard a ringing sound somewhere behind the door. They waited and soon heard the tap of footsteps approaching from inside. The door handle began to turn. Fred stared at it, and suddenly, everything was moving in slower motion as dread welled up from his stomach and nausea took its place. The door slowly opened, and a woman in a fancy apron appeared, looking a bit shocked.

"If you've come to remove the fountain in the backyard, you need to come around back. The mistress does not want workers tramping through the house," she said, looking them up and down.

John began to speak, "We are here with business and would like to speak to the gentleman of the house. I believe this is the Lynn residence."

"It certainly is, and if you will remain here, I will inform Mr. Lynn. Whom shall I say is calling?" she asked.

"John Whalen and son if you'd please."

The woman turned, disappearing into the home. In Fred's mind, this was all moving too slowly, and time seemed to drag on. He didn't have any idea as to what was going to be said. He prayed that his father would control the temper that he had been the object of on more than one occasion. Looking up at his father, he noticed the seriousness of his attention on the closed door and wondered if he, too, should be looking in the same fashion or down at his scuffed shoes in shame. Heavier steps approached on the other side, and the handled turned again in slow motion, the door swinging open to reveal a smaller portly man handsomely attired.

"I'm Richard Lynn, and I'm told we have some kind of business relation. Do I know you, sir?"

"You do not, but I believe your son knows mine." He put his hand on Fred's shoulder; he looked back to Mr. Lynn. Continuing, John suggested it might be helpful if his son joined them.

Mr. Lynn turned to the woman standing a short distance behind him, waved his hand, motioning her to do as requested. In short order, Dick appeared at his father's side.

Mr. Lynn began by asking if this was a school matter, wondering if the boys were classmates.

John assured Mr. Lynn that he didn't know of any school relation and began explaining the situation that brought him to his home this day.

"My wife and I are opposed to gambling in any form, especially when it involves money. And it appears that our boys were involved in a pool game here in your home in which my son, according to his version, won this metal box filled with money. If this is the case, I would like to return this to your care and suggest that we both work to see this does not happen again."

Lynn took the box and opened it. He turned toward young Dick and looked at him. "This is yours, isn't it!"

The boy only nodded and continued to look down. Mr. Lynn looked down at his son, closed the lid, and handed the box to him. Telling his son to wait for him in the parlor, he turned back toward Fred's father, looking up at him. He held out his hand and thanked John for bringing this to his attention, assuring him it would not happen again. John took his hand in return. Fred noticed that Mr. Lynn looked at his father's hand as they shook, noting the difference in size. Fred could tell Dick's father was not used to touching a workingman's hand. Lynn knew this hand could crush his but was surprised that it was only firm in a way that inferred that John Whalen did not want to have to repeat this visit.

The men turned from each other. Richard Lynn entered his home, closing the door. The Whalens turned and stopped at the edge of the porch as Lynn's voice began scolding his son.

"If you ever put me in that kind of situation again, I will send you to boarding school in Chicago! Furthermore, you are not to associate with that class of people in the future! Do you understand me?"

John looked at his son. His green eyes penetrated his son's, letting Fred know that only the strongest of self-control prevented him from turning and doing something he would regret. He put his hand on Fred's shoulder, gripping it in a fashion that was enough to make the boy wince and at the same time telling his son everything he needed know.

His father relaxed as they walked back toward the train yards. Fred felt the tension release in his father's frame. It was an aura that radiated as a warning to those pushing his limits. As the space between them softened, John began to cough, lightly at first and then in a convulsive heaving that he soon tried to muffle. Fred feared his father's temper, but this put a new fear in him, one that would begin to grow in him. As his father dropped his fist, Fred saw a flash of pink moisture from his lips. John grabbed his kerchief and quickly wiped his mouth.

The following day, John Whalen left before light to make up the freight to Chicago. Winifred woke up Fred and fed him breakfast, and before he left to pick of his papers at the news dock, she handed him the jar of coins.

"Keep this to yourself. Burying it in the yard is foolish. If you must conceal it, put it with everyday things that don't attract noses."

Lessons Learned

THE WHALEN HOME ON Sixth Street was a modest dwelling of three bedrooms. Winifred's brother, Frank, lived with the family and shared the basement with Edgar, the oldest son, who at twenty-one was a plumber's apprentice. Beulah was sixteen in 1912 and was helping her mother as a seamstress. At fourteen, Fred was selling papers as he had for the last four years but had seen advertisements in the paper for a variety of jobs that would pay more than his newsboy route.

As John became more ill and his tuberculosis advanced, the family members began contributing more to the family's expenses. Doctor bills began weighing heavily on their finances, and it looked more and more as if moving to a dryer climate was somewhere in the future. Fred had begun spending more time at Brown's Hotel and had become more involved with billiards. Brown had taken a serious interest in the boy's natural ability in stroking the balls.

Brown began working with Fred on the more formal gentleman's game of billiards, teaching him speed and control over the cue and object balls as the game played out on the pocketless table. Fred preferred the game of pool and pockets but soon understood that Brown was teaching him fundamentals that applied to mastering a game that required looking ahead three or four shots. Once the boy had mastered the game of billiards, Brown moved him onto the pool table.

Fred had watched straight pool but had felt more excitement in the short games of eight ball and nine balls. Money changed hands more quickly in these games, and he had seen small fortunes won and lost at Casey's. He had respected his father's wishes regarding gambling but considering the circumstances viewed it as a way to fast dollars and helping ease the burden at home. His mother and sister were working well into the night to supplement the family. He knew he must do something even if it meant going to Chicago and finding a better-paying job.

At fourteen, he was tall and lanky with a shock of black hair that lay loosely on his head. He noticed the girls smiling and whispering to each other as he passed with his papers. Embarrassed by his modest clothing, he had never made any attempt to meet girls. He left school after eighth grade because he needed to make money for the family. His father was growing weaker and was bedridden for the most part. He admired Mr. Brown who dressed impeccably. He promised himself he would look as good one day and began haunting tailor shops and sifting through catalogs. One afternoon, Brown took him aside as he dropped his papers. He put his hand on his shoulder and looked him in the eye.

"I'm going on a business trip soon and was thinking of asking your parents if you can accompany me," he said. "You could be of great assistance, and I would pay you much more than you make hawking papers in Alton. How do you feel about this, and will your parents allow it?"

Fred was surprised at this offer and wasn't sure what his parents might say. Everyone in Alton knew Mr. Brown and considered him a pillar of the community, contributing to many causes and charities. Many women considered him a fine catch although he had never demonstrated interest in any of them. He was about five feet nine with a finely manicured mustache and well-combed hair. When out, he wore a fine hat, a waistcoat, and finely polished half boots. He was a gentleman's gentleman and greeted all he encountered with pleasantries and good wishes.

Fred smiled and hoped his family would approve. "Yes, I would like that!" he returned, trying to hold back his excitement.

"Well, then, I would suggest that you inform your parents that I will call on them tomorrow afternoon and propose to take you on as my assistant and teach you my business. Now, it's getting toward suppertime, and you should tell them of my interest. Nothing more and nothing less. I will lay out the details of your employment, and we'll see how this works."

He could barely contain the excitement as he ran up the porch steps and through the door. His mother was in the kitchen getting supper ready. He reached in his pockets and emptying them placing the coins and paper on the table.

Nan looked up and placed the mixing bowl she was using on the table. She looked down at the pile of cash and walked to his side, putting her hand on his shoulder.

"Well, it seems you had a good afternoon selling your papers."

She wiped her hands on her apron before picking up the money as Fred started to speak. She put her finger to his mouth and almost whispered, "Your father is asleep and has been asked to take a string of freight cars over to the grain yards to be loaded tonight. So whatever it is you want to tell us can wait till supper. Go wash your hands. They're black with printer's ink, and I won't have them handling my food across the table. And comb your hair while you're at it."

He politely said, "Yes'm," and went to the basin and cleaned his hands. He knew his mother was his ally in most things and needed her to plead his case for leaving home and chores for an opportunity to help his family now that his father's condition was worsening.

As the family sat down for supper, Fred's father looked at each one for a moment and began by informing them that his doctor suggest he go to a sanatorium in Oklahoma to rest and have his lung condition treated. He told them he would be leaving in the morning and that the family would have to pull together to make ends meet. To a person, they knew this was most likely the only hope for John to get better and that he was struggling to hide his feelings about leaving his family this way. Fred knew that this would make Mr. Brown's pitch to his parents much simpler, and with his father leaving on the early train, his mother would agree Brown's offer for the sake of the family.

Just before noon, Mr. Brown knocked on the door, removing his hat as Nan greeted him. Fred stood in the kitchen as the pair talked, and his mother got assurances that her son was in good hands and the two of them would return in three to four days. With a nod, she motioned to her son to enter the room.

"Fred, Mr. Brown has asked for my permission allowing you to accompany him on a business trip to St. Louis," she said, looking sternly in his eyes. "You are to listen to Mr. Brown as if he were your father. I trust he will take care of you while on this trip, and I think seeing the big city and the world outside of Alton will do you good."

Looking at Mr. Brown, she suggested, "If you don't mind, I'll put together a traveling bag for Fred and he'll be ready to leave in thirty minutes."

Brown nodded and said he'd return at the time suggested. They would leave on the afternoon train and return in a few days, and she should put her concerns to rest and he would treat Fred as if he were the son he wished he had. Fred turned and went to the room he shared with Edgar. Nan followed her son with a small cloth bag and began stuffing it with clean long johns, shirts, and socks.

"Be sure to brush your teeth and comb your hair out of your eyes," she chided. "Do what your told with a smile and always be ready to help Mr. Brown."

At two o'clock, Fred and Mr. Brown boarded the southbound train for East St. Louis. They would cross the Mississippi Bridge and go to Market Street.

Fred had been to Chicago with his father but only into the yards just to turn around and take another freight back. This was his first venture into a large city. His heart raced as they walked down Market. He carried his sling bag over his shoulder and narrow case of Mr. Brown.

During the trip south, Brown began giving him the lay of the land. He was to refer to him as his father, and he would refer to him as Junior. There was to be no mention of Alton or any reference to home. It was in these moments on the train that Fred would learn that Mr. Brown was known only as Tennessee Brown. No first names, only the two handles, Tennessee Brown and Junior. Brown reached into his breast pocket and handed Fred a clip of bills.

"This is for you," he said, looking him in the eyes. "You will put $20 in your shoe just under the tongue and laces. This is safety money. We are going into a rough part of town full of pool halls and gambling establishments. You will see men and women that conduct various kinds of business, most illegal. We never drink anything but water and always in a clear glass. Look these people in the eye with no expression. If approached and asked who I am, your answer is 'My father.' No more no less."

"What about the extra money?" Fred asked.

"At times, you will be approached by people asking you if you will bet on your father. You can say yes, but the bartender must hold the wager. Never leave bets on the bar or believe the person making the bet will approach you after they lose and pay you off. These people will move away from you and watch the game. The minute they realize they are losing, they will disappear. The only way they would come back is to collect. I don't lose!"

"The barman will put an empty glass on the bet," he continued, "and will remove it and handed it to the winner."

The boy looked out the window as the train clipped along toward East St. Louis. The countryside passed by his eyes in a glaze of light and color. Soon, his mind wandered to another time only two years before.

*****

It was the winter of 1910, the wind pierced the clothing of the young boy who moved in and out along the storefronts peddling the papers he held close under both arms, trying to insulate his body from the chilling cold. He'd rather be playing pool, a game he'd picked up when he was nine, but he and his family needed the money. His father was sick, and every dollar helped now; besides, his father was against pool playing. Even though it was in his blood, he felt he owed his father that much. He'd play only enough to keep his hand and stroke in, that wouldn't hurt too much.

As he walked down the street, he anticipated his final stop, Brown's Hotel, where he would sell the remaining papers. The owner,

Mr. Brown, would buy what was left and put them in the lobby for the guests. But there was another reason to finish his rounds at the hotel; the most magnificent pool table he'd ever see was in the parlor, and sometimes, there were big money games. Some nights, he'd watch for hours, and in the two years he had been selling papers at the hotel, he'd never seen Mr. Brown beaten. The man was his idol, and he'd practice some of the shots he saw Mr. Brown make.

Mr. Brown had a standing rule—never to play his guests for money or fun—but now and again, a young kid or a passing hustler would try Mr. Brown for big stakes. When a game was on, the parlor would fill to capacity, and side bets were the rule. Often, the games went until morning or until the money dried up. Once in a while, the young boy's paper earnings would double in a fast afternoon of pool gambling.

The paperboy entered the rich lobby through the frosted crystal-glazed doors onto the plush wool carpet and up to the desk clerk. The man at the desk would nod to Mr. Brown's location or would purchase the papers if Mr. Brown were out of town on business. On this particular night, the owner was in the pool parlor, and as the boy approached, he could see a big game was winding up. It was a $500 game, and Mr. Brown was shooting out.

"That's it, my friend," said Mr. Brown, "it's been my pleasure."

"Let's go again!" fired the loser, walking toward his host.

"No thanks, you're too easy."

"What's that supposed to mean!" he snapped.

"Just what I said," returned Mr. Brown as he put his cue away.

"Bullshit! You were lucky," he cried.

"Luck had nothing to do with it, sir, and your play is as foul as your language. Besides, the child could probably beat you."

The young boy was caught up in the emotions of the moment, and without thinking, he spoke out. "I can beat him!" he blurted.

The only man who didn't laugh was Mr. Brown. He walked over and smiled at his paperboy. The owner took the usual remaining papers—plus the especially nice one that the boy always kept aside—paid him, and put his hand on the boy's shoulder.

"How do you know you can beat him, son?" asked Mr. Brown in a fatherly manner.

"Because you just said a kid could do it," answered the boy, "and besides, you should know, you're the best!"

Mr. Brown looked into his eyes and nodded. "I'll bet you can!" Mr. Brown whispered confidently.

"Look here, Carter! To prove how bad you really are, I'll bet this boy can beat you. Now, if you beat the boy here, I'll return your losses," offered Mr. Brown.

"Fair enough!" replied Carter, reaching for his stick.

"It's a deal!"

"The game is straight pool, call your shots with fifty points the winner!" said Mr. Brown.

The balls were racked, the opponents lagged for break with Carter taking the honors. Carter's shot sent the ball to the cushion, leaving the cue ball near the cushion opposite the rack. The boy stepped to the rail and called the only ball outside the rack. The shot dropped the object ball with the cue ball spreading the pack. From that point on, the next thirteen balls were easy. It was time for the next rack.

The boy shot, exploding the rack but missing the break shot. Carter jumped in and proceeded to put away three racks until over-confidence signaled a miss. The score was 42 to 14 as Carter smiled to those around him. One miss by the boy and he would run eight and out.

The boy chalked up and began running balls, one rack then two until he only needed one ball to make fifty. The only shot was a bank into the side; he missed. The men in the smoke-filled parlor moaned. Carter laughed. The man ran the next six. The boy thought it was over, but Carter's overconfidence struck again. While shooting the forty-ninth ball, he followed it in with the cue. The spectators roared.

With his stick chalked, the boy placed the cue ball behind the line. He had a choice of two shots, the scratch ball at the rack point or a bank shot to the ball behind the line. His best chance was to cut in the scratch ball and try to avoid a scratch himself. He watched the cue ball roll down the green field toward the object ball, clicking into it and sending both balls in opposite directions. The ball bounced into the pocket as all eyes watched the cue ball rolling toward the other corner. Collectively, they expelled their breath as the cue ball stopped at the edge of the hole.

The young boy had won, and the parlor became a bedlam of shouts and screams. Men started shaking his hand, patting him on the back and congratulating him. As he looked around, Carter had vanished, but at the end of the table was Mr. Brown who smiled with approval.

When all had left, Mr. Brown walked over and offered his hand to the young victor, who extended his hand eagerly. The young boy felt something in his palm, and he pulled it away to see a folded bill—$100. He stared at his hand unbelievingly. When he looked up to thank his benefactor, he realized he was alone; Mr. Brown had left.

The next day before making his usual rounds, he returned to the hotel and thanked Mr. Brown. Mr. Brown motioned to the boy to follow him into the parlor, sliding the doors behind them.

"You're very good young man!" he said, resting his hands on the table rails.

"Thank you, sir."

"What's your name?" he asked.

"Fred Whalen, sir!"

"How old are you?"

"Twelve!"

"Do you play often?" asked Mr. Brown.

"When I can," Fred answered.

"Would you like to be better?"

"Yes, sir!"

"Well, Fred, your first lesson begins today." Mr. Brown set three balls on the table, one in front of the side pocket, the cue ball directly across from it, and two balls adjusted in between.

"Looks impossible, doesn't it?"

"Yes, sir, it does!"

"The first thing you must have is faith. Believe in yourself. Many shots that look impossible are simple, and some shots that are impossible can be made if your hand is fast enough."

Brown leaned over and made the shot with a stroke that was both fluid and quick. He then showed him the same shot in slower motions. Magic! Fred practiced this shot every day and in different variations from all points of the table until it was effortless and natural. The trick was stroke speed so quick that the human eye could not detect a double stroke.

Market and North Broadway

NORTH BROADWAY PARALLELED THE river. Market Street ran perpendicular and ended at the river. Union Station was the center of the world on Market. It was along here where the action was. Gambling, prostitution, and all forms of illegal activities took place. The area has since become Gateway National Park.

In 1912, it was as seedy as they come. Even worse was East St. Louis on the Illinois side of the river. It was mostly black along that side, and many of its residents worked in St. Louis and hung out along Broadway and Market. Racism was very apparent and particularly bad in these areas. It was a lot to take in at fourteen years of age.

There were many nuances to learn. Fred learned basic idioms of the time, things done and not done, things said and not said, and Code of the Canon.

The Code was a language of its own. There was double-talk and misspeak. Words not used in polite company were strewn like pebbles, and rough rowdy behavior was the norm. In some ways, it was exhilarating and in most terrifying. Brown had warned him on what to expect, what to look for, and what to avoid. It was raw life as only big cities and the times purveyed. The ride began here, and the infection began with a small taste, a flavor of a life that would be hard to leave.

During this first trip, Brown kept to the river area around St. Louis. Blacks mostly haunted the poolrooms there. At first, Fred would sit at the bar and watch Brown engage in games for $5 to $10. Brown told him to study the opponents as much as he watches him. Brown worked the table close to the bar so Fred could hear every word because table talk was an important part of the hustle. The other tell was sizing up the competition's abilities, usually apparent by the way they approached the table and their addressing the cue ball. Their hand position on the stick and the quality of their stroke spoke volumes. In straight pool, positioning your next shot separated fair players from those that have mastered the sport.

Fred watched ten games. In his head, he kept track of Brown's winnings and thought in three hours or so his sponsor had tucked away well over $100. This was far superior to the ten cents per hour he made cleaning at Casey's.

He became eager to try his hand. Brown walked to the bar with his stick.

"Here you go, Junior," he quipped, handing Fred his cue. "Let's see what you've got. Take your time, there's no hurry. I think most players in this place are looking for an easy mark, and you fit the bill. Let them suggest the bet. If it's more than five dollars, you let them know that it's too rich for you. They will misjudge your confidence and feel they don't have to try as hard. You start with eight ball. Straight pool is for later when you've put some games behind you."

The last man Brown had beaten was racking the balls and looked up at Fred as he chalked his cue. The Black man was younger than Brown and definitely older than he.

"Your father says you're pretty good!"

"I have a lot to live up to," Fred returned, picking up the white ivory ball, yellowed from years of hard use.

"Your Pap said he'd lend you five dollah to play eight ball?"

Fred reached in his pocket and pulled out the bill, placing it on the rail next to his opponent's five, setting a chalk cube on it. He handed the man the cue ball and stepped back from the table. To Fred's surprise, the man looked at the ball and walked over and handed it back.

"You break, boy." He chuckled. "You gonna need a head start!"

Fred looked at the ball for a second and then placed it on the table offside of center. He walked to the rack and looked at it, making sure all fifteen balls were frozen. Walking back to the cue ball, he moved it slightly and bent over to make the break. The ball struck the pack and reversed direction, stopping near the center of the table. One striped and one solid dropped into the leather pockets. The remaining balls came to a halt. Fred walked the table assessing their positions and started shooting in rotation, choosing the solid balls as his targets. Each succeeding shot left him his next until only the 8 and 3 were left for his attention. The 3 ball was blocked by the 8 with no way of safely performing a shot. He had watched this man play Brown and knew he could possibly run the table to finish with the 8 ball. Fred looked at Brown for a second. Brown was sipping a glass of water and was expressionless. Fred knew this situation was a test.

If he were going to play safe, he'd have to shoot the 8 and position it in a precarious spot near one of his opponent's striped balls. He scanned the table, noting all his opponent's balls. The 12 was near a corner pocket and would be the man's most obvious first shot. He judged the distance from the cue ball to the 8 and measured his stroke, putting the cue ball into the rail first, rebounding into the 8 and sending it to the corner rail, leaving it near the pocket and blocking the 12. The cue ball touched his 3, sending it toward the corner opposite the 12. The 3 touched the rail and moved in front of the pocket, blocking it. The result, actually, pleased Brown, and he shifted in his stool looking intently at Fred's opponent.

"Well, isn't this a shit load a beans!" he moaned, chalking his stick. "I'll be fucked if I ain't peticular shootin' this out!"

Since the obvious 12 was blocked, he began picking off striped balls in the middle of the table until there were only three stripes left, the 12 at one end near, the 8, and 2 at the other end near the side rail. He could make a bank shot, putting one of the two in the side, leaving the cue ball on the rail behind the other ball. This would leave a long shot down the rail, squeezing the object ball between the rail and 8 ball. He had to run the cue ball just behind it down the rail, coming off to touch his 12 toward the opposite pocket where Fred's 3 was setting. He made the bank and left his ball a bit behind the other ball along the rail but not touching the rail. He studied the upcoming rail shot. He bent and slowly pumped his stick, trying to judge strength of stroke and proper English. His arm moved forward, and the cue ball hit the object ball down the rail toward the pocket. The cue ball ran with it but slightly started moving away from the rail. The object ball cleared the 8 and dropped into the pocket. The yellowish cue ball rolled lightly into the 8, slowly sending it in behind the previous ball.

"Damn nation, I swear you da luckiest som bitch eva!" said the Black man, leaning with both hands on the table.

Brown left his stool and stepped to the table, picking up the two bills under the chalk cube. He put his hand on Fred's shoulder and with the other retrieved his stick.

"You can't be leaving jus now! Eyes need a chance to gets my money back!"

Fred hadn't noticed that evening had come on. The darkness of the billiard hall with its pools of directed light over the tables made it easy to put passing time in another part of one's brain. Concentration and purpose took over, and time didn't exist outside the 5×10 green felt arenas. The swirling mix of cigar, cigarette smoke, and spilt beer permeated the stale air that was moved only by the bodies circling the tables. The coughs of chain-smoking patrons intermixed with swearing exclamations of triumph and disappointment were the sounds that would eventually become white noise. Short of a gun going off, and that was always a possibility; no one paid much attention. Drunken fights were more common than not, and the only time anyone moved quickly was when the paddy wagon was getting close.

All these things were previously out of Fred's realm of experience. Outdoors, the gaslights were being lit, and sounds of St. Louis were beginning to define the night. Carriages and wagons were still in use, and automobiles were just getting into fashion. Crossing to the other side of Market was an exercise in itself. Horse droppings had to be dodged in the uneven cracks and crannies of cobbled thoroughfares. Anything left on the streets had to wait till early morning before the cleanup was attempted. These things all played on Fred's senses. He wondered, *What could possibly be next?* They continued to walk, leaving the pool halls and saloons behind.

"It's time we checked into a hotel," Brown commented as he turned and reached for a pair of beveled-glass doors. After you, young sir!"

This was an entirely new experience for Fred. He'd been in Brown's Hotel in Alton, but the scale of the lobby and furnishings were completely foreign to him. In looking at the patrons, he felt embarrassed in his homespun. He hesitated for an instant but felt Brown's arm over his shoulder and immediately looked at the man.

"Don't worry, Fred! Tomorrow, we will get you a fresh set of clothes more in line for a young man on the town. After all, tomorrow we will visit the Fagan Brothers' Billiards on Olive Street. It's not tony, but it is a step up from where we were this afternoon. You need to see the difference between casual competition and serious business, small potatoes and high steaks."

"Speaking of which," he continued, "we must have a St. Louis cut sirloin after I check us in."

The desk clerk looked up and with a genuine expression of delight, recognized Mr. Brown, and welcomed him back, saying that it had been a few months since his last visit. He produced a ledger from behind the long desk and opened it, handing a pen and inkwell to Brown.

"This is my son's first trip to St. Louis," he offered, "and I would like him to sign with me. Here's the pen, Junior, sign Frederick Brown."

Brown took the pen after Fred's signing and handed it back to the clerk.

The man replaced everything and handed him a key, stating that it was his usual room and he would have the floor matron bring extra linens. In the passing of the key, Fred noticed a greenback in Brown's hand during the exchange. The clerk acknowledged the gesture and thanked him.

The pair turned, and Brown directed Fred toward a grand staircase across the lobby. As they walked, Fred noticed the high velvet winged-back chairs, the fine wool carpet runners over the marble tile floors. Once upon the stairs, the artistry of the oak balustrade made Fred wonder if he'd dare to touch it. At the broad landing, they turned and walked to one of the hallways that sprung from either side of the landing. Electric wall sconces lined the wide hallways.

Rich green velvet fabric in floral print ran along the walls above a warm stained oak wainscot.

"Here's our room," he said as he unlocked the door. "We'll wash up and retire to the dining room downstairs. Then we'll order the best steaks on the menu and turn in for the night."

Fred could only nod in response as the gilt and glitter of such a place was going crazy with his senses. The boy washed his face and hands and changed his shirt.

"Is this going to be alright for downstairs? It doesn't smell of cigars and cigarettes, but it's all I have."

Brown smiled. "You look just fine, and your clothes will do for tonight."

They went downstairs to the dining room and ordered two 16 oz. porterhouse steaks. Something the lad had never had but seen in the store at Cowsley's in Alton where he helped out for extra money. They finished dinner and returned to the room.

"Fred, I'm going to leave you here this evening for a bit. I want you to get some rest because we will start playing on Market and Broadway at places where the Blacks like to play. You'll be getting some good training with players I believe aren't up to your natural ability. Oh, here's that ten dollars from this afternoon. Put it with your money clip. Remember, keep your money in your front pant pocket. There are grifters out working people who look like easy marks. Pickpockets don't usually hit kids, but after tomorrow, you won't look your age. Nobody is light enough to reach into a front pant pocket to lift a man's clip. I'll be back later. I have some business to look into. By the way, while you were playing today, I took your opponent's friends for a little over two hundred."

Brown turned to the door, and looking over his shoulder, he said, "I almost forgot. We're going to my tailor tomorrow morning and get you outfitted for your new role as my son."

As Brown reached for the door, Fred blurted out, "You made all that money betting I'd win? I could have lost! How did you know?"

"When you played the safe shot blocking his 12 ball," Brown returned, "that was the tell. You figured out your best chance of saving the game and took it rather than try to make a bad situation into a losing one." Brown laughed. "When his friends believed it was all over, they doubled up! The greedy bastards thought they had an easy score. From playing that guy, before I gave you the cue, I knew he could make rail shots but couldn't control the cue ball. I knew he'd most likely scratch the 8."

"Fred! Close your mouth," he quipped. "You'll catch flies!"

With that, Brown closed the door and disappeared into the hallway. The boy looked perplexed. He wondered how Brown could be so confident and cool. He decided that he wanted to be as sure as Mr. Brown. He would make every effort to study his mentor's every action and word. There was exhilaration in the thought that billiards, a game he loved, could provide a living if you were good enough. At that moment, he decided being called Junior wasn't bad, and he would dedicate himself to being better than good enough.

Playing the Part

FRED NEVER HEARD BROWN return. The next morning, they had breakfast and left the hotel. Brown hailed a carriage, and they traveled into the center of St. Louis. It was a busy place with people going about their business and not seemingly paying attention to one another. Fred felt anonymous and expected a person could be lost in such a sea of humanity. In Alton, most people knew each other or particular persons of standing in the community and commonly acknowledged them. This seemed unfriendly somehow to Fred. He thought this might just be the people were in a hurry to get indoors. It was early May, and the heat and humidity were both starting to rise. Brown paid the man generously, and they stepped onto the sidewalk and made their way up a few doors into a tailor's shop. The bell on the door tinkled as they entered. A very well-dressed gentleman appeared from behind the curtain, separating the back from the front of the shop.

"Mr. Brown! It is so good to see you," he exclaimed. "It's been a while since I last took care of you!"

Brown took the tailor's extended hand and proceeded to introduce Fred as his son, adding that he felt it was time the lad began dressing as a young gentleman. The smaller Italian man then rigorously began shaking Fred's hand. He rang the praises of Brown's taste in clothes and the fact that he was one of his favorite customers.

"What would you like to see him in, Mr. Brown?" he politely asked, with a sweeping arm gesture toward the racks along the wall and the counters filled with shirts and accessories.

There were dressing forms displaying various types of suit jackets, waistcoats with vests, and other accoutrements. Starched collars, tiepins, and neck wear were assorted in glass cases. The forms along the windows on either side of the door cast headless shadows along the red oak floor. The air had a pleasant spicy scent to it and a very clean feeling. Fred had gone at times with his mother and older sister to linen goods shops but none of those in Alton compared.

"Anthony, I would like to get some ready-made clothes today that are appropriated for a man of his age," he suggested, looking toward one of the dressing forms. "Not overly stylish but something comfortable and loose around the shoulders. Some nice-cuffed shirts and trousers that works with half boots."

"I understand completely, sir, and I believe have just what is in order," he returned. "Let me show you some items that most young men his age wear in more casual settings nowadays. If you can leave him with me for the next hour, I will measure him completely and have him ready to greet society in the most comfortable fashion."

"Excellent, Anthony." He chuckled, putting his hand on Fred's shoulder and continuing, "I leave you my boy and expect when I return to see a young gentleman."

With that, Brown retreated out the door, ringing the little bell again as he left. Fred was a bit taller than the Italian tailor and wondered what exactly would happen next. He was used to his mother fussing over him to make his clothes but never a man. Anthony walked over to a basket and pulled out a tape and began to measure Fred's waist. The next measurement really got Fred's attention as only his mother had put hands anywhere near his crouch. He jumped back a number of times as the tailor tried many times to get an accurate tape on the boy. Finally, in exhaustion, he just asked Fred to go behind the curtain and hand him his pants. This Fred did but still felt very vulnerable. What if for some reason or emergency he'd have to vacate to the street? He looked around, seeing mostly spools of fabric until he saw what looked like an overcoat, which he quickly put on.

A short time later, Anthony stuck his hand through the curtain holding a pair of trousers. Fred took them and replaced the coat, quickly donning the pants. He realized the trousers were too long and said so. Anthony parted the curtain and walked over to Fred.

"Please stand still while I roll the legs up," he asked. "I need to pin these so the cuffs will break properly over your boots. I have no attention of touching you anymore than I have to."

Fred complied, and the tailor finished pinning the cuff.

"Please remove the trousers and I'll hem them," he asked. "Then we'll pick out some nice shirts, a belt, and fit you for a day jacket. By the look of your socks, we'll get a few pair of those also."

Fred looked at his feet and realized his socks were very shabby, embarrassed that a couple of his toes had almost worn through. He knew he had a freshly darned pair in his duffle, and he should have put them on before leaving the hotel. He had always admired Mr. Brown's impeccable appearance and decided that he would start taking better care of his overall image from this day forward. Brown had coached him at dinner and breakfast on table etiquette and reminded him that he should stand when approached by a lady or group of ladies. He told him to wait for the lady to offer her hand, otherwise, smile and nod. All these things flashed before him in his mind, and he tried to hold on to all that Brown offered.

Anthony returned with the trousers and motioned him to come out front where he could start matching him up with the rest of his clothing. Anthony used the word "repertoire" and seeing the confounded look on Fred's face explained the French word and just said, "The rest of your wardrobe." Anthony picked out three banded collared shirts, noting that at some later date, he might want to add starched button on collars. He buttoned one on so as Fred would be able to accomplish that in the future.

"You may need to attend a more formal dinner or afternoon event with your father and need a couple of these," he advised the lad.

This was all coming at Fred so quickly that he worried he would not be able to put it all in order when it came time to use the information being imparted. He had never had store-bought clothes. Everything on him was either made by his mother or handed down from his brother. He walked over to the full-height mirror on the wall and looked at himself. For a moment, he didn't recognize the person looking back. Something had changed. He didn't see the newspaper boy that he knew. He was somehow different, and he wasn't sure, for that moment, just who he was. Fred saw himself as young man even though manhood was a term he never contemplated in the past. In that moment, time had slipped, and he wasn't aware of time passing. As he turned away, he realized that Mr. Brown had returned and was standing alongside of Anthony, both smiling as if proud parents.

Brown turned to Anthony and said, "Now that's the young man that was hiding under all that!" He pointed to the pile of clothes on the bench nearby.

"You've done a fine job, Tony, and the items you've selected suit him well."

"Thank you, Mr. Brown!" he returned. "I'm sure these garments will stand him well in your company. What would you have me do with his former attire?"

"I'll send someone from the hotel to pick up his new wardrobe," Brown replied. "And box everything up, including his old clothing. We have to tend to a little business now that Fred is attired for the day at hand. Fred, I'll join you outside as soon as I settle with Anthony."

Fred turned and started toward the door but couldn't help glancing at himself as he passed the mirror. After a slight hesitation, he continued leaving the shop. Outside, the bright sunshine offered a better light in which he took stock of the transformation that had occurred. The crispness and smell of new clothes filled his senses. The sun reflected off his shiny new boots, and for a second, he was blinded in the sun that filled the street beyond. The shop's entry bell sounded again, and Mr. Brown was beside him looking him over. Fred looked up to an approving smile and was comforted by the thought that his mentor was satisfied with the new look.

"Thank you so much, sir!" he exclaimed in pure exuberance. "I hope I can repay you in some way for all that you've done for me!"

"Not to worry, young man," Brown quipped. "You and I will recover this investment and more in the next few hours. Just remember how we played it yesterday. We will be doing some of the same today and tomorrow with a bit of variation. I think you are a natural and a quick study. In the months ahead, you will gain knowledge and confidence in reading our opponents. This is by no means a career but a supplement to a life you may choose in the future. It can also be dangerous, and timing with some these players is crucial. One has to be aware of a man's ego. After all, this game of pocket billiards requires individual skill. A person in this game for money is putting his ability up against yours. You first watch the mark and assess his ability in light of your own. For now, I will rate the men you play. You understand me?"

"Yes, sir, I do!"

It was almost noon. The two turned and walked toward the river. They passed a number of café-type places, and Fred wondered which one Brown would jester to enter. To his surprise, Brown turned and held open the door into what was obviously a saloon of sorts. It was poorly lit, and Fred's eyes were slowly adjusting to the layout before them. A bar stretched along the wall with a few men, with bent elbows, resting against it drinks in hand. The sound of conversation filled the room punctuated, now and then, by the familiar click of ivory from the rear of the place.

Brown motioned to the bartender and pointed to a table near the edge of one of the many pool tables. The man nodded and dried his hands on his apron as he came out from behind the bar. Fred and Brown sat down as the man approached.

"What'll it be, gentlemen?" he asked.

"We'll have two of your roast beef sandwiches and some potato salad," Brown replied, "and I'd like a beer and the young man will have a Coca-Cola."

"I'll get it right out," he said and turned back to the bar.

Brown looked around to see what was happening around the pool tables. He got up from the table and almost disappeared in the smoke that was wafting around the gaming area. The bartender returned with two plates, utensils, and cloth napkins. He sat down a jar of horseradish and walked off. A few moments later, Brown returned and sat down, repositioning his chair watching the playing area. He took a swallow of beer and a bite of sandwich, ignoring the horseradish. Fred started to reach for the sauce, but Brown stopped him.

"That stuff will be on your breath all day," he warned. "And as the place warms up, you'll perspire its scent through your clothes. The same thing with garlic."

Fred withdrew his hand and grabbed the sandwich and made quick work of it. In between bites, he forked in some potato salad and washed it all down with coke. He was beginning to get anxious, remembering how much he enjoyed yesterday's activities. He looked toward the tables for an instant and turned back toward Mr. Brown to find him watching him intently. He felt a bit foolish for a while and gave an expression of presupposed guilt that he shouldn't have looked away from Brown.

"It's fine that you looked to see what was going on!" Brown said, realizing that Fred had felt awkward at that moment. "I want you to pay attention to our surroundings. Not just the action on the tables but also the entire scene and those occupying the place. As I mentioned earlier, this can be dangerous at times. There are men and women that haunt these rooms looking for an easy touch. Pickpockets? Yes, and even worse! You win even a small amount, and there will be people wanting to relieve you of your cash and worse! Look at everyone and assess him or her. People that watch your playing too long could present a problem. Notice if they are communicating with someone around the place, a look or sign."

Fred nodded in understanding but wasn't sure what to look for. He trusted that what Brown imparted was gospel. He began to realize that this was not an easy way of work but a craft that had many facets.

"There's a man in here I've seen many times before. I've not played him but have studied him and his choice of opponents. He is constantly looking for someone who has a lesser sense of security in his ability than himself. Don't misconstrue what I'm saying. This man is good and has been successfully separating his marks from their money. He plays eight ball because most below-average players are comfortable with that game. It's a quick moneymaker if you're good. It's even a better system if you can make it look as if you were just luckier than the mark. This man doesn't play that scam, and I doubt he is a player with that ability. His ego tells him to show off his skill in a fashion that humiliates his competition."

Fred again nodded his head and asked, "Is there a reason you haven't challenged him yet?"

Brown looked at Fred and answered, "He is a perfect teaching example at this point in our relationship. I will slow play him in a way that will give him the confidence to double down his bet, believing I'm just lucky. He will continue to bet until he's broke or realizes he's been snookered. Speaking of snooker, that's another game. You won't be playing it, and I'm not teaching it to you."

Fred took a stool near the pool table when Brown put down $5 on the rail. The mark was just finishing off his current opponent and looked up to see who had placed the bet. He had noticed Brown and the kid when they walked in and thought they were father and son. He decided that this man was just showing the boy another side of St. Louis life because they both were overdressed for the place.

He looked up and said, "I'll be right with you as soon as I drop this eight ball."

Brown returned, "No hurry. I'm just showing my son what goes on in saloons like this."

The eight was called, and the man put into a corner pocket and shook hands with his opponent, saying, "I hope there are no hard feelings. You are a fine competitor. Maybe we can play again sometime."

He then walked over to where Brown and Fred were sitting and out a matching $5 on top of Brown's challenge, placing a chalk cube on top.

"Is eight ball alright with you, sir?" he said as he walked the table, digging balls out of the leather pockets.

"I think that would be fine," replied Brown. "Do you mind my son watching? He's never seen a pool table, and I thought a quick game would give him some sportsmanlike entertainment."

"Sure, why not?" the man returned with a nod toward Fred. "Every young man should acquaint himself with a gentleman's game."

"My thoughts exactly," Brown said, taking a cue from the nearby shelf. "Please rack the balls. I hope my small side wager isn't offensive?"

"Not at all. I'm happy to accommodate you and your son."

"Should we flip a coin to see who breaks?" Brown asked.

"I usually suggest we lag to see who comes closest to the rail," he offered.

Brown nodded and said, "Please you go first."

The man placed the cue ball and shot, passing the rack and returning the ball close to the rail. The man put a dime where his ball stopped and handed the cue ball to Brown. Brown took his time pumping his cue stick, making it look as if he had not done much in billiards before today. He sent the ball to the opposite rail, and the rebound fell very short of the man's dime.

"Looks like I'm up for the break," said the man, grinning.

The man broke the balls trying to put anything in that might just go. The balls rolled all over the felt but none dropped. Brown saw an easy shot and slopped it in sending the cue ball around the table to finish in a safe position. The man was not impressed but could only try to make a very difficult shot, which failed. Brown now approached the table like an amateur, not examining the field before him and shot. He missed but did so that the object ball stopped in front of the pocket, blocking it. This left the mark with only one option, and he shot a striped ball into the side pocket. His next shot was another to the opposite side pocket that required him cutting it in. It fell, but the cue ball continued down the rail, knocking in Brown's previous missed shot.

"Thanks, I need all the help I can get!" exclaimed Brown.

The man's following shot missed and left the remaining balls in vulnerable positions. Brown dropped two very easy shots and missed following shot but left his solid balls in easy positions, including one in front of the corner, again blocking a pocket. The cue ball rolled and froze against the rail. The mark shot, dropping another strip, but failed in his next attempt, leaving the eight ball in a precarious position near a side pocket. Brown put two easy shots away, taking his time. This slow approach to shooting reinforced the mark's sense that he was playing just a lucky hack.

The man eventually put in one more ball before missing, leaving Brown with just one ball and the eight remaining. Brown's last solid dropped in, and his shot at the precarious eight was a gift, and to make it seem really sloppy, he rolled the cue toward the corner as if to scratch but stopping just short. Brown thanked the man for the game and picked up the $10 as he headed to the cue shelf.

"You can't leave without giving me a chance to at least break even!" he suggested. "After all, you got some pretty lucky breaks this game."

Brown stopped and pulled his pocket watch from his vest and looked at it. He then looked up and agreed to another game. The mark proposed they play double and put $10 on the table where the previous bet had rested. The bet was matched, and the man gathered and reracked the balls.

"I believe it's your turn to break," he said to Brown as he chalked his cue.

"I'll do my best. Just this one game as I promised my wife that we wouldn't be gone too long this afternoon," asserted Brown.

Brown then broke the balls with an exaggerated thrust of the stick. Balls careened around the table, and two solids fell into a corner pocket with another stopping close to the side. With his break and second shot, he had sunk three of his balls. His third shot left another easy miss in front of another pocket, denying his opponent its use.

The mark ran two balls and inadvertently knocked in another of Brown's solids. Brown had three balls left, and the mark's last shot had left Brown with easily made shots. The eight was buried in a cluster of striped balls. Brown decided to call the eight in a corner pocket, knowing it couldn't be made. This was a setup shot that allowed Brown to play safe and move the eight into a better position. The mark then made an easy bank shot into the side, still leaving four balls and the eight. He sunk one other and missed, leaving Brown with a lengthwise bank shot, calling the eight into the corner pocket. Game over!

Fred could see that Brown's "lucky play" was anything but. He watched the mark become continually frustrated by the positions Brown left him in. The man believed that Brown was an unaccomplished pastime player that had run into a two-game winning streak by happenstance.

As Brown picked up the winnings, Fred watched the man mentally squirm, telling himself that he was the better player. He knew he could beat Brown at any time. It was just lucky rolls of the balls that made the difference. If he could just persuade Brown to play one more game for $40, he'd come out on top. The hook rested deep in the mark's mouth.

"You can't leave now!" he exclaimed. "After all, I'd think you'd agree that you've had a run of luck."

"I have to admit that I've never won two straight games at any time before this afternoon," Brown offered. "I would be pushing it to continue after a streak like this. For me to play one more game, I would have to have a lot of incentive."

The mark reached in his back pocket and pulled out two $50 bills and slammed them on the table. Brown looked at the bills and then at Fred.

"I don't know!" Brown said, letting his voice crack a bit. "If I lost this kind of money, his mother would have my head examined. I must say I'm tempted. What do you think, son?"

"I won't tell if you won't," Fred replied, "and if your luck holds, you can get mother that contraption she's been pestering you about."

Brown reached into his front pocket and brought out three crisp twenties and laid them on the C note. He chalked his cue and gave the man the honor to break. The balls damn near left the table the mark hit the rack so hard. One striped and one solid fell. The man took the solids as his balls and was able to made a third. Brown approached the table and slowly repeated the prior game plans, achieving the same result. The man threw his cue on the table and stomped out, muttering to himself. After the man had left the building, Brown turned to Fred.

"His ego won't let him believe that his loses were just an opponent's lucky play," Brown said, handing Fred one of the fifties. "He'll be back here tomorrow or the next day recovering his losses from some wannabe hustler."

Fred stared at the greenback in his hand. He had never seen one, much less hold one. He had twenty in his boot, a bunch of fives and tens in his pocket, and a $50 bill in his hand.

"Don't look so surprised!" Brown cautioned. "You'll be seeing those and more if my hunch about you pays off. The play you saw is the safest way to stake yourself before you go after the big money players."

Olive Street and
Tennessee Brown

BROWN AND FRED LEFT the Market Street pool hall and headed toward Olive Street where the better class billiard rooms were located. While they walked, Brown continued his lectures on the world of pocket billiards and hustling. There were many nuances in the game of pool. Fred was eager and wanted to please Brown. He repeated in his mind every sentence, especially those that were emphasized. He saw this as an opportunity to made significant dollars and help his family's financial burdens.

The couple reached Olive and turned up the street. Looking ahead, Fred saw a sign announcing The Fagan Boys Billiard Room. Brown had told him previously that this was one of the places haunted by the best players. It was at Fagan Brothers that John Layton and Bob Cannefax played on a regular basis. Layton was one of the world's greats. He went on to win the World Pocket Billiard Title in 1916, and he was to be the Three-Cushion Champion in 1919. Brown wanted Fred to meet these players and watch them closely and eventually play them. Brown had emphasized the need for Fred to practice straight billiards in order to learn ball control and the overall geometries of the game.

As they entered the building, almost everyone turned toward them. Soon, all were greeting Brown. Those not engaged in active games made their way from the bar and tables to come shake Brown's hand and give him cordial pats on the shoulders and back.

"Good to see you, Tennessee!" said the man behind the bar.

"Tennessee Brown! It's been a long time!" yelled one man looking up from a table in the back.

The older of the Fagan brother came up and asked, "Who's this tall drink of water?" He referred to Fred.

"Gentlemen, I'd like to introduce my son, Fred," Brown proudly announced to the assembled crowd. "I thought it was about time to bring him along to see St. Louis and meet some real pool players."

With that, everyone was shaking Fred's hand and greeting him in the same fashion they greeted Brown. One thing that Brown hadn't mentioned was the fact that he had a moniker, Tennessee Brown. Fred thought about it and decided he liked it. It had a special flare to it.

"Watch out, boys! This young man will make his mark in billiards someday. Mark my words. He's beaten me!" Brown announced to all gathered.

Fred noticed a man slowly making his way from a table in the back. As he got closer, Fred saw that he had a wooden leg. It was Bob Cannefax. Brown had told him that Bob was one of the great players of the time and would actually pawn his leg so that he could play for money if the need arose. He had a passion for pocket billiards and great confidence in his ability to always recover his prosthetic from the pawn.

Johnny Layton was expected to come in that evening, and Brown mentioned that he wanted his son to meet him. In the same breath, he suggested that some of the clientele should play Fred. It seemed most were eager to give Fred a go. It wasn't long before Fred was involved in contests. Brown staked Fred at $5 a game. As the evening approached, more men and a few women had entered Fagan's and got caught up in the action when they realized it was Brown's son playing. As usual, Brown made side bets as he rated the players that challenged Fred. If he thought it was going to be a route, he even gave odds.

Fred won all his games except his first one with Cannefax. The first game was close. Fred lost by four balls in straight pool. The second was completely different, Fred ran fifty balls right after Bob missed his twenty-fourth shot. It was an impressive showing for a boy of fourteen against men that had been playing for years. Many said he was a natural, and with a little more experience, he would be tough to beat.

At six thirty, Brown decided it was time for supper and they should return to the hotel and freshen up. After dinner, Brown decided to return with Fred to Market Street and the pool halls along there and Broadway. These halls were predominately Black hangouts. Missouri had been a slave state since 1821 and was a point of contention during the civil war as it was considered a border state. Black Americans were still being treated as second-class citizens in and around St. Louis. Many had menial jobs that paid little, and a good number lived across the river in East St. Louis.

Small-time White hustlers would frequent these haunts, hoping to skin their Black opponents. Most were White trash and were marginally good. Such was the mark Brown had taken earlier in the day. Brown felt Fred could do well on his own after his showing at Fagan's. Over dinner, he exposed his plan for that night. It amounted to Brown playing whomever he could enlist and knowing when to quit, suggesting to more enthusiastic players that they might fare better playing his son. In which case, he could maximize the betting on the side.

Brown looked at Fred across the table and said, "I want you to take what I'm telling you as seriously as if your life and mine depends on it. These rooms can be tricky and dangerous as some losers can get ugly. When we go in and sit down, I want you to ask the bartender where the restroom is, usually in the back by the rear door. Check the door to make sure it's not locked. Then check the crapper to see if it has a window. A window a man can get through if the need arises. Some of these guys are not the good-natured Negroes you may be familiar with in Alton. They'd cut you up as soon as look at you. We played early in the day this morning. At night, more folks will be in these halls. Most are off daywork, so they have fresh dollars to gamble and drink. Drinking makes many men ugly, and losing just adds to it."

Fred had been in schoolyard and ball field fights, but this was a seriousness he'd not seen in Brown before. He remembered the problem with Dick Lynn's father and the anger demonstrated. He took every word to heart and was very attentive to this part of the training. He knew gambling was a serious business and debts especially.

"How will I know when the situation has become dangerous?" Fred asked.

"I will pull on my right ear," he returned. "This is when I'll hand you money and send you to the bar to get me a drink. Order the drink and pay the man and say you'll be right back from the restroom. Leave by the back door or window and get away to wherever we are staying. In St. Louis, it's the hotel or Fagan's if it's closer. Tell the boys you met today that I might be in trouble and bring them running. I've been in tight places before, but I wouldn't want to face your parents if you were hurt in some way because of me. You will have most of our winnings and be safe and able to get home!"

"What will you do?" asked Fred.

"I'll miss my next shot," he said. "And then while the mark is shooting, I'll excuse myself saying that I wonder where my boy and drink are. With the bet on the table, I have some options. I can go back and lose or gracefully extract myself from the potential confrontation."

Fred nodded, and they finished dinner. They left the hotel and made their way to Market Street. Entering the same place they had been earlier, Brown picked out a table and paid the bartender for its use. The place was starting to build a crowd as the two began playing eight ball. The light from outside was fading fast, and the smoky air became more obvious under the table lights. Brown acted as if he was teaching his son the game and both were playing way below their abilities. This was a ploy Brown had used in the past when hustling with the boys from Fagan's.

Men wandered by the tables looking at the play. Some were just curious, but others were looking for what they perceived as an easy mark. Brown and Fred were making their play a very obvious opportunity. It wasn't long before the pigeon that had circled the room came back to the table.

"Are you boys open fur friendly wagering?" the heavyset Black man asked. "Or are you's just playin' fur fun?"

"I was just showing my son what it is like to play in a billiard hall," Brown offered. "We have a 4×8 table at home, and these bigger tables are a bit more challenging."

This narrative fit well in this environment. Their dress was far above the folks that patronized this place. In this instance, the obvious difference made them a shiny object that looked ripe for the picking.

"Well, would five dollahs be awright?" he offered, reaching into his overalls.

"That suits me," Brown quipped. "I don't like my boy gambling at his age."

The money was matched, and the play began. Brown started by losing the first game handily. The mark, thinking he could press the gent, wanted to double up. Brown agreed, and the hustle was on. Brown began the lucky routine he used earlier, and the games proceeded with the Black man thinking it just wasn't his day. After losing four games and the better part of $60, the mark was down to his last five. He looked longingly at the greenback and slowly sat it down. Brown matched it and let the man barely win.

"I's betta stop furs I's cleaned out!" the man moaned. He stuffed the two fives in his shirt pocket, turned, and left the building.

Brown told Fred to keep an eye on the door in case he comes back. He also told Fred to go use the toilet while he racked up the balls. Fred returned a few minutes later.

"You practice some while I go relive myself," Brown said, heading to the bar. "You hold the kitty while I'm gone."

Brown returned, and by ten o'clock, they had amassed almost three hundred, and it was time to move on. They left the joint and walked to Fagan's. On the way, Brown informed Fred that it was usually this time of night that the big money players dropped in at Fagan's.

"If there's an opportunity, I'll play for one hundred or so a game. You watch and study how it goes. We'll head home tomorrow."

The evening passed, and they headed back to the hotel about 1:00 a.m. Brown had added an additional $600 for the effort. The train to Alton didn't leave till eleven fifteen. They had plenty of time to have a late breakfast and make the train. With the past two days swirling in his head, Fred nodded off as soon as he hit the bed. He had absorbed a great deal of information and skills he planned to practice when he got back. He also was carrying $300 that he could help the family with. He looked out the window and thought how special trains were. They were a means of coming and going. He had watched them every day pulling in and out of Alton, especially the passenger coaches. People were going somewhere. He knew he had itchy feet and he needed to see more. The trip to St. Louis was his tipping point. He would travel and never slow down. For now though, he was content to daydream. He thought back to when he was twelve.

*****

For as long as he could remember, trains were part of his life. He viewed them as a means of getting away and seeing new places and people. His mom called it the "itchy foot." The only problem with trains was the rails. One could only go where they went. He decided there were too many places that trains didn't go, and those were places he wanted to see. Trains were heavy and bulky, and he wanted to travel quickly and light.

In 1910, the Model T Ford had been on the market for almost two years, and the motorcar was slowly replacing carriages and horse-drawn wagons. One day, before heading home, he passed a new business that had opened. Inside through the glass doors, he saw the shiny bright object that would soon take possession of his fancy, a Model T. He stared at it so hard that he lost track of time. It was light and racy in his mind. He thought, *Now here's the real freedom to travel wherever he wanted!*

He would visit the showroom as often as he could, running his hand over its body parts. Eventually, the man inside approached him.

"Are you wanting to buy an automobile?" he asked, smiling at the young lad before him.

"Yes, I would!" Fred expelled in a breath of enthusiasm. "How much?"

"For you, ten cents," he returned.

He was amazed that it could be so affordable. He wondered why more people didn't have one. He plunked down his dime and ran out the door. He was surprised that an adult would give him such special treatment. He hurried to the vacant lot he and his friends played ball on, looking for as much help as he could gather to help him retrieve his new possession. He returned with three other boys. The salesman was nowhere in sight, but his dime was on the desk. He opened the parting glass doors, jumped behind the wheel as he and his helpers pushed the auto into the adjoining yard and out into the street.

They had pushed the car about one hundred feet when a policeman stepped in front of them and raised his hand.

"Hey! Where are you taking this?" he inquired, exhibiting a frown.

"Home!" Fred answered in excitement. "I just bought it!"

"Really?" the officer returned.

"Yes!" he said, pointing to the showroom from which he had just left. "You can ask the man inside."

"Let's do just that, young man," he said, directing the boys in that direction.

As they entered the showroom, the salesman was coming through a door in the back. The officer hailed him asking if these boys had bought an automobile from him. Suddenly, the man realized something was missing. He looked outside and was astonished that his new car had moved down the street. Gathering from the two's conversation, the salesman had jokingly told Fred the car was only ten cents. The officer chuckled and saw the dime on the desk as he bent over laughing.

He handed Fred the dime and said, "This man wasn't serious as much as you were serious about buying it! I hope you both have learned something!"

He then turned to the salesman and said, "Go get your car out off the street and stop teasing impressionable boys!"

Fred was mortified. He would be the butt of his friends' humor for days over this incident. He gave up playing baseball for a few days and kept a low profile, waiting for the entire escapade to blow itself out. He vowed that he would have an automobile as soon as he could afford one.

*****

The train pulled into Alton. Fred thanked Brown and headed for home. He was excited to show the family the money he had made helping Mr. Brown on his business trip. He had rehearsed his story when asked to relate exactly what he had done for Brown. He told them he helped Brown distribute sundries of a nature that supplied the higher-end hotels in St. Louis. It satisfied all concerned, and the extra dollars came at a good time for the family. His father's trip to the Oklahoma sanatorium had been expensive and had taken most of the family's savings. After two days in Oklahoma, John Whalen missed his family and realized no amount of rest and therapy was going to make a difference in his condition. He checked himself out and returned home. Fred's mother was happy to see her son well and successful in his business venture with Mr. Brown. His father had just been back a day and was resting in the bedroom.

"What's all the excitement over!" he asked as he left his bed.

"John, Fred is back from his trip to St. Louis where he helped Mr. Brown with his business," she explained.

John nodded his approval and hugged his son. Fred helped him to a nearby chair and expounded on his trip to St. Louis. He described the hotel and the things he saw. He especially talked about the dinners and how Mr. Brown dealt with the people he met. All this had been rehearsed in his mind so that the explanations were seamless.

"Will Mr. Brown need your help in the future?" asked his father.

"He thought that I might accompany him in the fall when he expects to resupply the hotels with soaps and other items," Fred responded.

He started feeling bad about the tale he was offering because he'd always been truthful with his parents. He consoled those guilt feelings by telling himself that it was for the good of the family and they needed the dollars more than the truth. That became his truth and lessened the feeling of being ashamed that had welled up in him as he expanded the lie.

John soon went back to work, and for the next few weeks, everything seemed normal. Fred began looking for other work as he had given his lucrative paper business to a close friend. He had thought about being a salesman, and after all, that was a profession that supported the story he had given his family. He saw many ads in the newspapers that gave the impression that sales were a good moneymaker and would be easy to master. In fact, some even went as far as suggesting that one could make large sums of income if one worked hard.

Fred's mother's brother, Brad Twyman, was a professional gambler. He generally played poker in all its various forms and was quite good at it. He was a handsome and generous man who, when visiting, would give his sister and him $5 to spend at the nearby amusement park. He was tall and well built with white hair and fine clothes. He had a look of distinction and reminded him of Mr. Brown. Fred decided that he wanted to be like him, traveling to many places and living a life of many adventures. Mr. Brown had given him a good start and a foundation in the art of gambling on one self's abilities.

Fred and his older cousin, Junior, decided on a moneymaking venture involving apple trees that were growing in various parts of his father's farm. His aunt would gather them to make pies and such, but for the most part, they would just rot on the ground. Uncle Ben told them to have at it. They gathered some bushel baskets and began sifting through fallen apples and picking good ripe ones still hanging in the trees. They would sell the apples along the residential streets, door to door. They got $1 per bushel. On one street that was two blocks long, they had our best sales. This was Pissel Street, Alton's red-light district. Fred realized it was a particularly adult place with a lot of traffic coming and going. In some cases, men sat on the porches of the houses there, smoking and pacing back and forth. They found that they could sell apples at a nickel apiece to the patient clientele, some sitting in their automobiles.

Fred had known about Pissel Street, and it was a curiosity that most boys his age had. After baseball games, the boys would dare each other to go down to Pissel and sample the wares. The boys would even suggest chipping in the funding if any one of them would take the plunge, so to speak. None of the boys had the nerve to consider the offer. They would listen to older men on the sly just to hear the goings on behind the porch doors of Pissel Street.

This wasn't Fred's first trip onto the two-block stretch. The thought of what was going on there did give him a reaction that seemed quite pleasurable, similar to what he had started to experience in his sleep. The feelings that rose up were a bit embarrassing, and he wondered if it were noticeable. He and his cousin would always go there last with any leftover produce they had.

The two boys made many trips to Pissel Street but would just laugh nervously to each other when some patrons would suggest they drop the apples and venture into a particular place. It was on one of these visits that Fred developed a young man's passing affection for one of the working girls.

She was very pretty and wore white high-buttoned shoes. Soon every trip to the area required him to take his time going up and down the street with their apples, looking to see his new distraction. He knew the girl was much older than him, but still he fantasized meeting her even if not in a professional setting. It was during one of his forays onto Pissel that a woman emerged from the front door of the house he and his cousin were walking up to. As they reached the porch, she stepped forward and took Fred's arm. She pulled him, apple basket and all, through the front door.

"You come right in here, youngster, and let me take care of you!" she said, looking at Junior standing dumbfounded frozen on the porch. "I'll come back for you next!"

The room was dimly lit with the curtains drawn and light filtering through the window. The curtains wafted as the heated air rushed inside with the closing of the door. The woman was in a satin-like robe with loud flowers busting out all over it. She untied the cloth waist belt and took his hand into the gap that now exposed her breasts. She placed his hand over one as she reached to unbutton his pants.

"How does it feel?" she asked, still working on his buttoned pants. "I'll bet this is a new experience for you!"

Fred was tongue-tied for the moment trying to think of something to say that wouldn't sound particularly childish.

"Soft, isn't it?" she whispered, leaning into him next to his ear.

"It feels very nice," was all he could think to say.

By this time, his pants had fallen to the floor, exposing a very erect appendage bumping into her thigh. His face flushed as they both looked down at his excitement. The tips of his shoes protruded out from under his stacked pant legs, and for a second, he felt all the blood rush from his head. He wobbled, but she steadied him.

"Don' worry about your shoes, just hobble over to the daybed here." She guided him in the general direction. "It'll be just dandy, and it is a dandy!"

She sat back on the bed, pulling herself further on to it, dragging Fred down between her outstretched legs. He collapsed on top of her, shifting his hands from her breasts to the bed. He had awakened with erections before but nothing of this magnitude. It was so big it hurt. The woman was rather large, and he was cushioned on her stomach. He wasn't sure just where everything was, but he knew it must be close. In frustration, he tried to think of something to say.

"Put me in there!" he asked, not knowing really how to handle the situation.

"You are in there, honey!" she returned, smiling up at him.

With the realization that he was, in fact, THERE, it was over! He felt the release of the pent-up tension and all that went with it. He pushed back from the bed and quickly pulled up and buttoned his pants. He rushed out the door, passed Junior, and off the porch.

"Where are the apples?" Junior shouted, running after him.

"She can keep them!" Fred answered, looking back over his shoulder.

*****

The summer of 1912 passed as most did in small Midwestern towns. Earlier that spring, the *Titanic* had sunk, and there were still articles in the paper about the tragedy and the fall out about the peoples' lives that had been changed. The related stories were more about the rich and famous who perished and less about those regular passengers unless, of course, they were a person from someone's home area. Fred thought about the number of papers he had sold that April due to the sinking. He ran his tail back and forth from the printers because everybody wanted to read about it and probably wanted to save it for various reasons.

He was beyond paper hawking now. He would visit Brown's Hotel in the afternoons and play his mentor, refining his skill and gaining more confidence as he did so. Fred knew the big money games were 14.1 straight pool. He practiced running fifty or more balls every chance he got. The repetitiveness of the practice wasn't work. He truly enjoyed the game and the angular essence of it all.

Fall was approaching, and Brown mentioned that it was time to make another play in St. Louis. They would be leaving in a week, and he should let his parents know. John Whalen had been working most days through the summer, and there had been hope that he was slowly getting better. In mid-August, he collapsed walking home from the yards. As was Fred's custom, he met his father and walked with him home. John began a coughing fit and doubled over, blood oozing from between his lips. Fred grabbed him and slowly let him down unto the ground. They sat there a while as Fred wiped the perspiration and blood from his father's face.

"I guess I'm not as well as I thought," he choked, looking at his son.

"It's fine, Dad. I'll get you home and you can rest. You'll be better tomorrow," he replied.

"I'm not so sure, son!" he coughed.

"The doctors didn't want me to come home, but I couldn't bare being away from you and the family any longer," he continued. "I may have to go back to Oklahoma and see what happens."

"Don't worry about us," Fred consoled. "I'll make sure we're good at home. Just do what the doctors want and get better."

"I'm glad that you have a position helping Mr. Brown," he said, holding onto Fred's shoulder. "Your mother will need the help your wages have provided."

Once at the house, John was taken to bed. The family gathered about him and decided that the sanatorium was the best hope and that Edgar would get him resettled there. Winifred knew this was serious and that Oklahoma was his best chance of getting better even though she knew lung fever was never cured.

It was September and time to head to St. Louis with Mr. Brown. Fred kissed his mother and sister goodbye and left Alton with Brown. The train ride had a different feel this time. He'd changed since the first trip. He'd become more self-reliant and confident; he could make his way in the world as it now presented itself. He knew the plan and would react accordingly. He trusted Brown's judgment, and he knew he could hold up his end.

They checked into the hotel and began, as before, on Market and Broadway playing would-be hustlers and building a bankroll of cash. Between the table wagers and the side bets at the bar, Fred and Brown had compiled close to a thousand dollars. The afternoon sun was heading into its western climax when the pair left Market and turned to Olive Street. Just ahead was Fagan's Billiard Hall. The street was starting to fill with people leaving work, heading to a variety of establishments that made it a nighttime destination. It was a Saturday night, marking the end of the usual six-day workweek that was typical in the early twentieth century. A hustler could smell the money.

Brown had introduced Fred to the Fagan crowd on the first trip. This time, upon their entry, the patrons immediately called out Tennessee and began greeting Young Tennessee Brown, his prodigy son. Fred swelled with a sense of pride and the promise of greater success. Brown who nodded to him matched his enthusiasm with a wink. This was going to be their night. He would let his mentor select his challengers.

Fred warmed up on the good players until Brown directed the better players his way. The results were as predicted. Young Tennessee Brown made them believers. Johnny Layton hadn't come in yet but was expected around ten as he was prone to do. In the interim, Cannefax had arrived and wanted to give Fred another game for a hundred. Fred's cue was hot. He'd been playing for hours and was only gaining more experience and confidence. Bob Cannefax had just come in and may have been a bit cold. Although it was a contested match of 14.1, Fred was the victor, running sixty-one balls and out after Bob missed his forty-sixth.

As they shook hands and exchanged table talk, Layton walked in. This was his realm, and he knew it. Layton exchanged pleasantries with everyone and headed to the table he always played on. Brown remained in the back where Fred was playing, not wanting to attract unneeded attention to either of them. The man who had entered with him limbered up his cue, and it was obvious that the two men had planned to play this night at Fagan's. Fred looked over in Layton's direction through the swirling smoke that flowed under the table lights as players moved about their respective tables. Fred decided to make fast work of his current opponent and took a seat in the shadows watching Layton's play. He had to admit Johnny was a pool technician. Carefully analyzing each approach and shot. He was everything Brown had described. The most important aspect was that Layton had an ego that was easily bruised. He could be goaded into making mistakes because his temper matched his ego.

Layton was about to close the game with his imported opponent. Fred saw an opening to move past him as he was about to poise for a final shot. He purposely brushed Johnny's cue as he passed behind him. Layton became angry, and Fred was ready for a reaction.

"Get that boy out of here!" he ordered, looking in Fred's direction.

He then bent over the table and sank his last ball. Fred had taken a seat.

Fred sat down, pulled a wad of bills from his pocket, and began counting them loudly so that he became obvious to all around and especially, Layton.

The youngster was becoming an obvious distraction to all around Layton's table, taking some of the glitter off his recent thrashing of his quest.

"One, two, three hundred, four hundred…" Fred slowly peeled off bill after bill, snapping them for added effect; Layton had to respond.

"You've got a lot of money there, lad," Layton declared for everyone's benefit. "Do you think you want to risk it playing me?"

Fred answered the question as casually as it was asked, "I wouldn't mind trying my hand. After all, you're John Layton, one of the best."

Layton walked over and extended his hand. "You know my name, but whom do I have the pleasure of playing?" he asked.

"Freddie Brown! Young Tennessee Brown!" Fred returned.

Fred liked his moniker and was proud to exhort it in front of all within earshot. Everyone looked to Tennessee for a reaction, but Brown just smiled. Brown knew this had to happen and believed Fred had a good chance. He knew Layton would underestimate the kid, and that was Fred's edge and Johnny's Achilles' heel. The kid had already irked him with the cue brush and loudly displaying his money.

"How much you willing to risk here, son?" asked Layton.

"You tell me how much action you want," Fred responded. "I've got five hundred here. If I lose, I'm sure you won't waste another game on me!"

"Let's say four hundred," he suggested, concluding with, "you'll still have a hundred left to get home!"

"That suits me, Mr. Layton," said Fred, offering a tidbit of respect that caught Layton off guard but fed his ego.

"Why don't you break?" offered Layton. "Fourteen point one, first player to fifty balls takes the money."

The players handed their cash to Tommy Fagan and proceeded to chalk their cues. Fagan racked the balls, and Fred moved to the opposite end for the break. Fred controlled his confidence. He knew this was a pivotal game in his early career and that it would require absolute concentration. He knew his advantage was slight as Layton would be overconfident playing a beginner. Johnny had played novices before and had easily beaten them. This was going to be a repeat of past thrashings. He felt letting Fred break was his advantage. Beginners always over broke the rack, usually leaving themselves with a difficult second shot. Layton could then step in and run the table in continuous rack.

Fred's breaking stroke was close to perfection. He spread the rack and left his cue ball in perfect position. Layton acknowledged Fred's good leave and had to play safe. He granted the kid would sink his first shot. After the first ball dropped, Fred's use of the cue ball to further separate the pack while sending the cue ball into another great position was nothing short of great play. Layton, who had been standing close by the table, was expecting to start shooting after Fred's second shot. It wasn't to be. Layton took a seat, believing it was just a matter of time before Fred would miss.

Fred ran the first fourteen balls, leaving the fifteenth ball in a perfect break position for the next rack. Fred sank the break ball with an authority that blew the rack apart, leaving a plethora of possible following shots. Young Tennessee Brown never looked back. As Fagan racked the balls for the fourth time, Layton could hardly sit still. He writhed in the stool where he sat, watching this boy take the table apart. Fred reached fifty balls and back away from the table. The room exploded. No one had ever seen a player take Layton without him ever making a stroke, much less an obvious teenager.

Fagan walked over to Fred and handed him the pot. Eight hundred dollars! It was not only the largest gamble Fred had made to that point but one he would never forget. He turned to face Layton and thank him for the game, but in the commotion, Johnny had left the building. Someone said later, "He left with his cue between his legs!"

Fred was high with excitement. The entire place was rocking with the feeling that something extraordinary had unfolded before their eyes. Fred looked for Tennessee and found him standing along the wall smiling broadly. In his mind, Fred envisioned his father standing there and wished it were so. He wondered if his father would ever see him win, much less approve.

Brown walked over to Fred, patting him generously on the back and putting his arm over his shoulder. He nodded toward the door, and they moved with a bit of difficulty to the exit. People still wanted to shake Fred's hand and pat his back. Someone started chanting, "Young Tennessee Brown!" Fred reveled in his newfound fame. As they turned up the street, the hum of Fagan's was still in their ears. They were heading to the hotel when Brown stopped and told Fred to look back.

"Remember this night!" he counseled. "You will have many occasions to savor this kind of victories, but this one, at Fagan's, will stay with you until you close your eyes for the last time."

Fred paused and looked down to Fagan's, etching the scene into his memory. He appreciated the sentiment and wished he could have been a fly watching himself play Layton. He had been confident in his ability, yet he realized it could have easily gone the other way. He thought of Johnny Layton. How must he feel? Layton lost in his own church of worshippers without taking a shot. Fred trusted his ability but was aware that luck played its part. He would never take the outcome for granted. It was a contest of wills as much as talent. He had willed himself to win. He envisioned himself the winner.

It was close to midnight, and the streets were thinning out. Brown realized that neither of them had eaten anything since breakfast. He pointed up the street to a restaurant, turning at the same time to look back. They were being followed. Brown opened the door, letting Fred enter first while he watched two figures duck into the shadows.

The pair sat down at a small table and ordered steak and eggs. After the waiter left the table, Brown informed Fred of his suspicion.

"It might be nothing Fred, but I think we're being shadowed," he cautioned, passing a thick wad of bills onto Fred's lap. The money rested on top of Fred's napkin. The weight of it surprised him.

"This is a lot of money!" Fred whispered, looking directly at Brown.

"I took this table in back so as not to be as visible from the street," he returned. "I made twelve hundred betting Layton believers. In all, there's two thousand dollars there. I want you to take a sip of water and choke. Grab your napkin with the money wrapped in it, holding it to your mouth and cough your way back to the kitchen. Ask the chief for the back door and say you might be sick. Carefully leave and head to the hotel. I'll pay the waiter when I finish and meet you in our room."

Fred didn't hesitate. He sipped the water and began choking up the liquid, raising the napkin to his mouth and backing from the table and knocking over his chair. He made his way into the kitchen and was shown the back door. He looked both ways, but the alley was dark and wagons were spotted here and there along its course. He quickly walked to the end and turned away from Olive and put distance between himself and the restaurant.

His first thought was to go to Fagan's and get help, but he obeyed Brown's wishes and got safely to the hotel. He got his room key and made his way up the stairs.

Two men entered the restaurant and walked over to the bar. They looked around until they saw Brown sitting at a table in the back. Brown was alone, so they asked the waiter as he passed, "Didn't that gent come in here with a kid?"

"Yes, he did," he answered, "but the boy was choking and went to the sink in the back."

The men looked at each other, and the larger of the two walked toward the kitchen. Brown had been watching the two since they entered the place and decided he was correct in sending Fred out the back with the money. The waiter returned with the two meals, placing the plates on the table.

"Could you bring me the check and some butcher paper?" he asked. "My son isn't feeling well and probably returned to our hotel."

When the waiter returned, Brown paid the tab and asked him to wait a second while he tore of some paper and scribbled a short note. He tipped the waiter and handed him an extra $2.

"I see two friends of mine at the bar," he said. "Would you give them this note and a beer on me?"

The waiter hailed the bartender and ordered two beers.

"Compliments of your friend at the table," he said. "He asked me to give you this note."

The smaller of the two unfolded the paper and read it aloud to his partner, "Better luck next time, gents. That was my last two bucks!"

The men looked at each other and then to Brown's table. He'd had gotten up and was walking out with three men who had finished their dining and were leaving.

Fred was anxious about leaving Brown alone in the restaurant. He began pacing the room, trying to decide his best course of action. An hour had almost passed since his arrival at the hotel. He decided he would head back and try to find a policeman along the way. As he reached the door, he saw the handle turn. Stopping as he began to reach for the door, it swung open. There was Brown holding a wrapped paper bundle.

"Had the waiter wrap dinner up for me," he said. "I thought we'd better eat in our room!"

Brown took the package to the table, noticing that it was covered in greenbacks that had spilled from Fred's napkin. He smiled and moved the money off to the side and began unwrapping their meal. Fred sighed with unexpected relief and pulled up two chairs, throwing the loot on the closest bed. Fred was full of questions about what had transpired at the restaurant.

Brown answered each one, playing down the seriousness of the encounter. Fred especially enjoyed the part about the note and complimentary beers.

The morning arrived early. Fred was ready to continue playing in the St. Louis billiard halls, but Brown felt they should head back to Alton, leaving the boys at Fagan's with something to talk about. Brown knew that by the time they returned, the successes of the prior night would have been exaggerated into legend. The telling and retelling of his win over Johnny Layton will have circulated around the pool universe in a matter of days, making every would-be hustler a potential challenger of Young Tennessee Brown.

Farewell, Alton

AFTER THEIR RETURN TO Alton, Fred decided that it was time to find a regular-paying job. Alton was no St. Louis, and the chances of finding big money games there was not a possibility. He wasn't averse to physical labor and began answering want ads in the paper. His first job was at the Illinois Glass Factory pulling molten glass from the fire kilns. He tried this for a week but decided that it could be dangerous if his hands became burned or worse.

His uncle Billy was an electrician and needed a helper. He worked for his uncle for a few months and decided that pulling wire and the chance to be electrocuted was not for him. At fourteen going on fifteen, he felt that the last two jobs were more in an adult's job description.

His father was still in Oklahoma, and the money that Fred had brought back from St. Louis had about played out as it was directed to the sanatorium and his father's care. It was decided that he would go work for his uncle Ben and aunt Ollie in Upper Alton. It was the farm he and his cousin had gathered apples on to sell in town. He hadn't done farm work up to that point, but being around the greenery of the country and fresh air appealed to him. It was an improvement over life in town. The tainted air from the steel mill and the railroad became an unwanted memory of his past life. He thrived on the freshness of it all and grew a bit heavier and taller.

The few months at Uncle Ben's came to an abrupt end when he received word that his father had returned home. Aunt Ollie thought it best that Fred return as the prognosis was not favorable and that his father might not be with them for much longer. Fred hurried home to spend time with his father.

The lung fever had progressed to a point that caused frequent coughing spells that wore heavily on John Whalen's overall condition. Night sweats and bleeding up from his lungs slowly turned into pneumonia. It was at this juncture Fred and his father became even closer. They would sit together in the yard and porch talking and reliving memories of those days that meant the most to their relationship. Fred saw the strength of character and stature that was his father. He understood why those around him respected John for the man he was. His father's steadfastness was what Fred loved the most, his uncompromising devotion to take care of his family.

He knew his father was becoming disappointed as he grew weaker, that he could no longer care for or support his family. Fred would cover him with one of his mother's throws and assure him that he and Edgar would take care of the family. Soon, he was not able to leave his bed. Winnie sent for his brother, Uncle Ben, and the family gathered for John "Stormy" Whalen's last moments.

"Would you put the window down?" he asked, and soon after, "Would you put the window up please?"

This happened a number of times. Fred sat on the bed and held his father's hand as he passed away. Fred was not prone to crying, but watching his father struggle to stay with the living forced him outside where tears came in a flood, choking and gasping. The loss swept over him and consumed what energy he had left. He returned to the house and his parents' bedroom and looked deeply into his father's face. He sat with his father until the darkness outside matched the dark within. He promised himself he would never let his family or loved ones down. In this moment, Fred became a man.

The family decided that they could no longer stay in Alton. The house would be sold. Winifred and his sister, Beulah, would move to St. Louis where they could expect to find employment in the garment houses. Edgar had established himself in the plumbing trade and chose to stay in town. Fred returned to Uncle Ben's farm and worked another year. He would take leave when Mr. Brown traveled to St. Louis and visited with his mother and sister. Over that time,

Fred helped his uncle increase his fruit and vegetable business. They would load the wagon and set out to deliver fresh produce to the markets and hotels. In this way, Fred was always available to attend Brown's Hotel billiard games and keep his skills sharp. It helped that Uncle Ben would stop and play pool at Casey's.

By 1914, conditions in Europe were beginning to deteriorate. Fred had made many more trips to St. Louis with Brown, and his prowess in 14.1 and other pool games was well established. Young Tennessee Brown was the person to challenge. By then, Brown stood in the shadows, making side bets and marveled at how developed Fred's talent had become. Eventually, Brown moved on, letting Fred go his own way. It was time for Fred to move to St. Louis and begin to venture into the adult arena.

PART 2

The Wunderlich Farm

JUST A WAY OUTSIDE St. Louis was the small community of Pacific. Farms, large and small, dotted the landscape, creating a patchwork quilt of earth colors. Brown fields ready for planting, tan-colored winter wheat waiting to be cut, and green sprouting fields of corn and onions waiting for the summer heat to bring them on. At the town's edges, smaller twenty-to-forty-acre places made up a buffered ring, separating the larger plots of 160- to 200- and 300-acre larger farms from the central community. These small places had been larger in the past but overtime had sold off to neighbors as the owners passed and families moved to the big city.

The Wunderlich Farm was at the edge of Pacific and sported a large farm that had once contained a milking parlor and stalls for the horsepower once needed to operate a larger concern. Ferdinand August Wunderlich was a farmer by choice and a stone and tile mason by training. He had learned the skill as a young boy from his father while the family was still in Germany. Having come to America in the 1850s, the family settled outside St. Louis. Ferd and his brothers had settled with a number of cousins in the area and had steadily built their farms and craft trades.

The Wunderlich men were tall big-boned men, well suited for farm and masonry work. Ferd and his wife, Emalene, were a matched pair of draft horses, pulling in the same basic direction but fiery when separated. As with most farmers at the time, outside work kept the family a going concern, and like most farm families, the children were many. In this case, the offspring numbered sixteen. There were three older boys. Charles, Bill, and Jean were the first to arrive in that order. Next were two girls, Lillian and Florence, followed by August and George. They were followed by a set of mixed twins and another girl. As time went on, the family grew by another set of twins and four more after that. It was said that Ema would get with child every time Ferd unbuttoned his pants. The family joke was that Ferd laid Ema more than tile. Someone had said upon visiting Rome, "There's a list of honor scrolled on a wall in the Sistine Chapel declaring Ferd and Ema as Faithful Contributors to the Spread of Catholicism!"

The oldest boys, to help make ends meet, day worked for some of the larger farms around Pacific. During planting and harvesting times, the boys would be gone for weeks, staying at the farms they worked on. During those times, Ema would rent out rooms to travelers, operating a boarding house of sorts that included meals. Gus and George would do the farming chores, and Lilly and Flossie would help their mother around the house. This also meant taking care of the younger children once they were weaned.

Although the family was Catholic, they would sometimes go down to the river to participate in the baptisms and gospel singing that the local Black Baptist congregations would hold at lunchtime on Sundays. Ema had hired a Black woman, Cassie, to help early on after the first two boys were born. Cassie was a young girl of fifteen when she came to the farm. Through the years, she was like an older sister to Lilly and Flossie as well as Gus and George. She would often take them with her to Sunday services where they joined in the singing and praising the gospel. Cassie would help clean the rooms and serve the meals along with the two girls. She'd help put the boys back together after some of their misadventures, the most memorable being Brother George's trying to fly from the Brother Gus didn't take well as he had to double up on chores.

Cassie married a man named Charlie Parker when she was twenty-two. They lived in a small shack-like structure behind the livery in Pacific. Charlie was a blacksmith and eight years older than Cassie. He worked at the livery learning smithing and mechanics from his employer. He had put away money for six years and had courted Cassie for much of that time until he felt he could afford to marry. They tried many times to have children, but miscarriages plagued their attempts. Cassie doted on the Wunderlich babies as if her own. Every Sunday, Charlie and Cassie would take the livery wagon and stop by the Wunderlichs and pick up Ema and the children and take them to the meetings at the river. The children wondered why the morning Mass at the church wasn't fun. They thought the Black Baptist enjoyed their worshipping, especially because it was in English. Ferdinand never went to the river services. He thought one appearance before God was more than enough for any man, especially one who had done yeoman's work bringing so many children into the flock. If the Lord rested on the seventh day, then why not him; after all, he had done his part.

When Gus had spare time, he would walk into town and visit with Charlie. The one horse the family still had needed its hoofs trimmed every couple of months, and it became his excuse to see Charlie work on automobiles. These gas buggies were becoming more and more popular, and Gus was intrigued by the mechanical workings of them. The automobile was more refined than the steam-operated farming machines he'd seen working some of the larger farms. Sometimes, when Charlie had finished working on one, Gus would ride along on a check ride around Pacific. Gus tinkered with many things and found satisfaction in getting them in working order. The windmill on the farm was always breaking down until Gus figured out a way to prevent its periodic failure. There were days he spent too much time with Charlie and came home only to be tongue-lashed by his parents for neglecting his chores at home. Ema didn't like the grease worked into his overalls and made him help with the laundry.

As time went on, Ferdinand sold the farm. The older boys had worked hard and wanted to each have their own operations. With the money he got for the farm, he was able to buy a large house in St. Louis. His masonry business was becoming more involved in the city due to the massive expansion and building boom. Brick and stone buildings were replacing the older frontier wooden structures that had been the St. Louis of the mid-nineteenth century. He staked the boys with the leftover proceeds.

Ferdinand and Ema Wunderlich

Within eighteen months, Ferdinand suffered a heart attack, leaving the family with a serious loss of income. Ema had but one choice, and that was to take in boarders. Running a boarding house was not an easy task for a middle-aged woman with young children still at home. Twelve of the sixteen children were still at home. The house was large enough to add four boarders. These men worked twelve to sixteen hours a day in the factories around St. Louis, spent two hours at meals, and the remainder of the day sleeping. It was this same pattern that brought about Ferd's death.

The boarders that lived at Wunderlich House were steady, dependable men. Their board made the family continue as a going concern. Still, it was barely enough extra to keep the family from going under. The work was constant throughout the days, and on Sundays, the house was for the most part at rest. Flossie, Lil's younger sister, had taken a job in a factory near downtown. The extra money she contributed helped cushion the family when unexpected expenses popped up. George had found outside work and began contributing to their enterprise. Gus got on with Charlie's boss and soon was a mechanical wizard with an aptitude toward anything with moving parts. As the younger children grew, they began helping around the place and cared for those siblings below them.

The older boys would come in from the country every couple of weeks and bring produce from their farms. On occasion, they brought in a butchered pig or a quarter of beef to help their mother and the younger ones. All in all, the world was looking up.

Charlie and Cassie would continue coming by on Sundays, taking the family to prayer meetings at the river. It was during one of these trips that Lil and Gus noticed a flyer for an evangelist's revival being held outside of St. Louis at a nearby barn. They had heard of the meetings but had never ventured out to see one in the flesh. One night, when Flossie had returned from work, Gus asked her if she wanted to join them at one of these barn events.

"Hell no!" she exclaimed in her high-pitched voice. "I don't need to come all the way out there to witness one of these damn revivals. Hell, they have them right downtown in some storefronts not too far from where I work."

"What's it like?" Gus and Lil said in unison.

"Shit, I don't know!" she returned. "We're Catholics! Why in hell would I go there? We hardly go to Mass as it is!"

"I asked Charlie about them, and he said they were noisy and full of folks talking in some dern language that he couldn't make out!" Gus offered.

"He said that the people he saw leaving these things looked like they'd run ten miles!" added Lil.

"It's because they flop around on the floor and jump up and down praisin' the Lord!" said Flossie. "If you were to go, you'd probably leave all battered and bruised, sporting black eyes!"

"Sounds pretty entertaining, Flossie!" Gus proclaimed in a loud voice.

"Let's see if Ma wants to go downtown!" asked Lil.

"Don't you be draggin' Mother down there," warned Flossie.

August J (Gus) Wunderlich

St. Louis Blues

FRED ARRIVED IN ST. Louis in the same manner he had the many times he accompanied Tennessee Brown. He got off the train with his bags and eventually made his way to his mother's house. He had wired them a few days before to let them know of his plans. His sister and mother were happy to have him. They each said it was nice to have a man about the place, and they started right in spoiling him.

He thought he'd be in a better situation all around. He could play pool at night while he looked for some kind of employment. Winifred had subscribed to the *St. Louis Post-Dispatch* and received the newspaper at her home every evening. She looked for outside seamstress work to supplement her and her daughter's factory jobs. Fred went right to searching ads for something that would make sense with his plan to play pool.

The next morning, Fred was out walking St. Louis's busiest streets going door-to-door and shop-to-shop asking the same question, "Do you need a boy?"

It was nearly noon when he walked into G.W. Todd and Company. P.G. Henn was their district manager. He looked at Fred and said, "You're hired! You can start tomorrow morning! Be here at seven."

His first duty for the company was delivery. The Todd Company manufactured a device called a "check protector." After a few weeks, he became their repairman because he took an interest in how they operated and soon developed a better method for keeping them running smoothly. He would deliver new machines and take back the older ones. Normally, these older machines were junked. He knew he could repair them, clean them up, and resale them to new customers. Fred crossed the river into Illinois and sold the first one to a business in Collinsville.

A month later, the business owner in Collinsville called the company about the machine. Having seen the message about the machine, he worried and refused to go into the office the next day. Mr. Henn contacted Fred's mother and had her send him back to work. Mr. Henn was not angry and told him that he would be a great salesman someday.

Todd and Company came out with a check-writing machine that worked in tandem with the protector. The check writer would perforate a check for an amount, making it difficult to alter or increase the check. When the new machine came out, Fred mastered it quickly and impressed Mr. Henn. He was so taken by the boy's interest in the company products that he took him to the New York company that assembled the machines. The original machine was made with copper-type fonts for printing the amounts. These copper font types would wear down and become ineffective, allowing a clever person to alter the amounts. After demonstrating how one could alter a check using the copper, they replaced the type with steel fonts. Mr. Henn raised Fred's pay to $20 a week, which was a lot of money in 1915.

He began playing for money after a week on the job with Todd Company. His pool playing was bringing in an extra twenty to $30 a week. He was Todd's youngest employee, ambitious and confident in his skill as a pool player. Fred had never thought much of banks. He never had enough money around to even consider them. He now had and income of $50 or more a week and didn't spend any leisure time entertaining himself.

The money was piling up under his mattress, and he worried that some disaster might befall the house or even a break-in. After three months, he had quite a stash of cash. Mr. Henn suggested he open an account where Todd did business and save his money. Henn also explained interest earned and writing checks were a better idea than carrying around large sums of money.

Soon he had an account totaling over $1,900. Feeling flush, he decided that he'd take some time and look around St. Louis and all it might offer a young man in entertainment. One of the first treats for Fred was attending a professional baseball game. After all, it was his favorite sport. The St. Louis Cardinals were playing at Robison Field. This was a whole new experience and one he repeated often. Just up the street from Fagan's, he discovered at the corner of Olive and Cardinal a Pentecostal Meeting of the Holy Rollers. If he couldn't get a money game at the pool hall, he'd go and enjoy the excitement the religious folk provided. He was impressed with the collections that this place brought in. When the hat was passed, he noticed the pile of cash as it went by him. He thought, *There's big dollars in religion!* He placed that in his mind's money-scheme file.

There were other distractions in the city, and he wasn't averse to looking into them. The one thing he wouldn't do was drink!

Fred often played in a poolroom across from the Maryland Hotel on Pine Street. Ollie Miller owned the pool hall, and they became friends from the first time he entered his place. The majority of pool players in St. Louis knew Fred as Young Tennessee Brown. His triumph over Johnny Layton years before had solidified his reputation, and many believed he was Tennessee Brown's son. St. Louis was one of the principal hubs for serious pocket billiards, and many of the best players called it home and Miller's was where the best usually played.

Another pool hall was Charlie Peterson's at Sixth Street and Olive. Fred played Alfred DeOro at Peterson's. Charlie arranged an exhibition, promoting it as a one-hundred-point game between DeOro and Young Tennessee Brown. DeOro, at the time, was the World Champion. Fred beat him in a close match in front of a paying crowd. Each was given $75 for the match.

DeOro took Charlie aside and said, "Charlie, keep an eye on this kid. He'll be World Champion someday."

Miller held the Missouri State Championship at his place on Pine Street. The primus was whomever won the championship would meet all comers at Ollie's at eight o'clock on that next Saturday evening. The current state champion was a fellow named Jack Butterfield who had beaten Rickly recently, the former champion. Fred won the title, beating Butterfield badly. He then took on all comers for nine straight Saturdays. Miller paid him $25 per Saturday to play challengers. This was good money in 1915. It all came to an end after nine weeks when no one would challenge Fred. One thing that Fred had learned from his time with Brown was the side betting. For those nine weekends, Fred staked a shill to work the crowd making bets. He split the winnings less the seed money. Within three months Fred had amassed over $4,500 in his bank account.

At sixteen, he was considerably flush. He continued to see Anthony at the tailor shop and had outfitted himself with the best of clothing and accoutrements. His father had given him his gold railroad watch and fob. He now wore a vest and sported that watch when he played. There wasn't much he didn't have access to. There was just one more item that he promised himself years before, an automobile. He remembered the humiliation of believing he could buy one for ten cents. He was determined to make the incident right. He left on the Sunday train for Alton. He would stay at Brown's Hotel.

Fred arrived at Brown's a bit after noon. He walked into the lobby and asked for Mr. Brown. He didn't recognize the desk clerk and thought that his arrival would be a great surprise. Brown came down the staircase and didn't recognize him at first. As the older gentleman drew closer, he paused in his step and marveled at the young man now before him.

He looked to his clerk and said, "Harry, this is Young Tennessee Brown! One of, if not, the best pocket billiard players in the country!"

Fred smiled through his flushed grin at the pomp and ceremony just afforded him by his mentor and stepped forward to hug the smaller man.

"I see you've visited Anthony since we were last together." Brown chuckled. "I'd know his couture anywhere."

"You have to stop using those French words on me," Fred returned. "I only finished eighth grade."

"No one would ever know it by the presence you command."

The pair walked into the billiards lounge and sat down on one of the leather couches that line the walls. Fred caught him up on what had transpired since the time he left Alton. Brown acknowledged that he had heard about the young pool marvel that was beating the best.

"Why are you back in Alton?" he asked.

"Besides visiting you, I have some unfinished business in town," Fred replied. "There is a salesman that requires my special attention."

"It's none of my business, but I'm sure he deserves all you have in store for him." Brown sat back and looked at the first of the two tables in the lounge. "You've come at an opportune moment, Fred." Brown gestured toward the table. "I have a guest from Chicago who could probably use your attention rather than mine."

"Is he good?"

"He's above average and has heard the hotel hosts big dollar games."

"What time do you expect him?" Fred inquired.

"He should be coming down from his room around six."

"Why don't you take his money?"

"I would, but I think he needs a lesson that only you can give him." Brown continued, "You see, he feels that Chicago is the pocket billiard capital of the universe. He claims that he's run the St. Louis players out of his territory. I'm going to let him know that one of that city's best is here and only plays for one thousand dollars a game. I'll let him warm up with a couple of ten-dollar games. You can watch him and decide how you want to take him. I think 14.1 fifty balls should do the trick. A one hundred balls if you feel up to it."

"It's your mark," Fred said. "You make the call. Fifty-fifty split?"

"Like old times!" Brown said, handing Fred the key to his suite. "Get cleaned up and rest at your leisure. I'll be here getting the stage set."

Fred retired to Brown's rooms upstairs. He'd been sitting for a few hours when he decided to walk about the downtown. He wanted to walk past the showroom with the Ford motorcar in it. In two years, the cars hadn't changed that much. He'd seen plenty in St. Louis, and it was time he had one. Some motorcars now had electric starters. He had helped people crank start their autos in the past, and it was a pain in the ass if you had to do it alone. Some even broke wrists and arms using the crank.

When he got to the sales shop, he looked through the glass doors at the model displayed. Shiny and black, just as he recalled on that day he thought he bought one for a dime. He stood there for a moment and felt the embarrassment of the past wash over him. He would make everything right in the morning.

He walked into Casey's Pool Room, seeing that not much had changed since he hawked papers there and first started playing pool. Thoughts of his father rushed into his head, and he became saddened that his success couldn't be shared with the man. He walked to an empty table and rolled a ball across it worn green felt. He turned toward the bar right into Casey, himself, standing behind him. He hadn't heard the man come up behind him, being lost in his thoughts of past times.

"I thought that was you!" Casey exclaimed, with a broadening smile. "You sure have grown into a fine young man."

"Hello, Mr. Casey," Fred replied, reaching to shake his hand.

"Good firm grip. Just like your father," he said. "The place hasn't been as clean as the day you left it."

Fred looked around and had to agree. He had worked hard to keep Casey's trust and patronage. Now he just wanted to pass some pleasantries and shoot a few balls.

"How much for an hour, Casey?" Fred asked.

"On the house, son, you've more than earned it." He smiled. "In fact, you can play here anytime, no charge. You were like a son to me."

"Thanks, Pop!" Fred smiled, watching the smile on Casey's face grow larger.

Fred turned as Casey patted his shoulder and walked over and selected a cue. The sticks weren't the best, but one would do for now. He began shooting 14.1 and ran four racks, counting nearly sixty shots without a miss. He replaced the cue and racked the table. He had done it so many times before when he worked there that it was just an unconscious movement.

He waved to Casey as he left and headed back to the hotel. Tomorrow, he would buy his first motorcar and savor a bit of redemption. For now, he would concentrate on the task at hand, helping Tennessee Brown skin another blowhard.

It was four o'clock, and the hotel lobby was more active. He looked toward the Gentleman's Lounge as proclaimed on the etched glazed doors. He could see that there was quite a bit of activity within its mahogany confines. He smiled and thought the hustle was on! He continued up to Brown's rooms.

At five, there was a knock on the door. As he went to answer, the doorknob turned, and a Black woman in a maid's attire pushed in a rolling silver-trimmed cart with plates of hot food and a pitcher of iced tea.

"Mr. Brown asked me to bring you a little something before he meets you downstairs," she offered, placing the dishes on the table. She turned to leave but Fred stopped her.

"Thank you so much," he said, taking a $5 bill and handing it to her.

"Oh no, Mister Fred!" she cried. "Mr. Brown would fire my Black ass if I took that!"

"I won't tell him," Fred said, "and don't you mention it either."

She gently took the bill in a manner that would make one think the damn paper was on fire. She quickly stuffed it down the front of her bib, blushing a bit and looking down.

"Thank you, Mister Fred! I won't!" She turned and left the room.

Fred ate lightly, not wanting to feel bloated. He had time to dampen his face and brush his teeth. He was combing out his jet-black hair when heard the door open. Looking into the next room, he saw Brown come in, carrying a small leather case. He stepped out to greet him as Brown laid the case on a desk that was over by the windows facing the street below.

"What have you got there?" Fred asked, focusing on the case.

"I was going to bring this to you the next time I was in St. Louis."

Brown clicked the snaps back and opened it, facing Fred. He looked down and saw a beautiful two-piece pool cue. It had a pearl inlaid handle and a finely lacquered shaft. Brown picked up the two sticks and slowly screwed them together and handed it to Fred.

Fred was tongue-tied in that moment. He held it like a fine piece of crystal, slowly turning it in his hands. As the stick turned, he noticed, written in script, Young Tennessee Brown flowing in black letters along the shaft just above the handle. It was light and balanced perfectly in his hand. The shaved tip was rounded to perfection, waiting to be chalked. His mouth dropped open as he continued moving it in his hands. It was a delicate expression of fine art as anything he could imagine. The motorcar now took second place in his mind to this instrument. Instantly, his mind began playing with it in an imaginary game. This all consumed him in less than a second. He gathered his wits about him and slowly returned to the moment.

"I…I can't believe this!" he muttered, try to gain some semblance of composure. "I had thought about having one made. I always admired yours but didn't know who to go to or what!"

Brown's smile could have blinded the pool gods. He reveled in the expressions that rolled like lightning across Fred's face. He could feel Fred's surprise and gratitude as he watched him roll the stick in his hands. It was better than Christmas for both of them. For Brown in particular for he had no family, no offspring, and not a person that meant as much to him as Fred. He often thought, if he had had a son, Fred would be the model.

"How can I ever thank you!" he said.

"You've thanked me often!" Brown returned. "You just weren't aware of it. You've made me proud by your accomplished play and made me realize that in teaching you, I have done something worthwhile! You, like no other, have taken my assistance to heart. Talent like yours is rare, especially at your age. There is one other that I've met that has what you have. Ralph Greenleaf is about your age. He's an Illinois boy and the only match for your talent. He plays around Chicago and will, most likely, play for the World Championship one day. I suspect you will meet each other one day, and I hope I'm around to witness it."

Fred slowly disassembled the cue and placed it back in its case. As he closed the clasps, he looked at Brown and hugged him. He thanked him again and ran his hand down the leather case.

"Don't try using it tonight," Brown cautioned. "You'll need to spend some time with it getting used to its weight and movement between your fingers when you bridge for a shot."

"I wondered," replied Fred. "I'm so used to the hall sticks!"

"Don't play anyone with it until you've gotten its feel and stroke."

Fred pulled his pocket watch, springing the cover. It read five minutes to six. He replaced the timepiece and nodded to Brown. They both turned to the door and left the room. At the top of the stairway, Brown turned to Fred and said, "Take a seat in the lobby while I go into the lounge. I'll see how things have progressed and meet you in the back by the billiard table in about five minutes."

Fred nodded and waited for Brown to reach the lobby. He slowly descended the stairs and took a seat as instructed. Passing the lobby desk, he grabbed a copy of *The Alton Evening Telegraph*. The headlines were mainly about the war news in Europe and conjecture about American involvement. He found some motorcar advertisements for various manufacturers and noticed the Cadillac ad in particular. It was a fine-looking automobile, and its published price was reflective of it. He liked it better than the Model T, but his wallet was far from anything except a Ford.

He sat the paper down and got up from his seat. He looked back at the headlines and wondered about the passage on possible *Conscription* should the US enter the war. He passed through the frosted glass doors and made his way by the men watching the play on the front pocket billiard table. He noted the man bending to make a shot and thought his dress was a bit obnoxious. The man was a bit heavy and sported a cravat with a stickpin of some stone. His coat hung loosely on his shoulders, and his collar looked quite tight as his neck glowed from the pressure.

Fred walked up beside Brown, and they both for a moment watched the shot and followed the cue ball to its next resting place. Fred looked at the abacus along the wall where one of Brown's employees was keeping the score as well as stating the count as balls dropped into the leather pockets. It was not a close game by any means. The Chicago Dandy was comfortably in the lead and would make fifty balls in a few more strokes.

Brown turned to Fred in a muffled tone, "I'll make the introduction when this game is settled. I put my best stick here on the billiard table for you. Warm up here, clicking some balls. I'll bring him over to you. He already knows the bet. I'd say he's taken a hundred or more from my local players. Most will stay to watch your game. You determine the ball count, 50-100."

"We'll lag for the break," Fred replied.

Fred limbered up on the billiard table while Brown took care of the front end. A few minutes later, Brown brought the Dandy back to where he was tapping balls. Fred was introduced to the man as Young Tennessee Brown from St. Louis. Brown mentioned the mark wanted to play the best player in Alton, and if a better player was available, he was up for a game. The mark was told that there was no relation between the young man and himself, just the coincidence that they shared the same last name. The wager amount was agreed on, and they thought fifty balls would satisfy both parties.

The mark lagged first, leaving his ball four inches from the reverse rail. Fred tapped his ball down the felt and returned it, stopping just in front of the rail. It was Fred's honor. Brown froze the rack, and Fred broke, leaving the cue ball in a perfectly safe place, sending one ball to the rail. The mark attempted a shot on the only ball viable, calling it into the corner. His English was almost perfect, and the ball ran the rail but slobbered around the pocket and bounced out. The cue ball caromed into the pack, breaking it up a bit more.

Fred took stock of the various ball positions relative to the cue ball and began picking off one by one. With perfect cue ball control, he further expanded the pack, creating good follow-up shots. As the field lightened, Fred chose his future break ball and dropped the outstanding remainder, leaving the cue ball in a preferred position to take down the future break ball while dispersing the rack.

The attendant called out the count, "Fourteen to null. Let's have the second rack.

Brown turned to the mark. "You may want to sit down," he advised. "I don't think you'll be shooting for a while."

"Twenty-nine to null!"

"Forty-four to null!"

"Fifty-eight to null!"

The game was called, and Fred walked over to shake hands. The man reluctantly offered his hand as he looked up to his taller opponent. The man began to put a viselike grip on Fred's outstretched hand. Much to the mark's surprise, Fred returned the favor until the man lightened up the handshake. Both men dropped their arms to their sides. The attendant stepped between them and handed Fred the $2,000 in wagering. The mark turned and scanned the crowd around the table, suggesting that he wanted to continue playing if anyone had the wherewithal to bet. Seeing no takers, the mark retired from the room.

Brown looked at Fred and smiled. "Easiest five hundred I ever made!" He laughed. "No, I take that back! I made more than that the night you stunned Layton!"

*****

The next morning, the two shared breakfast in the café across the street from Brown's Hotel. It had been an exciting reunion for both. They rehashed the good and bad times of their prior partnerships. Fred thanked Brown for all he'd done for him, especially the needed cash from their trips that eased his parents' expenses during his father's illness. He also thanked him for the custom cue that he patted on the table next to him. The men rose from the table, shaking hands in a half hug and headed to the street.

"Enjoy your new motorcar!" Brown called as he waved Fred on.

"I intend to!" Fred waved back.

Fred had more than enough cash to buy about any automobile he desired. The unexpected windfall of the prior night's game had boosted his holdings to the tremendous fifteen hundred. He knew the motorcar would cost $600 to $800 depending on the model. He had decided to get a touring model, thinking it was about time he explored his options on weekends. There were small towns around this part of the Midwest where pool halls were pastimes for most men. He could nickel and dime his way around the countryside, paying for everything he needed. He also wanted to take his check protectors and writers to sell at the same time. He needed a territory.

The car showroom was open, and Fred walked in making a point of checking out the car displayed in front of desk where a rather familiar man sat looking down at some paperwork. The doors were open, and the salesman didn't hear the customer enter. Fred slowly looked at every aspect of the vehicle.

As in his encounter before, he moved his hand over the machine as if it were a pet or object of fine sculpture. It shined as bright as the one from a few years before.

"Nice-looking, isn't it?" said the salesman, finally realizing he had a customer.

"Yes, it is!" Fred returned, still moving around the motorcar, floating his hand across the surface of its fenders.

When he reached the rear, he felt the spare tire, squeezing it to see if it were filled with air. This was a three-door Touring Model T. He could get plenty of machines in the back. He looked into the driver's area, and it pretty much looked like the interior of Uncle Ben's delivery model. Ben used to let him drive it to town for delivery, so he knew how to operate one.

"Is this one for sale and ready to go?" Fred inquired.

"Sure is! Just have to fill the tank. It'll run on gasoline, kerosene, and even ethanol. It'll do over 40 mph and runs about fifteen miles plus to the gallon."

"How much?" Fred asked.

"This here one is $725 out the door."

"I heard some kid thought he could buy one for a dime, a year or so back. I wonder why he would have thought that?" Fred queried.

The salesman now took a better look at whom he was dealing with. There was something familiar about this young man, but his mind couldn't grab it flying by. He stepped closer to Fred and found him staring directly into the man's eyes, daring him to figure it out. Fred reached into his vest pocket and placed a dime on the car's fender. All of a sudden, it grabbed him. This was the kid but so different. Taller now and dressed even better than himself.

"My word!" he half choked on. "You are quite the young sir now! I'm sorry you believed the price was a dime. I said that because I knew you would be disappointed if I gave you the real cost. Boys come in here most every day asking. I paid for that dime quote! I had to push that car back here on my own. Damn near killed me!"

"Wish it had!" said Fred. "I've had a hard time living that down!"

"I'll take it!" he said after a short pause.

Fred's declaration caught the man off guard. He didn't know how to respond at first. This wasn't the same boy he once embarrassed. Fred attire, stature, and bearing suggested that he was serious. The salesman wondered how a person of his young years affords a motorcar. He couldn't be older than seventeen. He could only give one response.

"Will that be cash or check?"

*****

Fred drove out to his uncle Ben's after taking delivery of his new Ford motorcar. They were surprised to see him and ask how his mother and sister were. After catching up on all the news and showing them the new Model T, they sat down to supper. Fred spent the night and drove back to St. Louis the next day, leaving early in the morning. As he crossed the bridge from Illinois, he looked ahead to the buildings backing up the river wharfs and thought it was time to make his mark. He would start by getting his own sales territory and work every day to prove he was the salesman Mr. Henn thought he could be.

He got to his mother's just as she and his sister were returning from work. He honked at them as they walked to the house. The women stopped and looked around, wondering what had made the offensive sound. Upon seeing Fred at the wheel of a motorcar, they both dropped their bags, raising their hands to their mouths.

"Fred! What have you done?" his mother shouted.

"Mother, he's stolen a motorcar!" Beulah exclaimed.

"Oh, mother of Mary, for heaven's sake! How in God's world did you get that noisy thing! Winifred asked.

"I bought it, Mother!" Fred answered. "With my own money!"

"Where did you get money like that?"

"I'm selling those check protector/printers like hot cakes. I'm getting a salary and a commission for every one I sell."

This wasn't the case yet. Anything to keep them in the dark about his pool playing would do for now. Besides, tomorrow he was going to ask for a territory and prove himself to be the Todd Company's best salesman. He had a plan.

"Go get dressed up!" Fred told them. "I'm taking you downtown to the best dinner in St. Louis! I'm driving my favorite ladies to town!"

Fred ran into the house after the women. He put his new pool cue under his bed and then went to his mother's cash can and put $100 in $10 bills inside. She kept the family cash in a baking soda can along with her other baking ingredients. It was out there for the world to see. She believed in hiding things of important in plain sight.

The family drove downtown, passed the pool halls on Olive, to Tucker Boulevard. It was the most famous hotel in the downtown area: the Hotel Jefferson, a twelve-story building noted for its fine restaurant and exquisite architecture. Winifred and Beulah felt out of place. Their attire was the best they had, made by their own hand. Fred continued reinforcing them and marched them into the restaurant, one on each arm. He tipped the maître d' a whopping $10 and asked for a nice out-of-the-way table so the ladies wouldn't be self-conscious. He refused to let them see the menu and ordered for them. He and Mr. Brown had eaten there often, and he wanted the best this evening for his family.

Needless to say, the women were enchanted by the opulence and eventually relaxed and enjoyed themselves. It was the first of many occasions of which Fred shared his success with his family.

The following morning, Fred reported to the offices of Todd and Company. He went to Mr. Henn's office in hopes of persuading him to give him a sales territory. Mr. Henn informed him the company had made a change, and he, Mr. Henn, had been promoted to the New York office. Fred's new boss was Mr. Steele. Henn introduced Fred to Steele that afternoon, giving Fred a glowing recommendation.

Fred told him that he worked three days in the office repairing machines and the other three days selling. Fred was making $25 a week for repairs and was taking the usual commission on the sales he made. Steele was aware of Fred's job description and his stellar performance. He asked Fred to see him the next morning as he needed to look over the entire operation. Fred appeared at Steele's door first thing on Wednesday.

"Good morning, Mr. Steele," Fred opened. "Where do I go? Where is my territory?"

"Well, Fred, you really want to be part of our sales force?" Steele returned.

"Yes, I do, very much!"

"I'm quite impressed by your enthusiasm, and you have contributed to the improvement of our product." Steele continued, "I'm going to let you choose an area. Where would you like to start?"

"Alton, Illinois, sir!" answered Fred enthusiastically.

Fred was sure that Steele knew he was from Alton and that he might have good reason to think it a safe place to start. His having taught other salesmen how to properly operate the machines and insights on how to make them operate better than covered in the manuals strengthened Fred's confidence. He was an Alton man.

Fred left the office and went directly home to tell his mother and sister the news. He asked them to meet him downtown after they finished work. He wanted to surprise his girls. The women meet him at the appointed corner in central St. Louis.

"What's this all about, Fred?" his mother asked.

"I'm taking you ladies shopping!"

"For what?" his sister asked.

"I'm going to buy you new clothes and take you around showing off my two beautiful ladies!"

Their mouths gaped in total shock as he grabbed their hands, stepping between them. As he stepped forward, he felt a tug as they were not sure he was really serious. They stagger-stepped after him and caught up. This day would become a family topic for years to come.

Lilly and Brother Zachary

HE DROVE TO ALTON on Thursday and began walking the streets. He made no sales that afternoon or on Friday. He was very disappointed and returned to his uncle Ben's farm where he was staying. The following day, Saturday, he found himself standing at the Market Street turn around for the trolley holding two machines in his arms. He was worried about coming into the office on Monday having made no sales. It was early still. Lunch was over, and the businesses were still open. He decided he would try once again.

By five o'clock that afternoon, he had sold five machines. He also sold two check writers. On Monday, he walked in to Mr. Steele's office and gave him the seven invoices and the payments for the same. Fred was beaming, and Steele could see the excitement in his eyes.

"Mr. Steele!" Fred asked. "I'd like to sell six days a week!"

"Fred, I appreciate your efforts and your success," Steele replied, "but we need someone to repair machines. If you are willing to continue on a three-and-three schedule until we can find a replacement for you to train, I think you can then move to sales on a permanent basis."

Fred agreed but was disappointed. The next three days were hard for him. His mind was occupied with the idea of sales. He made $25 for three days of repair work whereas in three days of selling, he made $10 for each sale.

The $95 he made the prior week was a big boost to his confidence and really helped the family. He would double his efforts this next three days.

Upon his return the following Monday, Fred walked into Steele's office with eleven orders. Fred was sure he would get a big territory based on his recent performance. He felt that Steele believed that his success in Alton was due to personal relationships in his hometown.

"Fred, I'm very impressed with your efforts," he said. "I'm going to give you a difficult area. The man we had working South Broadway has been disappointing. You can start in his place on Thursday."

South Broadway was where Amheuser-Busch Brewery was located. It was a challenging area, but Fred put all his abilities into the effort. In three days, he sold seventeen machines. The company began putting together a weekly booklet that was distributed throughout the Todd organization. In it, they spotlighted the best salesman of the week. Fred's picture was in the booklet every week. He was the company's leading producer.

While selling for Todd, Fred began expanding his sales area. During one of his forays, he ran into an evangelist he had met at one of the Pentecostal Ministry meetings he attended for entertainment. He hadn't gone to one of the Holy Roller events in months and was surprised to see him north of St. Louis. The man called himself Brother Zachary. Fred remembered him as a guest preacher at the downtown church. He had not been very well attired when Fred attended there, but now, he was pretty dapper.

"How have you been, Brother Zachary?" Fred inquired.

"Doin' well, Brother Whalen!" he returned, his eyes lighting up. "You seem to be prospering too!"

Fred explained that he was in sales and was making his way around Missouri and Illinois on a regular basis. As they caught up on what, where, and when, Zachary suddenly got very agitated and excited. He began telling Fred that he, too, was on the road in a similar fashion, selling JESUS to the saved and unsaved. Fred smiled and realized that Zach had found a lucrative niche. He had developed a following of washed-in-the-blood believers and was traveling around the countryside renting barns for revivals.

"You know, Fred," continued Zach, "I could use you at these prayer revivals on weekends if you're in the area. I could make it worth your while!"

Fred was always looking for a means of increasing his revenue. Besides, he had always enjoyed watching the antics of the believers at these meetings. Zachary handed Fred a flyer that listed all his upcoming revivals. He then laid out his plan for Fred. Fred had been selling for Todd for a year, and his seventeenth birthday had passed, and it was coming spring and things were warming up. So far, 1915 was becoming a good year. Adding another moneymaking scheme that filled his weekend nights became very attractive.

*****

The Wunderlich Boarding House was making ends meet with a little extra from the kids' factory work. The weekend was approaching, and summer was coming on fast. The Friday chores were close to done, the sun was falling off, and the boarders were enjoying the breeze across the front porch while they waited for supper. Lilly's mother was putting the final touches on the biggest meal of the week. The younger children were running around the barn, playing with the usual amount of noise, and Gus was running home with an unusual smile on his face.

As soon as he was within shouting distance, the air became filled with whoops and hollers. He reached the white picket fence that bordered the front of the house and the flower garden that lined and it hurtled it. He stumbled at the porch and sprawled headlong into the door, cracking the lower panel paint and knocking himself half senseless.

The men on the porch jumped up to help Gus as he rolled onto his back staring up at the porch's warped rafters. Lilly and her mother ran to the front door, leaving all in the kitchen to see what had shaken the house. When Ema and Lilly got to the door, Gus was sitting up holding his head with both hands as if he were trying to put it back into place.

"What is going on here, August?" demanded his mother, mixing rage and concern in her usual delicate manner.

"The reverend's back in town!" gasped Gus as he crawled away from the door.

"That's no reason to bring the house down!" continued his mother, beaning him on the lump that was rising from his head with her wooden mixing spoon.

"Now get washed up, the lot of you," she said. "Dinner's ready."

She turned and hurried back to the kitchen with Lilly. As Gus jogged passed, she collared him. "Now don't bring the reverend up in front of the young 'uns," she scolded. "I don't want them going to that. You and your sister can go, but be home early. Lilly, call the kids."

The dinner passed as usual except for the building excitement that could be seen bouncing back and forth between Gus and Lilly. Gus gulped his food down and prodded his sister from under the table to hurry. As everyone was excused from the table, Gus slid back his chair, catching his foot in the carpet and falling over his seat, splintering it to kindling. His mother sighed and hung her head in disgust, shaking it from side to side.

Looking up at her dumbfounded son, she yelled, "Get out of my house while I still have one!"

Gus and Lilly got to the Henderson barn at seven thirty and found people already lined up to go in. Banners hung from every corner proclaiming Brother Zachary's Holy Rollin' Revival. Children ran about, vendors sold special delights, while the old and crippled stood about awaiting their chance at salvation and good health.

The younger generation moved back and forth getting caught up in the noise of expectation that grew as the hour of revival approached. Followers of Brother Zach moved through the crowd, passing out pamphlets and gathering donations.

It was the height of the revival season, and the preachers were out in force renewing folk's souls. Just like the refreshed earth sprouting up its greenery, so were the evangelists reaping the green harvest of the faithful's pockets. There were talkers and healers setting up tents here and there, but the best of all was the Brother Zach's Holy Rollin' Revival.

Brother Zachary would come to town each spring and fill the largest barn in the area with singing, shouting, and shivering. Everyone would go, young and old. Standing room only was the rule, and the only exception being whether or not you could see it all. Saturday night was the best of all, the healings and the testimonies were something to be experienced. A person had to be in the barn early, and places in the loft went fast because it afforded a total view of the revival.

Soon Lilly and her brother were inside the large barn comfortably seated in the loft. They could see it all. As the time to commence drew near, people who were more reverent and gullible filled the floor below, with those who were scheduled for healing occupied the front area beside the makeshift stage. A portable pump organ had been strategically placed in the rear complete with a quickie choir. Bales of hay served as pews, with some guests finding a pointed thrill as they sat down. The noise steadily increased to a deafening pitch, and those who sat in the covered loft felt their ears ring to the sound.

Suddenly, the organ began to wale, and the choir hummed until at last the pressure was right and the voices were in tune. "Bringing in the Sheaves" built into a general accompaniment by all who got the feeling and a rhythm of hands swayed below the rafters. All was right now, and from behind a stall out jumped Brother Zach, dressed in white and looking fresh out of heaven.

His hair was blond, his eyes blue, and every move was enough to make a dancer jealous. In his right hand was a Bible, worn and tattered from the rears spent beating a dollar form the pulpit. His shoes were as white as his suit and as bright as his teeth. There may not be gold in heaven, but the flash of his mouth meant there had to be some in religion.

His hair floated as soft as a silver cloud when he moved from side to side. His eyes flashed a blue that made the sky a poor second. His arms waved like bird's wing in sweeping gestures that brought the faint of heart up from the hay. Yes, here was a hustler that would be hard to match. Even God was a little worried.

No one on earth could say the name Jesus the way Brother Zach did. He made a person jump with the "JE" and swoon with the "SUS." His hand was as light as a hook and as deep to the touch. One could feel him reach the soul through his or her collective pockets. Smooth was the style that graced every large barn in the fertile Mississippi Valley.

Brother Zach moved to the front of the stage. Every eye moved with him. The opening hymn ceased, and complete silence fell over the gathering. He stood there looking into the rafters, slowly raising his arms to heaven. Motionless now, his gaze locked on the ceiling. For the next five minutes, total silence. The crowd slowly began to look up with Brother Zach until all eyes were above.

Zach, sensing total control now, quickly lowered his head and shouted, "Glory be to Geee...suss!"

The congregation leaped as one startled body. Women swayed and men's knees quivered and babies cried. They were his.

"Geee...suss is here tonight!" he continued, opening his arms to collect the entire space around him.

"Good people, can you feel him?" he begged, dropping to his knees.

"Amen!" came the thundering reply.

"Alle-luu-yah! Geee...suss will touch you tonight!"

Still on his knees, Brother Zach bowed his head and clasped his hands.

"Let's pray to Gee...suss together," he urged, humbling him even more by rolling his shoulders.

"Dear Son of God, we praise you, we your humbled children, and ask that you..."

The prayer continued to an appropriate amen, and with that, Brother Zach jumped to his feet and delivered a fire, hell, and brimstone sermon, beseeching those wandering sheep to return to the flock and beg forgiveness. On this note, he again went to the crowd before him.

"Dear servants of Christ," he began, "I know there are some out there who are sinners waiting their chance to be saved, but fear and embarrassment has kept them from speaking out. Dear people, pray in silence with me so that this person might lighten his burden and come back to the flock. Geee...suss came to me last week in a vision and spoke that a young man would return like the prodigal son to the flock here in St. Louis. Brothers and sisters, let's pray that this man may step forward."

All bowed in prayer, except for those few in the loft that surveyed the floor, hoping to spot the man he spoke of. Gus and Lilly searched the congregation, hoping to pick out the sinner before he exposed himself. Five minutes passed, then suddenly, a man began to moan and move uneasily. Gus pointed the person out to Lilly, and both watched intently as the young man jumped to his feet and raised his hands.

"Oh, Brother Zach!" he begged. "Help me!"

"Speak thy mind, brother!" he joined. "Free thy soul of its sinful burdens! Step out and come forward!"

The man moved from his bale to the middle of the center aisle of the barn. The young man proceeded to tell of a most lustful, sinful life—the horrors of wanton women and pool playing depravity. Tears rolled from his eyes as he began to shake. He cried out, "Oh, I can feel Jesus coming into my body!"

With that, he fell on the floor in a fit, jerking and shaking. Soon, an epidemic of fits broke out. Men, women, and old people fell to the ground, rolling and flailing their arms. The organ and choir exploded into "Washed in the Blood." The show was in full swing. Rapture.

Almost as quickly as it began, it subsided. Exhaustion was apparent on many faces, including those who watched. Brother Zach, with tears rolling down his cheeks, asked an attendant to bring the repentant man to him. Two ushers in the rear moved forward, assisting the man to his feet and helping him move forward to Brother Zach. He then cleansed the man with his hands and told him to set to the side and meditate over his forgiveness and new life.

Zach looked back to the congregation and proceeded to remind that the Son of God had entered this man and that person's life has been changed from evil and put on the Lord's path.

"What's your name, young man?" asked Brother Zach.

"Fred Whalen, Reverend."

"Are you a sinner?"

"I truly am!"

"Do you accept Christ as your savior?"

"I do, Brother Zach!"

"Then in the name of Geee…suss, you are forgiven."

Brother Zach, obviously exhausted from his ordeal, retired to the side of the stage, head bowed in deep prayer. It was time for the money pitch. One of Zach's followers stood and praised the work Brother Zach was doing, citing the salvation of the lapse sinner who was now meditating outside.

"Come now, brothers and sisters", he called, "it's time to help the work of Jesus. Our brothers will pass among you and do be generous. Give till it hurts. After all, you can't take it with you. No pockets in a shroud!"

After the hat was passed, Brother Zach returned to the center of attention. Hymns and prayers were followed by the miracle healings. The only miracle that was evident appeared in the straight faces of all who participated in the healings. The meeting was closed with a final chorus, and Brother Zach moved among the crowd, people reaching out to touch him. By the time he made his exit, the only question to be answered was who touched whom the most. It was answered when the collection was totaled, Brother Zachary by a KO.

Gus and his sister made their way down from the loft. As they passed through the main doors of the barn, Lilly noticed the young man who had been saved. Breaking out of the crowd, she ran over to him. Not knowing exactly what to say, she stood silently looking up at him. He was a very good-looking sinner.

Lilly went unnoticed by Fred, who was busy counting the money he had just collected for his performance—Brother Zachary paid well.

"Are you really saved?" she asked, her eyes seeking his.

"What?" he returned, confusion marking his face.

"Have you repented your sins?" she asked. "The ones you confessed in the barn to Brother Zach."

"Oh, that!" He laughed, looking the girl over for the first time. "I sure have, at least till the next time."

"The next time?" she replied, shock replaced by wonder.

"Yeah, the next time he pays me to repent." He chuckled, patting his pants' pocket.

"He paid you to do that?"

"Sure did! He paid those people that were healed too. Sinnin's a profitable business."

"Well, I never!" she shouted, anger rising in her shapely body.

"Now calm down. It's not that bad. After all, it made a lot of people feel better and more comfortable about life."

"I don't like to be fooled," she said, turning to call for her brother. "Gus!"

Her brother was busy flirting with a local girl that had dominated his attention for the past month when he heard his sister call. Excusing himself, he ran over to where Lilly and Fred were standing.

"Whadda ya want?" asked Gus.

"This guy is a fake, and so is Preacher Zach!" she returned in an effort to educate her brother while exposing Fred.

"I know that, Lilly. Hell, Brother Zach is a money-hustling evangelist."

"How long have you known that?" she asked.

"Since last year," he said. "Old Turk told me. I thought you knew."

Fred smiled at her and introduced himself to Gus. As they shook hands, both men felt they would grow to be close friends. Lilly looked confused and bewildered, but the feelings were soon to fade.

"How about if I treat us all to some ice cream?" offered Fred, again tapping his pocket.

"Well..." started Lilly.

"Good, let's go into town, my car is over here." Smiled Fred.

"You own a gas buggy?" gasped Lilly.

"Sure do."

The trio walked to the other side of the barn where the automobile was parked. Lilly and Gus were more impressed than ever when they saw the vehicle, shining in the early moonlight. Its leather seats and spoked wheels told of luxury their family could never afford. Both Lilly and her brother reached out to touch the car as if in a dream, fully expecting it to vanish before their eyes. When it didn't, they smiled, looking at each other with amazement and delight.

"Come on, jump in!" encouraged Fred, taking Lilly's hand and pulling her unto the running board.

Gus leaped into the back as Fred ran back to the driver's seat after cranking the motor to life. They sped off, throwing dirt and dusk everywhere. Fred looked over to Lilly and for a moment letting the motorcar drift toward the ditch.

"Look out!" Lilly shouted, sliding across the seat toward Fred.

Fred snapped back to watching the road, but Lilly had become a beautiful obsession. He had a hard time not staring. The cool wind blew back her auburn hair, and the moon made her face glow. He had been doing these revivals with Zach for a few weeks and had seen lots of girls, but this one was special. He could tell.

"Where are we going?" Lilly asked, brushing the hair from her face.

"I think Carter's is open!" Fred yelled over the winds rush and the engine's exhaust. "They have the best hot fudge. It's just a few miles more."

The trio arrived at Carter's, and they ran inside. The counter was empty, so Fred offered Lilly a stool and sat down beside her. Gus sat on his sister's right, and they all ordered sundaes. Fred barely touched his. He was fixed on watching Lilly eat her ice cream. She could see him staring at her in the mirror's reflection and became a bit self-conscious.

"Eat your ice cream, you sinner!" she said. "Before it melts into mush!"

Fred looked down and took a spoonful. He went right back to his gazing. There was something about her. Maybe it was her unbridled spirit and the way she talked back. It was something, and he was willing to take as much time as needed to figure this out. Ice cream was too fast. He needed more time with this girl. He had an idea.

"Let me take you two home," he offered, knowing there was no other choice for them.

This way he would know where she lived, and he could plan his sales calls so that in the late afternoon, he could casually stop by.

They jumped back into the car, and Gus directed Fred back to the boarding house. When they arrived, Fred left the engine running and walked Lilly to the door. Gus was still looking the car over. It was pretty new and wished he had one.

"How old is your brother?' Fred asked.

"Just thirteen," she answered.

"He sure is a big one for his age."

"I've got three older brothers, but they stayed farming," she offered. "I'm the fourth oldest. My sister, Florence, came after me, then Gus and George."

"How many are you?"

"Mother had sixteen children."

"Busy lady!" Fred said. "Your father must have a great job," he added. This is a big place."

"My father was a stone mason. He died last year."

"Oh, I'm sorry!" he begged.

"We take in boarders. It helps us get by."

Before he could say anymore, Lilly's mother called, "You and Gus get in here now!"

Fred said his goodbyes and jumped into his car and left. Lilly ran to the window and watched him leave. She thought he was very good-looking and wondered if she'd ever see him again. Gus came in the house, shutting the door behind him. He saw Lilly looking out the window, standing very still.

"He's gone, Lilly!" Gus teased, knowing she had taken an interest in the sinner.

Ema walked in and asked, "Who was that that brought you two home?"

"Just a guy we met at the revival," she answered. "He was a big sinner, but Brother Zach saved him."

"You're only fifteen, Lilly," her mother reminded. "Your still an impressionable girl!"

"You married father when you were sixteen," she pleaded.

"And look what that got me!" Ema replied. "I got sixteen children, a husband that worked himself to death, and left me a widow holding the bag! I want you and Florence to have an easier life than I have had!"

"He seemed very nice, Ma!" she pleaded.

"You know nothing about him!" she continued. "How old is he? What does he do for money?"

"He's a salesman, MOTHER!" Lilly emphasized.

"Well, that's just the last straw!" Ema cried. "You've seen those types coming to our door all the time! They're here there and everywhere! They've got itchy feet and a girl in every little town they stop in!"

Gus just stood there, taking all this in. He adored his two older sisters and never enjoyed these heated exchanges between the girls and their mother. Both the girls were strong-willed and deliberate. His younger brother, George, was being picked on in school by a bigger boy, and Lilly hauled off and blackened his eyes and chipped his front tooth. Both girls were fighters and prone to tell you what they thought on any subject.

Thinking he could add something positive in Fred's favor, Gus volunteered, "He had a really nice leather case in the back seat. I opened it, and there was a pool stick in it. Really nice one with a name written on it!"

Ema's mouth dropped open, and she looked at Gus as if he'd just walked over her grave. She put her hands on her ample hips and really let loose. "That's the last straw!" she yelled. "Pool is the devil's game! It destroys a man's ambition and leads to gambling a life away! I'll have none of it in my house!"

Lilly got in her final say as Ema started up the stairs. "Mother, at least he's been saved!" she offered.

The next weekend, Florence went along with Lilly and Gus to another one of Brother Zach's revivals. They had gotten a flyer at the last meeting and planned their Saturday nights accordingly. Florence and Fred hit it off from their first encounter. Flossie could see that Fred was very taken by her older sister and realized the feeling was mutual. After about six weeks of these Saturday night excursions, Fred decided he would try to face Ema but not without flowers and candy. He not only brought them for Ema but something for everybody. Ema wasn't a pushover, but she started liking the Saturday treats. All the children adored him, and the boarders liked him too. He'd have to work on Ema for a while. He wanted Lilly, and no effort would be spared.

Emalene in the Side

FRED CONTINUED TO OUTPERFORM his fellow salesmen at the Todd Company. He had trained his replacement in the repair shop and was selling six days a week. Most salesman used public transportation and carried only two of each machine in a special case. Fred had a motorcar with a big back seat. He could get to places much faster and stay out longer. He would sell and take delivery orders for twenty-five machines a week. The $10 commission was putting an average of $250 a week in his pocket. If he stayed over in a larger market, he would hustle pool games at night.

He always was sure to return to St. Louis by Saturday afternoon. He'd purchase the booty he needed to keep his foot in Ema's door. He loaded the back of the touring car with something for everyone. The Wunderlich Boarding House was like a nest of baby birds. Lilly's siblings loved their Saturday surprises. Fred even began going to the Sunday river gatherings of the Black Baptist Church. Cassie and Charlie welcomed Fred to the summer ritual, and they would caravan down to the Mississippi.

In the beginning, Ema did everything she could to keep the relationship that was smoldering between her daughter and Fred from becoming a raging fire. Fred and Lilly concocted ways of secretly meeting with the help of Gus and Florence. Eventually, Ema found it harder to paddle upstream. She still wasn't convinced that Fred was a solid person. Fred had changed the balance in the boarding house, and the votes were stacking against her bias.

"Lilly! Lilly! Where are you, girl?" shouted Ema as she stepped from the kitchen onto the porch and into the yard.

"I'm with the cow, Ma!" came the shout back, somewhere from inside the barn.

As she crossed the burnt grass toward the barn, she muttered to herself and waved a wooden spoon at her side. She could often be seen in such a state, looking to the sky as if she were forgiving some-one for her burden. God knows it wasn't her fault. Upon reaching the barn, she planted her fists on her hips and her feet firmly in the straw, covering its dirt floor. Standing inside the parted doors, she blew the loose hair from her eyes and filled her lungs for her next burst of words.

"Lilly, come out here!" she yelled, sending her gray hair back into her eyes. Her daughter emerged from a stall back in the shad-owed interior. Bits of straw flecked her long auburn hair, and a yellow ribbon crossed behind her ears. She wiped her hands on the apron tied about her dress and shaded her eyes from the morning glare streaming through the open end of the barn.

"Where's your brother, Lilly?" asked her mother in a scolding fashion, motioning to the heavens with her spoon.

"He's not here, Ma," she answered. "He's gone!"

"Did Gus go to Alton with Freddie Whalen?"

"I think so!" she returned, dropping her eyes to her bare feet.

"You know so!" added the woman, spinning around with hands in the air. "He has chores around here. We need wood for the stove, and what does he do? I'll tell ya! Every time that smoothie Freddie comes over, he's gone. I'll be damned if I know what you kids see in him. He's bribed his way into this family, and I'm as guilty as the rest."

"Oh, Ma!" Lilly exclaimed. "He treats you real nice!"

"You tell your brother, Missy, that the next time he lets that cow go, I'll brain him with the bucket. And tell that pool playing son of bitch Whalen that if he ever drags Gus to those dens of filth, I'll shove that fancy cue stick up his ass! Now you get in the house and clear the table! I'll be in with the milk directly."

The woman walked into the barn, kicking the straw as she went. Lilly turned and started for the house. Suddenly, a yell and a conglomeration of foul language emerged from every cranny of the barn. Lilly turned and smiled. "The Lord gotcha, Ma!"

Lilly lifted her dress and ran into the house, ignoring her mother's continued thoughts on the damage done to her bunion and toe.

The morning warmed rapidly, the sun climbing higher until it was directly overhead. Inside the house, Lilly and her mother rushed from room-to-room cleaning and picking up. Most of Lilly's younger brothers and sisters were in school 'til noon while her sister, Florence, worked in a St. Louis factory ten miles away.

Running a boarding house was not easy, and Lilly's mother commented often on the difficulty that had befallen her since her husband died two years before. He had moved them from the farm in Pacific to the edge of St. Louis, buying a large boarding house and bringing enough of the farm along to make a decent attempt at city life. Besides having to accommodate thirteen of the sixteen children, the house had room for four boarders.

These were working men who spent sixteen hours in factories, two hours at the table and the remainder of the day in bed. It was this same type of work schedule that killed Lilly's father.

After cleaning the boarder's rooms, Lilly and her mother returned to the kitchen, the start and finish of each day. It was time to begin the evening meal as eighteen people had to be fed. As her mother began gathering the various paraphernalia, Lilly looked over from the sink where she was peeling potatoes.

"Mom, you didn't mean what you said about Fred, did you?"

"Well, most of it anyway," she replied as she started at the toe and bunion that began to ache at the mention of Freddie Whalen.

"He's not a bad boy. He's nice".

Her mother forgot her foot for an instant and looked over at her daughter. "Look, honey, Fred is no boy! He's a seventeen-year-old. And don't think I miss those flirty ways of his. Lilly, money comes too fast and easy with him. He's not a worker, he's a player, and pool at that!"

"He does work!" she returned, throwing a potato into the pot on the floor by her feet. "After all, he sells those check whoz-it machines. He has an automobile and nice clothes, and besides, he's cute!" defended the girl.

"Lilly, that may be, but travelin' around is no life for a girl like you."

"What's that supposed to mean?" asked Lilly, tossing the knife into the sink.

"Never you mind! Just peel those potatoes and tend to your work."

Lilly knew the conversation was over and continued peeling, watching the skins fall from her knife into the sink. She looked out back to the barn, her brown eyes looked on the loft, and her thoughts floated beyond the kitchen, to the first time she and her brother met Fred. She had enjoyed the attention Fred spent on her. She had never thought much about boys until recently. Most of her interaction with them was at the hands of her brothers and anyone that slighted them. Being one of two females between five brothers almost made tomboyishness a necessity. Still, every time she expected Fred, she would do everything she could to look like the pinnacle of femininity. Her brothers would say, "Lilly, you clean up real nice!"

It wasn't long before Ema came around. Instead of screaming at Lilly and Florence "Get rid of those sons of bitches!" she would nicely say, "Don't just stand there in the door! Ask them in!" She had given up on the idea of keeping the perceived "wolf" away from her chicks to "Let' see what's gonna happen!" And it happened!

Fred and Ema became friends. She allowed the two to see each other as long as it didn't interfere with the operation of the boarding house. Fred became a dinner quest on a very regular basis. Ema was surprised at the amount of food someone of his light frame could put away. She figured at six feet, it had to go somewhere.

Fred's proposal of marriage just erupted from his mouth one night, much to his surprise and Lilly's. It just happened. He wasn't sure if he could support a wife much less take care of another person. Lilly didn't hesitate accepting.

They went through the usual formalities, and he ran out to get a ring. Soon after, the marriage ceremony was held, and they were man and wife. Now what?

Lillian Ema Wunderlich-Whalen
Wedding at 15

His sales for the Todd Company were progressing well. He and Lilly moved in with his mother and sister until he could find other accommodations. With Florence working in St. Lois, another room was freed up at the Wunderlich Boarding House. Florence moved into Fred's room at his mother's. Cassie came on full time, and Gus and Charlie Parker pretty much ran the motorcar repair place.

Fred began looking for better players as he traveled around selling machines. He had pretty much run through the pool hall heroes that hung around the St. Louis downtown. Lilly got part-time work at a small hotel within walking distance of the house. On Saturdays, Fred would take Lilly with him in the morning selling machines and then come in to the office and give Mr. Steele the receipts of the week.

"Fred, it looks as if you are the top salesman again," he said. "Maybe you'd like to sell more today just to insure your position as number one this week."

Fred took Lilly's hand, jumped in the car, and spent the rest of the afternoon selling. At five, he returned to Steele and gave him three more orders. Fred did this often to reinforce Lilly's confidence in his ability to provide for them. It wasn't long before Lilly was pregnant, and the more money Fred made went a long way toward ensuring her feelings of security, knowing there would be a baby soon.

Ema was worried about Lilly having a child so soon after turning sixteen. She had had Charles at that age, and it was hard labor, but a little over a year later, she had William, and then by age twenty, Jean was on the ground and Lilly was on the way.

It was 1916, and the world was going to hell in Europe. The *Lusitania* had been sunk a year earlier, and the country was up in arms. The government had instituted The Conscription Act in January. Fred turned eighteen a month later and wondered what his future might be if inducted. Gus was fourteen and started going with Fred to the pool halls at night watching him play and hustle.

Ema and Lillian (Lil) 1918

It was late July, and Lilly had just confirmed her pregnancy. Fred felt he had to hustle more, both machines and pool. Fred and Lilly had left his mother's house and moved to the boarding house as

Lilly wanted to be with her mother. This made both women happy. Florence moved in with Winifred and Beulah, and she helped out in that part of the equation. Everyone in the family was reasonably settled, and it was a time of waiting for the baby and the war.

Fred went to Mr. Steele one Saturday hoping to get a $250 advance. Steele told him it was against Todd Company policy and that he would have to try and sell more. Fred became irate that the top salesman could not get this consideration after years of superior performance. He quit on the spot, without knowing how he was going to derive income from that point.

Not being one to waste time, he found a job selling coupons for the Murella Photograph Studio. An older salesman there told him he made $150 per week on average. Fred, after hearing that, knew he could do better. After all, he was making much more selling a very specialized machine. Coupons would be a snap. He had youth and confidence on his side. He made $250 his first week selling just around downtown St. Louis. He would start expanding his radius of activity and really produce. He decided that he could sell these coupons in smaller towns within reasonable traveling distance of St. Louis. He started in the known territory around Alton to test his theory. It worked, and he began hitting all small towns within a half days travel. Mr. Murella was very impressed.

In February of 1917, just three days after Fred's birthday, Lillian Virginia Whalen was born in St. Louis. Fred thought it was the most spectacular event of his life to date. He felt it was a special-ordered birthday gift arriving three days late. He doted over the little girl, and life was good. His mother-in-law was so happy to have a granddaughter for the first time. Her older sons had produced several boys over the last few years, but this was the first girl. This doubly endeared Fred to Ema. He could do no wrong.

The next two years ran smoothly for the Whalens and Wunderlichs. Florence had gotten married and had a baby girl a year after Lilly. Ema had two granddaughters now, and everyone was getting along. Even though Fred and Florence's husband were fathers and exempt, both men felt they had to join the military and do their part. They enlisted in August of 1918, and both were sent to train as ambulance drivers. This only lasted about eleven weeks as the war ended that November. They were both released. They weren't disappointed as army pay was not helping out at home. To make things crazy, the government passed the Eighteenth Amendment. Fred didn't care because he didn't drink. The rest of the family cried.

Roaring with the Twenties

FRED WENT BACK TO selling photo coupons until October of 1919. There had been a family squabble at summer's end, and Fred felt that he was not getting enough credit for supporting the family. He and Lilly wanted to leave the boarding house because all but a few dollars of Fred's income were left at the end of each month, and they wanted to be on their own with little Lillian. So as not to confuse the child with the use of Lillian around the boarding house, they decided to call the baby Bobbie.

Thinking that their prospects would be better in a bigger city, they left St. Louis and headed to Chicago. Gus thought that he might do better fixing automobiles and machinery there, so he jumped in the car with them. The trip took two days, and they stopped at a motor court as night started to come on. Bloomington was a decent-sized town, and Gus noticed a large pool hall as they looked for a place to spend the night. The boys only had a $175 between them. The opportunity to hustle additional funds was taken. They left Lilly and Bobbie at the motor court and made their way to the pool hall in downtown. It was a Saturday night, and the prospect of finding players with a week's pay in their pockets was a viable one.

They boys were successful in winning a number of $5 games and by ten o'clock had added $65 to their venture capital. There was something to be said in traveling through little towns and exploiting the hometown heroes. From that night forward, if on the road, they would pay expenses by plundering the community pool rooms.

In Chicago, Fred found a boarding house downtown. On Monday, he went out looking for a job. He walked into the Russel Photograph Studio on Jackson and State Streets. Dressed in his finest attire, he introduced himself to Mr. Russel as a salesman. At that time, all photograph studios were using the coupon method of attracting customers. Fred explained how he had previously worked Murella Studio in St. Louis and was their top salesman. He asked for the job and a $50 advance. Mr. Russel looked him over quite carefully and after a long pause handed Fred a fifty-dollar bill.

"I'm one hell of a salesman," Fred said. "You won't regret your decision!"

He came back that afternoon with well over the $50 advance amount in sold coupons. Gus had found work in a mechanic's shop, and all had begun on the right foot in Chicago. Lilly offered to help out at the boarding house, and the dollars rolled in. Mrs. Wood's Boarding House was on Division Street. The four of them stayed there for eight months.

Fred became the master of photo coupon sales. The coupons sold for $2 and entitled the purchaser to two 11x14-inch portrait prints. You paid $1 for the coupon and another dollar when you received the prints. The point was getting the people into the studio. Once there, the customer usually bought additional prints. Fred sold so many that the biggest complaint was the backlog of customers scheduling their portraits. His best customers were the women that worked in the office towers that were sprouting up all over Chicago. Fred was hard to resist. He was well-dressed and in some cases had to turn down various offers from women who were smitten. He did this at lunch hour when the executives went out for their noon meal, leaving the low-paid secretaries to their bagged lunches.

Fred began playing at various pool halls in the evenings. He sold coupons there as well as hustled pool games. In a short time, he began playing the better players in Chicago. He met Irwin Rudolph at Palace Billiards. Rudy was fresh out of the army and still wore his uniform. This fooled a lot of players into thinking he was just a rube, a fresh green kid from the countryside. Fred and Rudy began hustling together as they became good friends.

Although they made good money together as partners, Fred found it was better for him to leave Rudy. While Rudy was a great player, he had one habit that cost them both lots of money. He began betting marks too high and gave them an edge that would make himself and Fred such underdogs in games that they would lose most of what they had won some nights. It was a hard decision for Fred, but the break had to happen.

Fred moved the family to Roger's Park. Irwin followed and moved into the same apartment building. Charles Fagan from St. Louis joined them all at Roger's Park, and soon Fred found himself paying for three units. The Greek owner of the Palace, to encourage the better players to come in, was paying each of them $50. It became cheaper for Fred to give up the Palace than support Rudy.

Fred worked for Russel Studios for a year and then went to work for Melvin Sykes Studio. When he was offered the job, he didn't tell Sykes that he was also working for his competition, Russel. He also started selling coupons for the Block Studio, whom he didn't tell about the other two. He was getting $150 from Sykes, $100 from Russel, and an additional $75 from Block. Fred also recruited two other people to help increase his sales and was keeping all of them busy. One of his sub-salesmen was a boxer named Red Cole from the Pacific Coast and the other fellow was an acquaintance from St. Louis, Jerry Parker. They would sign Fred's name to their sales orders, and Fred would turn them in. This arrangement was very profitable for all concerned.

Fred didn't know that these photographic studios met once a year to discuss business in general, and in the course of the meeting, they began bragging about their best salesman. They each described this go-getter that had increased their respective business by leaps and bounds. They didn't want to mention his name, thinking the others would try to recruit the man for them. Soon it became obvious that they were describing the same person. The clue was the exceptional wardrobe and the gold pocket watch.

The three studio owners decided to have an additional meeting with one of the three, inviting his best salesman on the premise of taking him to lunch at the Drake Hotel. When Fred arrived, he was horrified to find his three current employers sitting at the same table. The studio owners were embarrassed but felt they were dealing with an extraordinary talent. They felt they couldn't keep the status quo and ask Fred to make his choice. His best deal had always been with Sykes. He stayed with Sykes throughout his Chicago days.

Chicago became the epic center of the period known as the roaring twenties. The Volstead Act and Prohibition wrapped around the Eighteenth Amendment, created an era of crime and violence that had never been experienced in the United States. Bootlegging became the source of great wealth for many outfits that began controlling parts of the Chicago environs.

Fred and his family along with close friends stayed on the periphery of the increasing crime that became a day-to-day activity in the Windy City. Playing pool and hustling were forms of gambling that the rising gangs didn't care about. Some pool hall owners paid protection money to the organized crime bosses later in the decade. It wasn't until 1922 that things began to get dicey in Chicago. Fred continued selling photo coupons and clipping other pool players during his evenings. Young Tennessee Brown was almost legend in St. Louis, but Fred's departure to the north dampened that reputation. He became a phantom in small town poolrooms where he ventured on weekends with the family in tow. By 1921, he had made a good sum of money hustling and selling coupons. Some pool halls in Chicago began selling bootleg alcohol out of their back rooms. As a gathering place for men, it was ripe for the trade. Flasks became ever so popular as glasses lifted so did women's fashion. Nineteen twenty-one was a good year for the Whalen-Wunderlich family, but the summer before had been a tight time. They took a break from Chicago to clear their heads. They stayed with Uncle Ben and Aunt Ollie. Fred's mother and sister had moved to the West Coast the year before.

Alton, July 1920

THE JULY SUN SEARED its path into midday, radiating heat throughout the river valley. The summer's humid breath touched all within the reach of the Mississippi's moist palm. Beyond the shallows, Alton basted itself in prostate surrender as the temperature continued to race the sun.

Morning gave way to the heat of noon, sending the town's inhabitants in search of shade. People moved slowly now, and less frequent, seeking the structures that lined the burning streets. A lone automobile crawled to a halt, its passenger escaping into the darkness beyond the open doors of an old brick building.

Above the entry the faded sign of a pool hall hung by its last bolts. The scent of stale beer generously mixed with tobacco smoke formed a curtain just beyond the threshold. Within the dimly lit interior, ceiling fans strained in the pea-soup atmosphere. Six rectangular islands stood spotlighted across the floor and around one moved two figures, bending alternately over a sea of worn felt. Ivory balls clicked and rolled toward the pockets. The men talked and sipped warm beer between shots, unaware that a stranger just off the street studied their play.

The man watched intently from his barstool seat, not paying the slightest attention to the beer at his elbow. Through the haze, he particularly noticed the larger of the two men who seemed to be having his way with the balls. The man was not a good pool player but was leading the other by making some very easy shots. The smaller of the duet hardly aimed in his effort to make a ball, an effort that rarely paid off. Although their conversation was lost to him, he sized up the situation and decided some easy money could be made on these two hicks. He sat patiently, awaiting his opening for the game was nearing its close.

The heavier on the two men was a tall blond-haired boy with a touch of farm in his dress. He was seventeen years to be exact and a husky kid at that. His companion matched his height but was darker and slightly thinner. He was a snappier dresser and about four years older. Both young men were more involved in their conversation than the game at hand for neither had much money, and they wondered where the next dollar would find them. The war had been over for months, and although they had enlisted, the end came so fast that they found themselves on the street again. President Wilson had brought home victory, but the economy began its postwar slump. Jobs were few, the times were lean, and talk was the cheapest commodity around.

"Fred, you're not even trying," said the blond kid, rolling the stick in his hand.

"I know, but money is on my mind, not pool, Gus!"

"Well, think about the twenty-five cents this table is costing us!" gripped Gus. "Shit, if there was money on the line, I wouldn't be beating you this way. You're not playing worth a damn."

"I know, but there's got to be a way of makin' some big money, Gus. Hell, I can't keep on selling these check-writing machines, and there's not much money in hustling pool. Besides, nobody will play me in Alton or St. Louis anymore unless they've never seen me before."

Gus bent over and made the next to the last ball and moved into position for the final shot.

"Fred, why not go back over to St. Louis and play some of those darkies along the river?"

"Because those niggers are as broke as we are, and anyone who's got some cash either knows me or is investing in a bottle. They get mighty thirsty on the river in the summer!"

"You know, I heard that some of those boys is stashing bottles in case the country goes dry!" returned Gus, moving back off the final shot.

"Well, if those prohibitionists make it, there'll be some good money to be made in bootlegging liquor. Go ahead and finish this game and let's move, Gus, there's no moneymakin' here!"

Gus made the last ball and turned to Fred. "Why don't we go to some other towns and play, isn't that what Brown was doing with you?"

"Yes! But he's gone now, and traveling takes money. Money we don't have!" said Fred, turning to finish his coke.

As he lifted his glass, he noticed the stranger for the first time. The man moved off his stool and came toward them. He was a well-dressed gentleman and very out of place in these surroundings. Nevertheless, he was impressed. The man approached Gus and nodded a hello.

"Excuse me, men," he began. "I'm traveling through town and happened in to escape the heat. I noticed you playing and wondered if I might join you in a few. I'd be glad to cover the cost of the table and a round of beers. I might even entertain a sociable get or so on the side! How about you, young man!" He looked at Gus.

"Oh no, sir, I only play for fun, and money is a little short..."

"I'd be pleased to, sir" chimed in Fred. "Though I'm only fair in the game, I'd give you sporting opportunity, especially since you're a stranger in town!"

"Shall we play for five, young man?" asked the gentleman, motioning toward the table. "I'd play for more, but it is only a sport to me, and I think we're evenly matched," said the man. "At lease, it'll be a pleasant way to pass a hot afternoon."

The balls were racked; Fred broke and gave the gentleman his first opportunity. The older man made one and missed on the next attempt. Realizing from the conversation that the stranger had observed his game, Fred continued to just miss balls until the game was near the end. His opponent played a fair game, but Fred could see restrained ability in the man's stroke. As the last ball dropped in, Fred reached for $5, the only bill in his pockets.

"Nice game!" said Fred. "You're good!"

"Nothing of the kind, you just had some bad luck," the gentleman returned. "I'll tell you what. I think we're a match. Now how about another for rrr...let's say...twenty?"

"That's awful generous of you, sir. I'll try you once more."

"Fred," cried Gus, "what the hell—"

Fred cut off Gus and took him to the side. "It's okay, I can beat him."

"But where are you getting the twenty if you don't?" replied Gus, turning away from the table.

"We're partners, right!"

"Right, but this is all we've got."

A crumbled wad of bills totaling $16 appeared in Gus's hand. Fred quickly relieved him of his green burden and turned to his opponent.

"I'll give my twenty to Gus here to hold just in case this country boy is being hustled if that's okay with you, sir?"

"Fair enough!" he replied, handing a new $20 bill to Gus.

The balls were racked a second time, with the stranger obviously giving Fred an opportunity. Fred continued his usual play just nipping his opponent in the end.

"The balls ran for you that time, son. You got your five dollars back plus a nice profit of fifteen dollars. I've got fifty dollars more here if you'd like to go again."

"I was lucky that time, but maybe it'll hold," Fred mused, reaching out for some fresh chalk and smiling to himself.

The gentleman gave a fifty to Gus. Gus looked at the bill and staggered into the wall, sitting down in the process as if the weight of the money he held was too much for his country legs. Fred smiled at Gus; the hustle was on.

"I believe it's your break, sir!" Smiled Fred, giving his opponent plenty of room.

The man moved over the cue ball and spiked it into the rack. Balls spread over the table, just missing the third. His opponent then stepped up, firing one ball after another until just the eight ball and one of his solid balls remained. His next shot was a deliberate miss; Fred looked at Gus and walked over to the wall where his friend sat.

"I think he knows that's all the cash we've got, and he's going after it," whispered Fred. "This is one hustler who is going to be busted."

Fred moved back to the table and chalked his stick. "Nice shooting," commented Fred as he moved for position.

"You just left me some easy shots," he replied.

"Well, I hope my luck holds out because you're almost done."

Fred looked over the field and began making shots—sloppy shots to make him look lucky and easy balls to make his play believable. Finally, three balls remained in play; the eight, a solid, and Fred's last striped ball. The thirteen sat square in the corner, but the cue ball had rolled to a bad position. His shot was blocked by the eight ball and the three ball. Fred knew a safe play would most likely be his last for the stranger was better than he let on. The only safe was to attempt the shot. Since it was do or die, why not ante the bet especially since the shot was obviously impossible.

"A nice run, but your lucks run out!" Laughed the gentleman. "The shot can't be made."

"I've another hundred that says it can," Fred taunted, moving to the wall.

Fred strolled over to his jacket and patted the lump in the pocket. Gus's eyes rolled, and prayer fled his lips. The stranger pulled his money clip out and threw a fresh one on the table.

"You're a smart-ass", he gripped. "And you don't have a chance!"

Fred picked up the hundred and handed it to Gus, who already had a death grip on the kitty. Fred stepped to the rail and chalked again, his collar wilting from tension and heat. His palms were moist, and cotton came to his mouth. He'd seen big money before and this was no different, but the shot was something else. As he looked over the balls, his mind wandered to another time. The second trip he made with Brown.

*****

Brown took Fred to St. Louis in September 1912. Since the first trip, the talk around the Fagan Brothers' Billiards often got to be about the fourteen-year-old son he brought in one night last June. They couldn't remember his actual name and began to refer to him as Young Tennessee Brown. The talk created a lot of interest in this boy protégé. Those players, decent and otherwise, began looking forward to his and Brown's return. Potential matches were already being anticipated. Much to Brown and Fred's surprise, they were heartily received the afternoon they appeared in the hall.

"Look who's here, gentlemen," announced the older Fagan brother. "It's Tennessee Brown and his son, the younger."

Fred and Brown looked at each other and smiled, both very satisfied that their last visit had been a memorable occasion. In fact, when the patrons were introduced to Fred, all Fagan could think of was Young Tennessee Brown. With that, both he and Brown accepted the moniker and continued to let it be known around the St. Louis bars and pool halls that they were a father-and-son duo.

*****

As Fred came back to the game at hand, he thought to himself, *I'm Young Tennessee Brown! I can't lose to this guy!*

The balls came back into focus. There it was, the shot that Brown showed him back in Alton. The shot he practiced every day at Brown's Hotel after dropping his last papers, the shot that taught poise and control. The balls were in the same alignment, only in a different spot on the table. It didn't matter. He had practiced this from every possible position. He just had to address the cue ball as he had done all those times before. Brown said it appears often and seems impassable. Stroke and speed were the only way to pull it off. There it was.

His stroke was perfect, his speed beyond comprehension of the human eye, and the ball dropped out of sight. He quickly called the eight ball. It was over. The game and the hustle were over.

The stranger threw down his cue, turned quickly, and walked to the door. A gust of hot air rushed into the poolroom as he left. The blast of heat reached Gus, and he opened his eyes wide.

"We were dead to rights going to lose. The shot isn't possible, but I saw it with my own eyes!" he shouted, jumping up from his high chair. I don't believe I saw that!"

"You didn't Gus!" laughed Fred. "Your eyes were closed for the last two shots!"

"No, I was just cringing," he declared pointedly. "I always squint my eyes when I realize something bad is about to happen!"

"Where's the money you were holding?" Fred asked, looking at the Gus's shock of blond disheveled hair.

Amazement turned to realization that in the excitement of jumping from his seat, the money had slipped from his death grip and fallen like a napkin from his lap onto the sawdust floor. He fell to his knees and swept the pile of cash into his large hands and made a fist with the wad and waved it above his head. He spread it out on the green felt and began dusting off every note.

Gus and Fred picked up their belongings and headed for the door, throwing a buck to the proprietor on their way out. In the doorway, Gus began counting the winnings as Fred stopped him short, looking onto the street to make sure the man was leaving. He heard a car door slam, and the man drove by them just shaking his head. It was obvious he didn't believe what he just witnessed. Fred smiled broadly as the car disappeared into the hot afternoon. Turning on to the street, Fred took the money from Gus and recounted it. While Fred counted, Gus loosened his starched collar.

"My god, we were lucky!" Gus panted as his collar button popped and bounced into the street. As he bent to get it, Fred stopped him.

"Don't bother with it!" Smiled Fred. "We won $165 big ones here. That'll cover a lot of collars."

"We have more than that," said Gus. "What about the hundred in your coat pocket?"

Fred reached in the pocket and pulled out an order pad for check protectors and waved it in Gus's face.

"You bluffed the bet?" cried Gus as shock replaced his smile.

"Yep!" Fred chirped, waving the pad over his head.

"You're truly crazy!"

"Crazy and fat with cash!"

Things picked up as summer crawled into fall. Fred was able to pick up a few big games at Brown's and took a few trips back to St. Louis to play at Fagan's. It was October, and the harvest was over. Uncle Ben had sold the farm, and the Whalen family decided to return to Chicago where Mr. Sykes was happy to have him back. The Palace Pool Hall offered Fred $50 to play exhibition pool games with his friend, Rudolf. Along the way, he continued to pick up big money games as more players made their way to Chicago. The idea of exhibitions on weekends was good money without the gambling risks. Fred decided to have posters made, advertising his appearances in small towns throughout Indiana and Illinois. Gus would take the posters to these towns and set the dates, which he'd printed in the middle in large letters.

In November, Lilly announced that she was pregnant and the new baby would arrive in May. Fred was delighted with the news and set himself to work harder to accumulate more capital. It was decided that Lilly would return to St. Louis in March and have the baby there with her mother and siblings. This would free Fred to spend more time working and handling road exhibitions.

During that time, he continued selling coupons and playing at the Palace Hall on Saturday nights. On Fridays, he and Gus would drive to a small town and play exhibitions. Gus found work, delivering alcohol at night from Monday to Thursday. He had returned to his mechanics job during the days. Fred's friends, Billy "Red" Cole and Jerry Parker, were recruited by Gus to ride as protection for the alcohol loads. The money was good at every end of their enterprises. In two months, they had put together over $10,000.

It was May, and time to head to St. Louis for the baby's arrival. Fred and Billy each bought a 1921 Hudson Super Six Phaeton. The cars were large enough for seven passengers each. With the remaining $1,600, they followed each other to St. Louis. Fred and Gus drove one, and Billy and Jerry drove the other. These cars were 76 HP and could hit speeds up to seventy miles per hour.

Arriving at the Wunderlich Boarding House, they were received as Homeric heroes returning from an odyssey. Ema ran down and hugged Fred, welcoming him home. It was a far cry from those first months, back in 1915, when he was a no-good, son-of-a-bitch pool hustler, making a living hunting revivals. Ema had become a believer. Lilly looked radiant and well cared for when she returned home to have her second child. Bobbie and her cousin, June, Florence's daughter, played on the porch as the greeted and greeters came up the walk. It was an occasion to remember, especially the rides in the new cars that followed.

On May 11, 1921, Jack Frederick Whalen was born. The entire family was excited, especially because the baby set a weight record at the St. Louis hospital. Jack was a monster baby, big-boned and chubby. Fred looked at his new child and swore that the boy would have more advantages than him.

As soon as Lilly and Jack were able to travel, the group returned to Chicago.

Fred continued to work and hustle but had doubts about having his family settled in the city.

He had not seen his mother since her move to the West Coast. Her occasional letters revealed loneliness and a longing to see her two grandchildren. In spite of the activity and the potential to earn a decent living, Fred and Lilly agreed they should move to Los Angeles. In the last year, Uncle Ben and Aunt Ollie had joined Fred's mother in California along with her younger sister, Louise. Fred's mother had gotten a job with the city library, and Beulah had gone to work in an office. The relatives had settled in Southern California and wrote that the weather was so nice, that they weren't missing winters in Alton. Uncle Ben bought a small orange orchard farm in the San Fernando Valley and was adding avocado trees, whatever they were.

By mid-August, they were ready to leave. Billy Cole and his wife had decided to join the move, and their small caravan of two Hudson Super Sixes left for the West Coast. Gus rode with Fred up front, and Lilly tended the two children in the back. Jack was only a few months old, so Gus rigged a sling that swayed with the car's motion, and Jack was quiet and happy most of the way. The travelers left Chicago with a heightened sense of adventure. They were heading into the new frontier, not knowing what to expect. Fred just hoped that pocket billiards had gone west too.

The party traveled west along the old route, basically following train tracks. This took them through Omaha, Lincoln, and to Denver. This road took them to the edge of the Rockies and the Continental Divide. From Denver, they headed south over Raton Pass into Santa Fe and on to Albuquerque. From there, the route straightened out. Route 66 made a beeline to Los Angeles. The early fall weather was ideal for traveling. They beat the winter in Chicago, and the summer sun was not as hot. Once west of the Mississippi, all realized the vastness of the west. Distance had a new meaning. Towns were spread out and much smaller than those they grew up in. The sky was open and immense.

Young Tennessee Brown
Fred L Whalen at 20

Even the larger towns seemed frontierish and more like outposts of civilization. It was new and exciting. The trip immediately familiarized them with cross-country traveling. Fred, Gus, and Billy would set up camp with tents and cooking pits while the two women looked after the children and broke out the picnic-like meals that they had packed and replenished along the way. Being in unknown places was a bit unsettling, but having Billy's boxing skill and Gus's overwhelming size reassured their confidence that they could tackle any adversity along the way. Fred didn't think his wispy tall frame gave anyone pause.

The hours of driving were made bearable by frequent stops for fuel and provisions. During these rest stops, Fred and Gus would locate a poolroom or saloon with a table. Fred was hardly challenged in the smaller towns, but $5 here and there added up to reduce the costs of travel. This changed when they reached Colorado Springs.

In Colorado Springs, Fred met Bunny Brunell. He was the Colorado State Champion. Bunny had spent some time in St. Louis playing and had heard the stories told about Young Tennessee Brown and Johnny Layton. As Fred and Gus walked up the stairs to the poolroom, they saw, along the walls, the printed results of an exhibition between Bunny and Tommy Hueston, the current World Champion. He had beaten Hueston badly with a score of 450 to 387. Fred was sure that Bunny was quite sure of himself and proud of his victory. Who wouldn't be?

"We may be in for a difficult time here!" Gus whispered to Fred as they entered the room. "He beat Tommy Hueston."

"It doesn't matter, Gus," Fred said. "The first one on the table to run balls wins!"

Fred was glad to hear someone whisper those words even if it was he. The room was a showcase for Brunell, and he wasn't hard to spot. He was playing a game with no particular enthusiasm, which foretold his enlarged sense of superiority. Gus and Fred knew they were being watched. Fred was carrying his cue case. The duo moved unobtrusively among the tables to a better vantage point. Both men were silent and did not speak to each other for a few minutes while watching Bunny shoot. Fred watched Bunny intently, looking for any weakness in his technique. Bunny was a damn good pool player.

"Fred! He's good!" Gus whispered.

"He's damn good!" Fred returned. "But I can take him!"

"My money's on you!" Gus cheered. "We can't afford to lose here!"

Fred continued watching as Bunny moved around the table. Bunny was getting ready to make a difficult shot and looked up at Fred. As soon as Bunny was facing in his direction and their eyes met, Fred said, "You're pretty good!" As he turned toward Gus, he said, loud enough for Bunny to hear, "Not good enough!"

Bunny didn't waste any time responding to Fred's accusation and returned, "You're pretty mouthy, aren't you?"

Fred smiled and didn't acknowledge Bunny's charge. Instead, he let Bunny's anger grow a little, working its way into his cue, affecting his shots. He missed an easy shot, and his frustration with Fred's comments grew. Bunny looked up at Fred. Fred's expression said it all, "I told you so!"

Bunny noticed that Fred was carrying a cue case and challenged, "Do you play?"

The room fell still as other players looked up from their tables.

"Where's your money to back you up, big mouth?" Bunny charged.

Fred reached into his pocket with practiced grace, exposing a folded wad of cash, his eyes not leaving Bunny's glare. He fanned $800.

"Any or all!" Fred responded, laying it out on the table. "Now or later!"

If Bunny was taken back by the display of cash, it was not obvious. He nodded and said, "Fifty for fifty!"

This was straight pool, 14.1 continuous rack. The game and bets were made. Fred laid $50 on the table, and Gus began covering side action. The preliminary rituals were begun as Fred removed his jacket. Lifting his case onto the table, he removed an assembled his cue. Bunny noticed the inscription, Young Tennessee Brown, on the handle as Fred screwed it together. Both men chalked their cues. Fred bridged and stroked the cue ball to get the feel of the felt and speed of the table. A coin was flipped, and Bunny won the toss. The game was set in motion with Fred's break.

Bunny was good. He ran the fifty balls. He relished his local followers cheering him on. He agreed to another game that produced the same result. Fred was down $100, not to mention Gus was losing all the while in side bets. Bunny was eyeing the door, but his worshippers were doing well on the sides and wanted him to continue. Fred could tell he wasn't a big money player and raised the ante to $200. The Colorado Springs boys had seen mostly $20 games in rare occasions, but this was ten times the pressure, and most hadn't ever envisioned seeing this size bet. Everyone swallowed hard and looked to Gus to double up on.

Gus looked at Fred with more than concern registered on his face. This was bottoming out their traveling money. Fred smiled, and Gus calmed down.

Bunny looked a little anxious, and the crowd felt it safer to spit out their chew. Spittoons were ringing throughout the place. Fred egged him on. He looked at Bunny and saw that his ego and fan base were on the line. He was committed even though he began to doubt his stamina for playing.

"Does two hundred dollars take you off the table?" Fred asked in a tone everyone understood.

Bunny lagged without saying a word. Fred won the lag, and Bunny broke.

Fred never looked up from the table running fifty balls and out. Fred barely moved the cue ball around the table. If it moved more than a foot, it was rare. Bunny took his defeat and declined further play. Gus circulated around Bunny's supporters, collecting the side. In all, they added $800 to the enterprise as the side bets netted more than the game.

"You're him!" Bunny said.

"Yep!" Fred replied.

"I heard about you in St. Louis," he continued. "You're better than I thought! You know how one hears stories and most seemed exaggerated. You're a good player but better at working your opponents."

The party packed up the next morning after Gus spent most of the evening telling the Bunny Brunell story. Billy had wished he'd been there but knew he was security for the families and accepted his role. The next stop was Albuquerque. The group spent three days there and turned west. While there, the girls wanted to walk around the town looking at the shops. Billy, Gus, and Fred began searching for a poolroom and a game. They walked into the first one that presented itself.

"Where are your twenty-dollar players?" Fred inquired.

There was some hesitation and most shook their heads. Others just put their heads back down and continued playing. A smaller soft-spoken gentleman stepped away from the bar and accepted Fred's challenge. The crowd seemed to approve, and Fred played the man. The man won, pocketing Fred's $20.

"Let's go again and double it!" Fred said.

"No thanks, but I'll play for another twenty," he offered.

The result was the same. Fred was now down $40.

"Well, now you've got forty dollars, so we can double the bet!" Fred said.

"I can't let you leave without giving you a chance to get even."

Fred got the best of the game and recovered his $40. No one wanted to make side bets, so Billy and Gus just watched. Fred suggested another game, but the smaller man declined.

"I know you're a player, and I'm smart enough to know when I'm outclassed and being hustled," he responded. "I'm no fool, and I can see from those fine cars out on the street that you'll have to find someone else to work."

He asked where Fred was from. When he heard Chicago, he said, "You're a long way from home."

He asked if Fred knew Irwin Rudolph. This questioned reminded Fred that Rudy had told him about a smaller man in Albuquerque known as Midget Dukes.

"Do you know Midget Dukes?" Fred asked.

"You're speaking with him," he replied.

"Rudy told me to look you up and that we could make some money together."

"After beating me in front of the crowd here, there's no way anyone would play you!" Dukes explained.

A moment later, Dukes took Fred aside and said that there might be a way to make some money in Albuquerque. He was pretty sure he could get a crowd to pay to see an exhibition.

"Tell you what!" Dukes offered. "If you can stay for a couple of days, I'll promote a match between you and me. They've seen me win a couple and would probably want to see me go again, especially if I bill you as the famous Young Tennessee Brown."

Fred agreed to do afternoon and evening matches for $250. The first four matches, Fred stalled by taking shots he would normally pass for better ones as they presented on the table. This allowed Dukes to win. Into the fifth match, Fred was down 180 balls when Dukes missed. Fred started to shoot, thinking that he would challenge himself to catch up. Fred started running balls at a rhythm that made Dukes nervous. It was looking like Fred would catch up and surpass Dukes. Fred was on fire. He couldn't miss, and some shots brought out oohs and aahs from the crowd. Fred pulled within seven balls and missed, much to his opponent's relief. They finished the sixth match, and the exhibition was over. Fred, Gus, and Billy packed up the families and headed west.

The closer they got to California, the fewer stops they made. They had been on the road for over three weeks and were anxious to finish their odyssey. Fewer stops meant fewer opportunities to make extra cash to offset the expenses. Once they arrived in Los Angeles, Billy and his wife went to a hotel. Fred and the family spent two days camping in Elysian Park until they joined his mother and sister. Winifred and Beulah were excited to have the children underfoot. Fred was happy to be spending time with his mother.

Billy and his wife stayed in Los Angeles for a month before going back to Chicago. He sold his Hudson for way more than he paid for it as West Coast delivery charges on new cars were high. Fred saw them off on the train from La Grande Station at Santa Fe Avenue and Second Street. The family stayed through the winter and watched it slip into spring. There was no comparison to the harsh Illinois winters, and they were glad to be in warmer climes. Fred's memories of Christmas hustling with Rudy to make money gave him a chill.

L-R Fred George Wunderlich Billy Cole with Wives behind each

They explored Los Angeles and its surrounding area. They found it small compared to St. Louis and Chicago. In 1922, the city was still very much surrounded by farms and ranches. They visited Uncle Ben in the San Fernando Valley and would take day trips with everyone in the Hudson out to the orange groves. This was their first exposure to Mexican food. They all enjoyed it, especially the guacamole. The sunny days were wonderful, but it still seemed very rural to them. They had become accustomed to the large cities but appreciated the climate and decided they would return east and somehow gather up Lilly's family and bring them back to California as soon as financially possible. The followed Billy Cole's lead and sold the Hudson for more than they paid and left on the train.

After arriving in Chicago, they experienced a rather chilly summer and felt their plan to bring all back to Los Angeles was the best decision. Fred went back to Sykes selling photo coupons and playing pool. He moved his play from the Palace to the Adams Street Billiard

Room. He was alone now hustling pool except for his brother-in-law, Gus. Fred still saw Rudy but declined partnering with him as he realized Rudy loved playing the game more than he loved the money that could be won.

Fred was making a living, keeping the family fed and warm. Lilly made most of the children's clothes and took in outside sewing from fellow boarders. It was not enough money to fulfill their dream of moving Lilly's family to California. Fred kept doing what he knew best, hoping that some opportunity would present itself.

While Fred was playing at the Adams Street Hall, he came to know a man he and Gus referred to as "The Candy Man." They didn't give him the moniker. The players in the room always referred to him as such. Years later in conversations reminiscing about the past, the family would refer to that time as "The Candy Man Time."

One early afternoon on a Saturday, around one o'clock, Candy Man approached Fred. He, in fact, was a candy manufacturer. He was newly made wealthy from his business and wasn't accustomed to the leisure time it afforded him. He had come to this station in life through sheer determination and perseverance. One could see that he was once a hardworking stiff that put his dreams to work and had made a success of them.

He was a heavyset man with heavy shoes with taps, and Fred could tell his dress was more in line with his roots. He did have a flare for dressing and was able to afford fine materials in his suits although the cut and shape would have made Anthony of St. Louis wince.

Fred was talking to Johnny Layton when the Candy Man introduced himself. He politely waited for Fred and Layton to finish their conversation. Fred turned as Johnny walked away.

"Can I help you, sir?" Fred inquired.

"Over the last few Saturdays, I've watched you play, and I must say I'm very impressed with your style and game," he returned. "I was wondering if you would play me?"

Fred agreed and walked over to rack the balls. He approached the man and wanted to make it clear that he did not play for fun but for money.

Candy Man was very sure of himself and responded, "I do understand and expect to wager when we play. Would twenty be enough to interest you?"

Fred nodded and indicted that it was his honor to break. They played 14.1 to 100 points. After a few strokes, Fred realized his opponent was very green. After reaching one hundred balls, Fred took the twenty and put it in his pocket. Fred did not ask if Candy Man wanted to continue, thinking the gentleman had learned a lesson.

"Please, can we play another?" he asked.

Fred agreed but felt he was taking advantage of the man. They played another game of one hundred. Fred won 100 to 30. It was like printing money. Fred then gave the man a twenty-ball advantage to make it more interesting. It was like handicapping. Twenties were disappearing into Fred's pocket as fast as he could shoot one hundred balls. He continued increasing the man' advantage until it was 100–50. Eventually, Candy Man reached his limit and thanked Fred for the games. Fred took a fistful of twenties home to Lilly and related the story of the Candy Man.

The very next Saturday, the Candy Man walked in asking for Fred just after the lunch hour. Fred was astonished to see him back for more. He asked that the games be rated 100–60. That was fine with Fred. Gus sat patiently, wondering why someone would knowingly play again and again with the same result. Fred thought it was refreshing that someone expected to only play for money and not for pleasure. Candy Man was as regular as the clock striking one every Saturday afternoon. Gus got so tuned in that he could hear the man coming because of the taps.

Fred never considered hustling the man for larger wagered games. He was content to pocket $240–$260 every Saturday. It wasn't long before the gentleman started showing up on Wednesday evenings. Eventually, Candy Man played Fred three times a week. He did improve, and why not, he was taking very expensive lessons. There were times he'd get to the hall before Fred and would turn down other players, saying he'd wait for Fred.

This continued for months. He began asking questions regarding Fred and his family. When he discovered Fred had children, he began bringing candy with him, handing the bag of sweets to Gus. He became curious about what Fred was doing with the money. Fred elaborated on his situation and told him the money was being put away so that he could move his extended family to California.

Slowly, additional members of the family migrated to Chicago. Lilly's brother, Georgie, came up on the train. He arrived wearing shoes that were so small Fred had to almost carry him to a taxi to get him home. As the number of family members increased, Fred rented a flat. It was a cheap building with no heat, and winter was coming on. It was already getting cold, and the wind blew through the cracks around the doors and windows. The children stayed in their bed while the adults wrapped themselves in blankets. It was more than Fred could stand, watching his family shiver. He made the decision to move the family back to California.

With the money they had put away from the Candy Man, Fred bought two used touring cars, a Doris and a Mormon. The cars had heaters and good tires. There was no reason to stay any longer in Chicago. The Clark Street flat was a miserable place. Fred said good-bye to Mr. Sykes who was sorry to see him go on one hand, but with Fred not selling, the studio could catch up. It was an easy decision for all concerned. Once the cars were loaded with their meager belongings, the family sprinted from the cold house to the warm vehicles.

Fred felt better about buying used cars, knowing that Gus was an accomplished mechanic; he could jump in and remedy any unforeseen breakdowns. They were a ragged band, but at least they were warm and heading south toward warmer country. Fred had enough money left over for gas and food to get them to the next few towns, but past that, he was going to have to hustle to make the trip west.

Although Fred had asked everyone to only take the essentials, he accepted the fact that the running boards were going to be used as shelves. The vehicles looked like they were held together with rope. Personal items were hanging from every possible edge plus loaded on the roof. The occupants within were huddled close together, not by choice but necessity. Gypsies looked better than the Whalen clan.

Gus drove the Doris and Fred was in the Mormon. There were four Whalens, and the rest were Wunderlichs. The cars moved slowly through the early November snow that covered Chicago streets. Traction was no problem as both cars were definitely carrying maximum weight and capacity. Lilly's mother had come to Chicago with Georgie a few weeks before. Her two hundred pounds afforded a soft pillow for the children. Fred laughed to himself as he pictured the group crammed into the cars.

Gus had Toots, Georgie, Rel, Bernice, Florence, her husband, and daughter, June. Fred's Mormon carried Lilly, Bobbie, Jack, little Peggy, and Ima. It dawned on him that they might have to go without lunch the next two days. The remaining dollars totaled fifteen. He decided it would be useless to worry. They were on their way, and the facts at hand were dire, but it was what it was.

The first stop was Davenport, Iowa. They drove down the main street, the women looking for a place to eat while Fred and Gus looked for a poolroom or saloon: any place that might have a table. Having spotted one, the caravan pulled off the street, and all got to stretch their limbs. Fred and Gus walked into the pool hall and looked to see if there were any money games in action. Finding the right table, Fred eased himself into a game of rotation. This was very popular in smaller towns. It was a game of luck to most players, but for a professional, controlling the cue ball made all the difference in the world. Since you were required to shoot the lowest numbered ball on the table, you needed to use the cue ball in the same shot to kick in higher-numbered balls. The first one to reach sixty-one points won. Fred's ability at caroming and confidence controlling the cue ball gave him the advantage. He, of course, made every shot that dropped two or more balls look purely accidental.

He had become an entertaining table talker while he played, feigning surprise and astonishment when extra balls rolled into the pockets. It wasn't long before he had won a number of games. Gus made some light betting side wagers, and between them, they put together $55 to further finance the trip. Fred and Gus caught up with the family in time to clean some plates and pay the dinner tab. Gassed up and reloaded, the caravan continued on.

They stopped for the night in Des Moines. They were around four hundred miles from Chicago and found a motor court for the family. Fred and Gus let out to find a pool game. They were not having any luck. The games they checked out were penny ante and not worth the time. They needed to find something. The next morning, Fred was up after a light breakfast and started down to a hotel nearby. While standing in the lobby, a man approached him. The afternoon, the day before, both Gus and Fred made it clear that they were looking for money games. The word must have gotten out to the right people as this man was out looking for them.

"I understand you, gentlemen, are looking to play for money?" the stranger asked.

"We are," Fred replied, looking to Gus standing off to the side.

"I'm Walter Wilson, and I like playing for money when I can!" he boosted.

"You've found a willing opponent!" Fred returned. "What's your pleasure?"

"There is a fine table hear in the hotel if that's to your liking?"

Fred nodded, and he and Gus followed the man into the adjacent lounge. Fred had heard of Walter while in Chicago, but the man was from an earlier generation. This would not be your typical hustler game. It would be matching his skills as a young player against a more seasoned player. It would come down to whom the game meant the most. Fred knew he was hungrier than Wilson but would have to draw on his own confidence in his playing ability.

"You've played in Chicago in the past, isn't that right?" Fred inquired.

"Yes, but not for years," he responded.

The amount was $25 for a game of one hundred balls. The amount wasn't important as Fred felt this was his first serious challenge to his ability after leaving Chicago. The game was close, but Fred prevailed. The second game was for the same amount, and Fred bore down, not wanting to risk wasting time and breaking even for the effort. Fred won by a slightly greater margin.

"I enjoyed our games, Fred!" Wilson said, handing $25 more to Fred.

"We could go again for fifty dollars!" Fred offered.

"It's difficult to play any serious competition here in Des Moines," he replied, offering Fred his hand. "Once in a while, a good player will stop in on the hustle, and in most cases, they are just good and I lighten their load. You, young man, are an excellent competitor and an accomplished player. You will do well."

"I enjoyed the play, Walter, and I hope we can do it again another time."

Fred and Gus left the hotel and gathered the family and continued toward Nebraska. In Omaha, Fred chose a Black restaurant that had eight tables in an adjoining room. While the family settled in to eat, he and Gus checked the action in the poolroom. Both men knew at once that this establishment was not used to an influx of White folk. It wasn't hostility, just curiosity. Fred had taken some of his candy money and bought a portable handpress before they left Chicago. His plan was to perform exhibitions if he felt outright that hustling wasn't an option.

The owner of the place saw that Fred was the obvious headman for the avalanche of whiteness that invaded his business. The man motioned Fred to come over to a remote corner to talk. The men sat down while Gus stood and surveyed the place. The man was straight upfront with Fred as he leaned back in his chair and made an assessment of this well-dressed White man.

"I'm a little confused why you and, shall I say, your family chose my place to dine," he asked, "considering there are plenty of White places nearby."

"The answer is this simple," returned Fred. "You have a poolroom which I would like to use for an exhibition this evening. I will play anyone, fifty or no count, for any amount of money, and afterwards, I will demonstrate forty-five exhibition shots with less than nine misses."

Fred continued in detail, telling the owner that he will place posters around Omaha publicizing the event at no cost. He emphasized the fact that he plays only for money and that the proprietor would be expected to enlist players he felt would play money games.

"If you are as good as you profess you are," he said, "I'd throw in fifty dollars to boot. Bring your people in here at seven o'clock to eat, and I will put you on at eight."

The deal was made. The men shook hands, and the family finished a late breakfast, having driven through the previous night. Fred found a motor lodge and rented three cabins. Everyone went to work printing the posters, and soon both Fred and Gus were driving the family around Omaha dropping of posters at businesses and tacking them to posts. The family was joyful, feeling of use in the family's enterprise, financing their trip to California. Fred went to other pool halls around town, giving the locals a taste of what was scheduled for that evening.

Seven o'clock rolled around, and the family had worked up quite an appetite as a result of hitting the town with posters. As the family dined, Fred couldn't help but notice a great number of people were drifting in and making their way to the poolroom portion of the restaurant. The bar was doing a brisk business even though Prohibition was in its early stages and hadn't been strictly enforced in some portions of the country.

The amount of folks that had come to watch was evident until Fred walked into the poolroom. Seven of the tables had been moved to the side walls and rear, leaving what appeared to be the best conditioned table in the middle of the room. The bodies were packed so tight that people stood on benches to look over others who had secured the better-viewing positions. Fred noticed the heat being generated by such close quarters.

Fred looked around the table and felt all eyes were on him. The place was full but not uncomfortable. The owner made a short announcement and gave the audience the schedule for the evening. Fred waited for an individual to be called on to begin the fifty-or-no-count portion of the exhibition. The owner hadn't motioned to anyone or called someone by name.

"Let me have that man, let me have him!" someone shouted from the doorway.

A ripple went through the crowd, and bodies began parting as Fred's opponent made his way to the center of the room. The crowd loved this man's spirit and began clapping hands in anticipation. Fred could not see his opponent as the voice continued and came closer. All of a sudden, a bubble formed in a direct line to the front door. A small Black man emerged and walked to the table's rail opposite Fred.

The crowd was silent as the two men eyed each other under the smoky light that illuminated the table. Both men did a double take as they recognized each other.

"That's the man, he's the one who beat my Black ass this afternoon!" he exclaimed. "He cleaned me out! He broke me!"

Since there were no other takers, Fred proceeded to play his exhibition and trick shots, not missing a one. He took his time as not to let anyone of the crowd feel they didn't get their monies' worth. The owner, at the conclusion, gave Fred $50.

"You may not have gotten a money game tonight, but it was a worthwhile performance. I enjoyed the opening the most. The little son of a bitch you beat this afternoon has caused more trouble in my place than I can recall if I had a week to do it!"

Early next morning, the vagabonds were on the road heading for Denver. They turned southwest at North Platte and slowly climbed to the front range of the Rockies and the mile-high city. Stopping for gas, Fred asked the attendant where one would find the most excitement in town. He was told to check out Curtis Street if he was a player. Denver claimed it had the most lit street in the country. In a way, they were right. There was so much light that you couldn't throw a shadow. The place everyone agreed on was Sarconi's Billiards across the street from Brown's Palace Hotel. All the people, to whom Fred and Gus talked, said Slim Harris was the one they thought of as most highly a money player.

Fred knew Slim from playing in St. Louis and Chicago. They found Slim playing on Curtis Street and suggested that a match between them would bring in a paying crowd. It was agreed that Fred would win, giving Gus the chance to make the most money of the evening with side bets. The game was to take place at Sarconi's because of its location across from the hotel. The posters were printed up and the game touted at $250. Gus carried the balance of the family's funds to be used side betting. Fred was barely known in Denver, so betting would favor the local talent.

Slim and Fred lagged to break. Slim won and Fred broke. Harris ran nine balls and missed. Fred ran twenty-three balls and turned the table over to Harris in order to make this look like a close game. Slim got a hot cue and ran ninety-one balls and out, not honoring the agreement. Once you allow the other player to shoot, you are in a good position to lose, especially against good competition. Since Harris failed to let Fred win, Gus lost all the side bets. Slim, without a word, picked up the $250 and walked out the door, leaving Gus and Fred broke. Fred was furious at being taken this way. They were virtually penniless and in a tough spot. Returning to the family, Fred asked Lilly if she or any member of the family had any money.

"I have fifteen dollars and some change," she said.

Ema had ten and Florence had twenty. Other than some other small change, the total came to $45. Fred took the money and grabbed Gus. They went back to the Black side of town and started playing games for $5. He was determined to build back a sizable stake in order to replay Harris. Eventually, putting together $150, he returned to Curtis Street. The players there had watched Harris beat Fred the night before and felt that they, too, could cash in. With Gus using fifty of the stake for side bets, Fred enlisted a number of $25 games, playing eight-ball and rotation, intentionally, keeping them close. By the end of the evening, they amassed a kitty of $375.

Fred and Gus found Slim at Sarconi's and confronted him.

"You ran out on me without even an apology for reneging on our agreement!" Fred said. "You cost us all our side bets too!"

"I just got carried away!" Slim offered. "I was shooting so well that I just couldn't stop! I wasn't keeping track of the balls like I should have."

"We're going to set up a rematch for five hundred dollars tomorrow night!" Fred said. "You're going to break, and I'm gonna run one hundred balls and out!"

"I don't have that kind of money!" he said.

"You've got my $250!" Fred returned. "Bring it, and we'll let the balance float! A five-hundred-dollar game will draw a bigger crowd, and Gus can recoup our losses from the other night."

Harris agreed. The family printed up another bunch of posters and went around Denver, dropping them at businesses and every poolroom they could find. They gave the desk staff at Brown's Palace a handful plus a couple of dollars to promote the event with their guests. After all, the show was just across the street. The match was billed to start at 7:00 p.m. at Sarconi's. The crowd that assembled was almost two times larger than the first. The Seventeenth Street pool hall was so crowded that overflow tried to watch through the windows in front.

The two players made their ways to the table. The manager announced the match and what the stakes were. The crowd applauded, and as Harris bent to break, Gus shouted, "My money's on Whalen!"

This time, the locals stood in line to bet on the hometown player. Harris broke. Fred played safe, leaving Harris without a decent shot. Slim missed and sat down. Fred ran one hundred balls and out. Gus had made bets in excess of their available cash, but it didn't matter. They left Denver for Albuquerque the next morning. They had more than they needed to get the rest of the way.

L-R Fred Gus Bobbie Lil and Ema Arizona 1921

They stopped in Albuquerque but didn't look for Midget Dukes. They wanted to get to California as fast as they could. The road was wearing on everybody.

The road west to Gallup was no more than an improved trail. The road, which eventually became Route 66, hadn't been paved yet, and the dust and mud in places was a nuisance. Some of the road was no more than planks covering soft spots. Just outside Gallup, the two vehicles came to a river that was for the most part a dry bed. Water was running in a one-hundred-foot swath through the middle between the banks. Fred and Gus pulled onto the flat beyond the washed-out bank and looked across where a group of Indians were waiting with horses. The Indians were waving them on.

Gus looked at Fred and said, "This looks like a scam to me!"

"I think you're right!" he agreed. "Let's just wait and see what they're up to!"

In a few minutes, another car pulled up. Gus had seen them coming and lifted the sides of the engine compartment as if he were working on a breakdown. Fred's Mormon with the kids, and Lilly were in line right behind the Doris. Gus waved the new arrivals around them. The Indians waved the car on, and it plowed into the river at full speed and sunk to its hubs about halfway across. The Indians rode in to the river and roped the car's bumper and pulled it out, collecting a fee as they did.

Soon, another car arrived but turned and drove up stream to the north about two hundred yards. There the car crossed with no problem. Fred dropped the engine covers down, jumped behind the wheel, and led the cars across, waving to the disappointed Indians as they rejoined the road on the other side. The whoopin' and hollerin' made the children and their grandmother laugh so hard it rocked the overloaded car.

Gus began having trouble with the Doris, and Fred decided to push on to Gallup with Lilly, Florence, Peggy, and the four younger ones. Ema and the rest stayed with Gus while he fixed the overloaded springs. Fred drove through the day into night and became so tired he fell asleep driving. Florence grabbed the wheel and pulled them to a stop. Fred got in back with the children and went right back to sleep, not waking until Gallup. It was early morning, and they found a campground and would wait for Gus.

Fred decided to create posters again and play an exhibition that night, hoping Gus and the rest would make it sometime the next day. That evening, Fred was still tired and couldn't keep his eyes open and lacked concentration. He lost the match and barely made it to the campground before falling asleep. He slept the entire day. Gus arrived in the afternoon with all repairs completed. When Fred awoke, he cleaned up, and he and Gus went around Gallup looking for some action. They had been in a pool hall for an hour when a well-heeled gentleman approached them. He identified himself to be a local banker and suggested a proposition.

"I know where you can play for some decent money here," he said. "I would like to back you if you are interested."

Fred and Gus could not believe their luck. It was déjà vu! Another Candy Man had presented himself, and the play was on. They followed the banker to a poolroom at the edge of town. Upon entering, Fred noticed the clientele were playing on 4×8 tables. Playing on 4×8s instead of 4.5×9s or 5×10s was a good deal easier. A good player can run a lot of balls as long as one controlled the cue ball's position.

In less than an hour, Fred skinned the locals for $300. It went so fast that Gus barely had time for side bets, which dried up after the second match.

The trio walked outside, and Fred reached in his pocket to reimburse the banker and split the $300 he'd won.

The banker took the $450 and gave the split back, saying that he wanted to watch a real hustler work a room.

"It was barely an hour, but it was the most entertaining evening I've had here in months," he confessed.

The next morning, the two cars crossed into Arizona, but before leaving Gallup, Ema found a photo shop that allowed the entire troupe to be photographed as cowboys and Indians. They printed the picture, and Ema got three copies for $2. This became the most popular memento of the crossing to California.

The caravan made some quick stops for fuel and food. They pushed on into Flagstaff where they found a campground and pitched their tents for the night. The next morning, the girls printed up posters and made the rounds promoting another evening exhibition. Gus would act as the announcer during these exhibitions. Fred would run fifty balls regularly, and Gus would say, "Mr. Whalen just ran fifty balls as claimed by his advertisements and now will demonstrate some very fine exhibition shots!"

After the exhibition shots, a man approached Fred, wanting to play him fifty or no count. He said the owner would back him and pay Fred the fifty just for playing him. It would be an easy $50. Fred could not run fifty balls. He'd run forty-eight, forty-nine, and the man defeated him eventually. The owner was related to Fred's opponent and refused to pay because Fred had not won. The crowd started booing the owner and his relative until the man relented and handed over the fifty. There was a catch attached to the $50. He wanted Fred to rematch his relative for an additional $50. Same deal, Fred had to run fifty or no count. The relative broke and never got up from his stool. Fred ran fifty and took the $100 to the cheers of the crowd.

The roads were good from Flagstaff west. The weather was exceptional as they started into the mountain range separating Arizona and California. The road through the mountains was not the easiest to traverse. It was tricky driving as they dropped into the mining town of Oatman. Ema and most of the children refused to ride down the grade. They left the two vehicles and walked to the bottom. Oatman was still mining gold. Gus was in the lead and took the Doris through the first series of bumps which were part of a deep ravine that flash flooding had created. Fred and Gus waited at the bottom for Ema and the kids to remount. Once in, they started through the town, and in five seconds, they were out of it; it was that small. It was a line of small buildings that reminded everyone of the western towns one sees in movies. Fred stopped and decided to turn around and drive back through the short stretch of street that the buildings were on.

Fred parked and started walking the street because, in passing, he thought he notice a saloon with a pool table not far from the front windows. He walked inside and approached the man behind the bar.

"You look like you've been traveling awhile," he said. "Maybe you could use a stop here before heading on. I noticed your two cars as you went by. By the looks of things, you are probably like most moving to California."

"That's right!" Fred returned. "I imagine we look pretty ragged! I'm a salesman and a pool player. I usually play exhibition games to help with the cost of moving the family west."

"Well, you've come to right place," he said. "This town ain't much, but the gold miners do enjoy that table. Some even fancy themselves good players, and they always bet on a game."

"What time to things start poppin' around here?" Fred asked.

"By five o'clock, this place will be roaring!" he responded. "If you can stand the smell of hardworking stiffs, you'll make at least a one hundred dollar."

"It's three now," chimed in Gus. "We can get the ladies and kids fed and be ready to go. I'll get them started on a couple of posters, not that we'll need too many!"

Fred walked over to the table. It was in poor condition, but as long as there were six pockets, he could make it work. Gus got the ladies going, and in short time, they had ten posters ready to go. They walked to the few storefronts of Oatman and placed them by the doors. The only concern Fred had was the tears in the felt. He asked the owner if he had any paste. Getting some, he wet the edges of the tears and smoothed the paste lightly until the edges were relatively flat. The really bad ones he could jump the cue ball over.

The proprietor brought in some sandwiches for the children and some chili for the older members of the family. A couple of loafs of sourdough bread to sop up the chili and all was good. Fred offered to pay for the meal, but the owner wouldn't have it.

"The food's on me!" he said. "I'll make it up and lots more tonight if you put on a show. There isn't much to do hereabouts. You'll bring 'em in by the wagon load."

Fred said he had about forty exhibition shots that should entertain the customers. In fact, some are so fast they won't believe they
were makeable. He then limbered up his cue and made some example shots that told the owner this was no ordinary pool player. The
man sported a grin from ear to ear. His smile couldn't have been
bigger if his throat had been cut.

"Look! If you don't make at least one hundred dollars, I'll make
up the difference!"

At four thirty, the saloon started filling up. By five, the place was
standing room only. Gus figured the entire town and its surrounding area had descended on the place. The girls took seats spread out
around the room.

The four children were sitting on the end of the bar. Ema held
Jack in a sling, sporting a mug of beer in her hand. All were set and
ready to go. Gus made his usual introductory remarks, asking if there
were any cash players.

"What games will you play for money?" a man in the crowd
shouted out.

"Any that you might suggest!" Gus returned. "Eight ball, rotation, 14.1, etc.!"

Fred started a fellow with $20 in rotation, making it look as if
he got lucky with slop after hitting the object ball. Gus called the
game after sixty-five points on Fred's side were made. This went on
for about an hour until one miner wanted to play 14.1 to fifty. The
man put a $50 gold piece on the rail, and Gus matched it in cash.
The damn thing glowed in the light and was very distracting. Fred
broke, and the man sunk one ball and then missed his following shot.
Fred ran fifty and out. After that, there were no more takers.

Fred began his exhibition shots as everyone gathered closer to
the table. He was knocking balls around in near-to-impossible shots.
Shooting balls over blocking balls into the pockets. It was vaudevillian! The crowd hummed with the entertainment.

"That about wraps it up, ladies and gents!" Gus expounded.

The words had barely left his lips when gold coins started landing on the table. It looked like a golden shower! The girls jumped to
their feet and began gathering them up, putting them in places Fred

and Gus never knew existed. Fred had no idea how many coins the girls retrieved, but they hovered them up. Ema was even tipped while holding Jack. Coins were dropped in his sling, and the big-breasted woman even found some stuck in her corset.

They decided to drive into Needles on the California side that night. It was flat desert, and the heat had left for the night and the heaters were turned on.

The girls got out the flashlights and started counting their gold coins in the back seats. Fred and Gus never knew how much they gathered, but when they left Needles for San Bernardino, they all had new dresses and shoes.

Fred continued to get action along the remainder of the trip, stopping for fuel more than for food. The orange groves were easily picked, and more fruit was eaten than anything else. They drove on, finally arriving in Los Angeles. This would be the new family headquarters.

PART 3

Cleaning Up California

FRED AND GUS DROVE the cars to Elysian Part. They had camped here during their earlier trip to Los Angeles. It was raining, and the entire park was mudholes and wet grass. Fred could have taken Lilly and the children to his mother's, but after weeks on the road surviving together, all voted to stay in the park. It was the main campground in Los Angeles for new arrivals and hadn't changed much since their first trip. Fred's mother and aunts pressured them to at least let the children stay with them, out of the wet weather.

It was decided to move the kids in with their grandmother, and Lilly's mother joined them. In a few days, the caravan was spread out among Winifred, Aunt Lou, and Uncle Ben. Everyone was placed, and everyone immediately sought employment. Jobs were easy to find. Southern California offered a variety of employment. The silent-movie industry was still in its infancy with westerns being made at the studios along Wilcox Avenue. The family combined their extra dollars to keep everyone together. By the end of 1922, everyone was well established in Southern California.

Fred opened up a millinery shop for Lilly and her mother on Union Drive just off Sixth Street. They were excellent seamstresses and were supported by Winifred and Beulah when they had to increase stock in blouses, underwear, and slips. They also sold hats by Borodine and Royal. The family lived in the back of the shop, and their success was gratifying.

Gus had gone to work driving for a man who ran a small boot-legging business. Gus would drive at night, picking up five-gallon tins of alcohol and dropping it at the man's home. There, it literally became "Bathtub Gin."

Eventually, Gus began helping his employer mix the juice and bottle it. One afternoon, Gus went by the millinery shop and told Fred what he was doing.

"This guy's car was broken down along Sunset, and I stopped to help him," he related. "When I got him going again, he asked me if I was available to work for him driving a truck and taking care of his vehicles. He offered me fifteen dollars a day. I agreed and followed him to his place where he told me he was bootlegging gin."

Fred said, "Why aren't we doing that?"

Fred could see that selling whiskey and gin was a big money-maker. His sister-in-law had married a man named Jess Navarro. Jess had a home in Seal Beach where they'd take the family swimming. On one occasion, Fred noticed Jess making a lot of trips to the front door. Every time he'd return from the living room, he was stuffing his pockets with cash.

"What's going on at your front door?" Fred inquired.

"I've got a still in Boyle Heights."

During that time, Fred watched the California Hotel being built on Bonnie Brae and Sixth. Across the alley from the hotel was an open shop on 1919 West Sixth. Fred leased the space for a cleaning shop. He called it Day-and-Night Cleaners. The hotel entered into a contract with Fred to do their clienteles' clothing as part of their room service. Fred knew nothing about cleaning clothes. He hired a man who did. He set him up running the operation, which had taken off due to the hotel business.

"Jess! Can you deliver ten gallons of your stuff to me tomorrow at the cleaners?" asked Fred.

"No problem!" he replied. "I'd rather sell large quantities than risk the door-to-door business."

Fred loaded up the children and Lilly and headed back into Los Angeles. He found a place that sold bottles and a printer to make labels. Fred started selling whiskey and gin out the back of Day-in-Night Cleaners. It was the first drive-up-window business in Los Angeles. Drive-ins had started in Texas but hadn't migrated to the

West Coast. Fred offered window service for cleaned clothes, so why not booze? The first week opening the shop, clothes came in as fast as the booze went out. Fred had hired his operator from Old Fashioned Cleaners and started charging outrages prices for cleaning, thinking that would cut down the foot traffic. The hotel business was good, but foot traffic was even greater.

Across the alley from the back of the cleaning shop were the Colonial Apartments. They had an elevated dock that facilitated bring furniture into the building. Gus thought it would be a great place to store the hooch. He built shelves and covered the open front of the ten-foot dock with planks between the street and the loading deck. Fred didn't want the alcohol in the shop.

People would call in an order or come to the counter and pass a note with the quantity listed. Gus would collect the money, run out the back, put the order together, wrapping it in blue cleaning paper, and hand it to the driver as the car drove down the alley. On occasion, the business was so brisk both Fred and Gus were running. Fred and the family were bottling the liquor at home during the night. This was clear alcohol. They made gin by adding water and juniper berries for flavor and smell. The whiskey and scotch were a bit harder. There was a pharmacy at one end of the alley, and the owner wasn't blind and guessed what was going on. During Prohibition, the only way you could get legitimate whiskey was by prescription. The pharmacist agreed to sell Fred the pints established under the law with the government stamp.

These pints went for $2.50 each. For every five gallons of alcohol, Fred and Gus mixed three pints of the real thing. This gave it the color and taste needed to pass muster. They would then bottle the mixture in pints and fifths. At that time, 12 oz. was called a pint. Only Scotch and rye were sold in fifths. Each five-gallon batch would be caramel colored with a flavoring to give it a more authentic taste. The gin took a bit more mixing. Equal amounts of alcohol and water were mixed. Fred and the family would take turns blowing air into the mixture using a rubber hose. This would agitate the mixture and blend it. They would trade off blowing because it made them light-headed. The pint bottles went for $3.50 out the back door.

Each five-gallon tin plus thirty-six ounces of the real thing produced fifty-six pint bottles. The batches would gross $196. This netted around $160 profit. The family sold over two hundred pint bottles a day, more on weekends. The money coming in on a weekly basis was in excess of $4,500 on pints alone. More pints were sold because they were easily hidden on one's person. The labels read "Old Ontario" with a bogus bottling address in Canada. Many thought it was imported because the Canadian distillers were selling to smugglers. The majority of the population hated Prohibition. The Volstead Act only intensified the alcohol demand in the United States. Fred and Gus considered it a bad law and were just supplying the demand.

The business became so brisk that the cleaning had to be farmed back to Old Fashioned Cleaners. Fred kept racks of clothes up front behind the counter for appearance's sake. The family couldn't help but learn the cleaning business by osmosis. The amount of traffic generated down the alley attracted the wrong attention. The police decided to check the business out. Two detectives walked in one day and asked to look around. Gus happily obliged and gave them the tour. Finding nothing out of the ordinary, they left the premises. Blue pressed shirt bundles, with tags, were shelved by the back door. The help was passing the bags to motorist as they presented their receipts. If a booze customer handed the attendant an order, he would just look at it and say, "Not quite ready yet! Come back in fifteen minutes." This was done when they suspected someone nosing around.

The cash was piling up. Fred spread a lot of it among the family members that needed it. Still there was so much money that Fred decided to buy a lot in Beverly Hills. He bought the lot from Carl Rosenberger. It was on Ladoux Road. Fred thought he was probably the only pant presser living in the exclusive area. He had a home built and moved the family in. It was Lilly's dream.

Since they now resided in Beverly Hills, Fred decided to purchase one of the most powerful road vehicles on the market. The Stearns-Knight was a luxury touring car that seated seven and was touted as having a top speed near one hundred miles per hour. Frank Stearns was an engineering genius. Unlike Ford and others, he operated out of Cleveland, Ohio. He was the first automaker that used a dual-throated carburetor.

Fred was still leery of banks. He found while working in St. Louis that access to your money was dictated by the working hours of ten to five. When he needed money, he needed cash. Playing for money meant at any time you could be beaten for every dime on your person. Since weekends were the best time to hustle, banks were closed. Soon the family had accumulated over $250,000 in cash. Homes were broken into on a regular basis. Under the mattress or behind a pillow wasn't going to work. Installing a safe called attention to you. Fred called the family together for a Sunday dinner at the Ladoux Road home. He knew writing checks left a paper trail, and the only trail he would leave went in and out of pockets, not banks.

"Lilly, take the kids out to the backyard, please," Fred asked.

With the children out of earshot, Fred began explaining, "We've accumulated thousands of dollars and nowhere safe to put it!"

"There's always a bank," Ema offered.

"Mother Wunderlich, in our business, we may have to leave in a hurry!" Fred added. "We can't wait until the bank opens the next day!"

"I told you when you were little, if you want to hide something, put it out in plain sight!" Winifred said.

"This kind of money won't fit in a cigar box or flour tin on a shelf!" Fred explained.

"Well, if it's large? Why not put it in a laundry basket on the back porch near the clothesline?" Fred's mother suggested.

It was so simple Fred was speechless. Gus voted for the idea, and all agreed it was the answer.

"Just remember," Fred cautioned, "if we have to run, grab the laundry!"

The cleaning shop continued humming along. Even the police decided that bootlegging was not the biggest problem in Los Angeles. Besides, they like to drink too. Fred got involved in law enforcement charity events as well as various religious outreach efforts. California was growing rapidly. Many folks were still camping out at Elysian Park and most were in dire straits.

A man approached Gus at the cleaning shop asking if he might buy the business. Fred thought about it and decided the illegal operation was hands down a better cash cow. Actually, the cleaning business was more work than it was worth and not very exciting. On the other hand, it was a great front. The man kept stopping by, and Fred finally agreed to let it go. For the next month, Gus gave out new instructions to the liquor customers and gradually moved the pick-ups to an apartment house on North Alvarado Street above Beverly Blvd. Joe Lanahan became the new owner of the cleaning shop. Fred had bought the ten-unit building and moved family members into it. Gus had slowly elevated the rents until the current residence moved. He then closed the building and did some remodeling, especially on the back stair.

Gus was a mechanical genius. He took out the bottom run of steps and installed the replacement on hinges so that it would rise like a drawbridge. He left a thin gap between the first riser and the first tread. There he had two thin metal plates connected to a battery-operated spring latch. Just slide a pocketknife blade between and complete the connection.

The under stair became the warehouse for the booze. The front apartment was furnished as if Gus lived there. Clients would drive up and meet Gus in the front apartment. He would seat them and go out to the back, trip the stair mechanism, and return with the order. All family members were trained, and when the lobby doorbell rang, it rang in the other units. Whoever was in the building would go to the front unit and serve the customer. This was the first example of Gus's ingenuity. The only thing that needed changing was the car battery that ran the stair latch.

The apartment building was in an excellent location as it was close to downtown. At the time, most people lived around the city center and took the railcars to the outskirts. Most of the growth was moving west toward the ocean. Driving was still quite a luxury, and those people commuted to downtown in their cars. Many of them stopped once a week at the Alvarado Arms.

Return to Sender

FRED AND LILLY ALWAYS felt a bit out of place in California, especially in Beverly Hills. They were Midwesterners, and their educations had only progressed through the eighth grade. In the early twentieth century, an eighth-grade education covered quite a bit more than just the basics. In fact, some people, having received their education later in that century, would be hard-pressed to pass the general knowledge test given to both Fred and Lillian. They were self-made successes even though their means was south of the accepted norms of polite society.

The bootlegging business brought them in contact with many of the famous personalities of the time. It could be said that they grew right along with the newness of Hollywood's limelighters. After all, these new stars were a product of the burgeoning studio system. Hollywood parties were not serving tea. The Whalens and Wunderlichs supplied the fuel the roaring twenties made famous. Life had sped up, and the small-town life they left seemed so much easier to them.

After talking it over with the members of the two families, Fred and Lilly decided to travel back to St. Louis and Alton with their children. They would take the Stearns-Knight and travel leisurely back to the Midwest.

Fred left Gus in charge. Emma would stay at the Ladoux Road home with Lilly's younger siblings. They didn't have any set schedule and could not say when they would return. The original cleaning business had been sold, and the family was living in force at the Alvarado apartment building.

The trip back east was faster than before and uneventful. Fred stopped a few times and hustled some pool games, but his desire to play with his usual concentration was not there. He had made money in Los Angeles faster and easier than at any time in his earlier days. He built a new home and owned properties that were self-sufficient. His newfound wealth allowed him fast cars and better everything. Life wasn't a struggle as it was before. They both wondered if the trip was just a way to show off their success. They weren't sure. Everything they created was being shared throughout the family. No one really wanted for anything.

In St. Louis and Alton, they haunted the places of their earlier lives. It was not as gratifying as they thought it would be. Not much had changed in the years that had passed. In fact, it seemed to them the people weren't growing but staying in place. They both felt they were no longer comfortable with small-town life. They decided to move on to Chicago, hoping that would legitimize their desire to return to their past.

Fred was excited to see the rush of life that Chicago embodied. The movement was a stark contrast to Alton and St. Louis, even Los Angeles. Fred walked the streets, reacquainting himself with Chicago's sights, sounds, and smells. He non-intentionally was comparing it with life in Southern California. After a few days, they both realized they had completely embraced West Coast life. They decided they would return home having only been gone less than two weeks.

The day before their expected return west, Fred, while walking the downtown, noticed an animated crowd standing in front Marshal Field's on State Street. He crossed the street and made his way to the front of the display window. To his surprise, he recognized the man in the window. The man was imitating a robotic manikin, an advertisement gimmick that was very popular at the time. His face was expressionless, and he moved rigidly in slight jerks. The idea was if anyone in the crowd could make him laugh, that person was given a new suit or dress. It was Al Blake, an old friend from his earlier time in Chicago. As Fred stood there smiling, Al locked on Fred's grin and broke up. A new suit of clothes and a meeting with a friend.

Al immediately left the window, waving Fred into the department store. They greeted each other, and Al had hardly finished with the usual salutations when he began talking a mile a minute.

"Fred, I have a great moneymaking idea!" he offered.

"Well, I'm ready for adventure as always!" Fred replied. "What do you have in mind?"

"Are you here alone?"

"No. Lil and the children are with me."

"That's even better!" he said. "That's even better! How much money do you have?"

"A few hundred, but I can wire for more if need be."

"No, that's plenty!" he continued. "Let me go to the office and quit and don't move! You're gonna love this!"

Fred waited near the door, refusing offers to help him, waiting for Al's return. He thought it must be pretty good if Al's quitting on the spot. In ten minutes, Al returned with some cash in hand and a certificate for having made him laugh.

"I've been doing this for two weeks, and you were the only one to break me up!" He laughed.

"So what's the play?" Fred asked.

"What are you driving?" Al asked.

"A Stearns-Knight."

"That's even better!"

"Better for what?'

Fred was getting impatient, but couldn't fault the man's excitement.

As they turned the corner, Al began explaining his idea. He proposed that they go to a uniform shop just down the street and get him fitted as a chauffeur. Fred told him that he and Lilly were planning on heading home to California. That was fine with Al because the whole plan centered on leaving Chicago.

Standing in front of the mirror in his new uniform, Al placed the cap on his head and turned to Fred and asked, "How do I look, sir?"

They left the shop and drove to Al's apartment. He ran in and twenty minutes later returned with his wife and their luggage. They then drove to the Drake Hotel where Fred gathered Lilly and the children with their bags.

The Stearns-Knight pulled away from the hotel headed into the rural countryside on the outskirts of Chicago. While Al drove, Fred explained the scheme to Lilly and Al's wife. Fred was convinced Al's idea was a moneymaker and would add excitement and adventure to their travel.

L-R Al Blake Gus Fred Lil Bobbie and Jack
on the road in the Stern's Knight

An hour later, they drove into a rural town and stopped in front of a poolroom. Al got out of the car and lifted the hood, acting like something needed repair. The proprietor did not notice immediately, so Al went inside and ask to borrow a screwdriver. Fred waited a minute and walked in after Al, looking around at the pool tables.

Fred asked the owner, "Could you direct me to the nearest Western Union office? Oh, and, Alfred, I'll be waiting in the car."

"Yes, sir!" Al returned. "I should be able to effect repairs within an hour."

Getting directions, Fred exited the building, returning to the car, thus giving Al the opportunity to set the hook. Al struck up a conversation with the owner and insinuated that his employer was a California millionaire. He confided to the man that playing pool was his boss's favorite pastime and that he wasn't very good.

"My boss is nuts about the game!" Al added. "He has me play with him, and I can usually beat him. He likes to play rotation for twenty or fifty dollars. If you can get your best players, I'll slow down fixing the car."

The owner went right to work enlisting any players willing to play the California gentleman with the fancy car. In a matter of moments, he had a couple of pigeons. Everyone inside followed Al to the door and looked at the Stearns-Knight parked in front. Al knocked on the rear window, and Fred looked out.

"Sir?" Al began. "The repairs will take an hour or so. If you'd like you may want to go inside and have a refreshment and play some pool?"

"That would be excellent, Alfred!" Fred responded. "I can use the break from sitting all morning. Thank you!"

Al opened the rear door, and Fred stepped out, wearing his finest. Al showed him to the door and proceeded to introduce him to the owner. The owner, in turn, did the introduction to the player he was to engage. In a small-town setting, the idea of a $20 game was rare, but a $50 game was an event everyone in the place wanted to witness.

Once Fred had established the bet and money placed on the rail, he went right to work. In rotation, the rack is ordered one through fifteen with the one-ball at the apex of the rack. Fred always let the mark break. The victim typically would hit the one and pray that some ball would drop in a pocket, hopefully a big-numbered ball. Fred showed no mercy. He'd sink the object ball and send the cue after another high-point ball. Fred made the entire match look like he was just so lucky picking off the higher balls by accident. Most victims believed it was luck and would try to recoup their losses. One or two games at most. Sometimes, the owners would back a player and fall victim themselves.

"Thank you, gentleman," Fred would say while picking up the wager. "It's been an enjoyable hour and thank you again!"

He would leave the building, and Al would open the car door for him and they'd be off to the next place. They decided to head south. The chauffeur game worked flawlessly from Chicago to Fort Pierce, Florida. The play was a big moneymaker and paid all the expenses and more.

In Fort Pierce, Al got a game in an upstairs pool hall with the chief of police. The chief was not a gambling man, but the owner was. He offered to bet a hundred that the policeman could beat the rich Californian. The owner had gone to the window with the chief to look down at the car. They watched Al go through the same antic he had perfected on the drive down. When Fred found out he was playing a policeman, he did everything he could to get out of it. Al could not resist the money. He made the bet in setting up his boss with the stipulation that he be paid 10 percent for arranging the game. While looking for the exit, Fred noticed that one of the patrons was wearing an Elk's ring. Being an Elk himself, Fred asked the man if he would have any trouble if he beat the chief.

"No!" the man replied. "The chief is a stand-up guy."

"What shall we play?" Fred asked.

The chief said, "Fourteen point one, a hundred balls for one hundred dollars."

The chief broke, and Fred ran nine balls and missed. The chief then ran forty-two balls before he missed. Fred ran ninety-one and out. The chief walked over to Fred and shook his hand.

"You are a fine player, but I'm not in your class!" said the chief. "It was a nice game!"

As Fred and Al were leaving, the owner ran over and asked, "What's the most balls your boss has ever run?"

"Sixteen!" answered Al without hesitation.

"Were you blind on that ninety-one?" he exclaimed with an incredulous look on his face.

While traveling with Al, Fred played exhibitions. Al would get out of the car and go into his mechanical-man routine. He'd walk around stiff-legged with precise movements with each arm and head gesture. It always attracted a crowd, and the wives would pass out flyers for that evening's show. They would assure the folks that the mechanical man in the chauffeur's outfit would also appear. The combination worked out well as the audience would put tips in Al's cap when he finished.

On the way back north, they stopped in Nashville. This was the only time that Fred and Al were caught and exposed. While Fred was being shelled to the poolroom patrons, a person outside looked into the back seat and saw an unrolled flyer. The girls were at the hotel, and the car was unattended.

Fred had gone to the restroom while Al made his deal. He failed to notice the person that entered soon after Fred. While Al went to the back to get Fred, the new arrival handed the poster to the owner behind the bar. Fred came out and began playing the mark. After a few balls, he noticed a number of policemen entering from the rear door. He became uneasy, wondering if someone had recognized him or this type of hustle. He played on in spite of his suspicions. After winning, Fred scooped up the cash and was about to turn and leave.

"How about an exhibition?" called out the owner from behind the bar.

"I don't do exhibitions!" returned Fred, noticing that the police had moved in front of the bar alongside the owner.

"This says you do!" he said, holding up the poster.

Fred put on one hell of an exhibition, doing around forty-five shots, without a miss. The place brook out in applause, and the police enjoyed it too. They continued north all the way to New York City. They ran into Johnny Layton, and they teamed up. Johnny and his wife followed in their car, and they slowly made their way back to Chicago, each taking turns as the chauffeur. When Al was in the uniform, he added the mechanical-man routine while Johnny and Fred wowed the crowds with exhibition matches.

Reaching Chicago, the traveling hustlers parted company. Fred, Lilly, and the children had had plenty of road adventures and wanted to return home. Layton and Blake continued the play around the Midwest.

The Rum-Running Navy

ON FRED'S RETURN TO Los Angeles, he jumped right back in where he had left off. Gus had continued the bootlegging operation during the four months his brother-in-law was gone. Money was piling up, and the satellite shop on Bonny Brae and Third Street was operating at full capacity and not just with liquor. The men in blue jackets had been stopping by on a regular basis. They were drinking on the sly like everyone else. The only trouble with having them around was they didn't know when to leave. It got to the point that they took turns directing traffic to the back of the store. While Fred was away, Gus put Lanahan, who bought the original cleaning shop, out of business. There was something to be said about customer loyalty. Fred was worried about how open the Bonnie Brae store was, but the local officers assured him that he nothing to worry about. The officers liked Fred and Gus and eventually nicknamed the place the Station House.

The operation was really taking up a lot of time. It was hard to dismiss it, but the place was a cash cow. Gus was occupied at the Alvarado apartments, and the family members that weren't watching the youngsters all had jobs.

Bobbie was almost ten, and Jack was turning five. It was May of 1926, and things were going good. Bobbie was in fifth grade and doing well. She was a pistol just like all the Wunderlich women. Fred and Lil decided that at five, Jack should go to kindergarten. This would free up Lil and allow her to help out while Bobbie was in school. Since kindergarten was half day, a friend recommended Urban Military Academy. This school changed its name in 1928 to Black-Foxe Military Academy.

Fred met with Maj. Harry Lee Fox and toured the facilities. At the time, Jackie Coogan and Alan Hale Jr. were also enrolled there. Fred felt if big actors trusted their sons to Urban Military, he could too. It was this relationship with Black-Foxe that eventually introduced him to many of the capital officers in the US Military. Fred also volunteered to give pool lessons to the older cadets if interested. He and Lilly attended fundraisers and many of their sporting events. Jack would remain there through high school. His socialization with many of the fathers enlarged his scope of business activity.

Rum Running Navy

Jack F Whalen at Black Fox

It was at one of the fundraisers that one of the fathers approached Fred. The man was aware of Fred's activities and was one of his best customers. During their conversation, the man suggested that Fred was in the wrong end of the liquor business.

"Fred, you're in the wrong business!" he said.

Fred replied, "How so?"

"You should become a smuggler," he replied. "It doesn't take much money to get into!"

"How much?"

"You just need to get a boat," he returned. "You can get the whiskey on credit!"

Fred was very interested. His friend took him down to Wilmington and a boat builder, a tight-fisted man named Ashbridge. They talked about the type of boat that would be needed and how much it would cost. Fred agreed on a price and in a few months launched himself into the rum-running business. It became the next phase of his romance with Prohibition. There was a certain pride in owning fast fancy cars, but a plain boat?

Ashbridge suggested that Fred go to the war surplus depot and buy Liberty engines. These were the motors that powered American aircraft in the last "War to End All Wars."

"Put these babies in a boat and the Coast Guard won't be able to catch you!" Ashbridge told him.

The idea of speed really got Fred's attention. Fred grabbed Gus and one of his delivery trucks and arranged to pick up a couple of the engines. The war was over, and these things were still in crates. They brought them down to the boat works, and soon they were mounted and adopted into the boat tagged the 1365. It was thirty-eight feet long with a round bottom hull. Fred and Gus took it out for a trial spin, and the damn thing nearly left the water.

It was painted a dark dull gray and resembled a larger version of a Chris Craft pleasure boat. It could haul 150 five-gallon cans of alcohol. Now, he just needed to line up a supplier.

Fred didn't have a clue as to how to become a successful smuggler. He and Gus had the nerve and the guts to jump in body and soul. After all, there was something romantic and adventurous about the whole idea. He had a large family to back him up, big farm boys from the Midwest and some old friends from hustling days, all of whom were economically in some ways dependent on him. Breaking into the smuggling business wouldn't be easy.

This was a closed secretive group of players that didn't think there was room for one more. These guys were inherently dangerous and loaded to the gunnels with armament. Gus felt twelve gauges were the best investment in protection. He shortened the barrels.

With persistence and a big money incentive, Fred and Gus drove down to Mexico. They contacted the owner of the Red Top Distillery. Pete Baker had opened up the distillery the day after Prohibition took effect. He was a tough older man who would later sell the business and become a partner with Fred. He had been in the Tijuana area since 1919 running this show and missed the day-to-day good old American lifestyle.

Not knowing anything about sailing or caring for boats, Fred began looking for a captain type to operate the 1365. He found a retired Coast Guardsman who was looking to make some extra money and who knew the ins and outs of their operating schedule along the coast. Fred and Gus were the original crewmembers and were quick studies of everything nautical.

Fred and Gus worked every day of the week. Alcohol was selling for $65 for a five-gallon can in Los Angeles. They were buying from Red Top for $17. One hundred and fifty cans netted Fred $7,200 per load per day before expenses. The captain got $200 per load, and the doryman was $75. For the most part, the receiving and transportation crew were a family affair. Gus and his brothers-in-law, along with a couple of friends from St. Louis, made up that end of the chain. The operation was close-knit as all had known each other for years, in some cases childhood.

The 1365 left Wilmington boat works in the morning with the captain and doryman. The boat would arrive in the late afternoon at Rosarita Beach on Charlie Quavas's ranch about eighteen miles from Tijuana. Charlie was a willing partner and made this a safer operation with less chance of exposure to curious eyes. Fred designed a chute to slide the cans down to the beach. Charlie built it and unloaded the Red Top trucks at the top of the slope. The cans were loaded into the dories and rowed out to the 1365 lying off the breakers. The boat would then head up the coast to a pre-positioned location, depending on Coast Guard activity and current weather conditions. The most used point of delivery was just north of Laguna Beach on the Irvine Ranch. The Irvine family knew nothing about this as they only had a small cottage near the beach. If the cottage were being used, Fred would unload at another location. The huge ranch had roads running through it, and there was easy access to the beach. The truck had a six-man crew. Fred and Gus would stand on the beach waiting to see the 1365. The other crewmembers were spread out watching the entire area for possible intruders. The boats hull would give off a phosphorous reflection that could be easily seen on the horizon. The crew would line up waist deep in the water to aid the dory in landing. The dory kept its bow seaward to ride the breakers and not be swamped, upsetting the load. Alaskan dories could carry one hundred cans, but for safety, they made two trips of seventy-five each. Each crewmember would carry four cans, one under each arm and one in each hand. The crew wore high-top sneakers, tightly laced, to prevent sand from getting in and slowing them down.

The run to the truck was usually sixty feet, and carrying four five-gallon cans over sand was exhausting. The only break was when the dory was headed back for the second load. One had to be in top shape to do this every day. At first, the loading was slow until everyone got conditioned.

Once loaded, the truck and lead car would get onto the Pacific Coast Highway to Westminster and on through Compton to Los Angeles and the storage plants. As the operation grew in size, Fred added trucks. These were green dairy trucks with a big brown cow painted on the sides along with the words Milk, Butter, and Eggs in large letters. The name on the door was "A1 Quality Creamery." The drivers would wear white coats and caps.

As business increased, it became necessary to provide a lead car and a trailer car. Hijacking was always a concern and, in some cases, deadly. Gus sawed off more barrels. The police were never a problem. On one occasion, the caravan drove through Inglewood and found a traffic control policeman had been added to a busy intersection. The officer waved the lead truck down, and all were stopped. Fred was driving the lead truck as the man in blue approached.

"I've seen you guys driving through town here on a regular basis," he said. "It would be great if you would leave a little something. We could stop traffic and let you drive on through without delay!"

Smiling, Fred answered, "That would be great! You'll find milk, butter, and eggs left behind that billboard sign on the corner over there."

The officer tipped his cap and waved the loads through. Fred now was pressed to create cartons and labels in quick time for the next morning's load. He went to the Challenge Cream & Butter Company and ordered six bottles of milk, four dozen eggs, and six pounds of butter. He had new lids made with A1 Creamery stamped on them. The rest took care of itself. Every time through that intersection, the last truck would pull over and drop the goods.

After six months of smuggling, Fred was convinced he had made the right move into the world of high-volume alcohol. He went down to see Ashbridge and ordered another boat. He named it the *Aconcagua*. Everyone laughed at their collective inability to pronounce the name. It was patterned after the 1365 and sported Liberty aircraft engines. With advanced round hull design, the boat could fly through the water fully loaded.

The fleet now consisted of two boats. Business boomed, and the operation became more efficient. Pete Baker sold the Red Top Distillery and joined Fred in partnership. This altered the nature of the operation. Initially, he brought in pure, distilled alcohol. It was of such high quality it was used to make perfume. With Pete's connections, Fred started bringing in the real thing. Baker had friends in the Canadian-based distillers, such as Consolidated, Brothmans, and Rifles. Through these various companies, Fred was connected to distributing of European whiskey, gin, and Scotch.

The distillers had offices in Los Angeles, and with Pete's assistance, orders were placed and contracted. This changed the game a little. The 1365 continued working out of Mexico and the Red Top. The *Aconcagua* became the boat that met tenders out beyond the twelve-mile limit. These tenders flew the Canadian flag and carried six thousand cases of bottled spirits. They would lay off the Mexican coast at fifty miles. The smugglers would send their boats out to take on loads. The company agents in Los Angeles would process the orders and give the smugglers one half of a torn Canadian bill. At the tender, the bills would be matched with serial numbers, and the orders would be loaded. The tenders got their loads from the mother ship, *Malahat*, ninety to one hundred miles off the coastline, south of Ensenada. The tenders were 150 or more feet long and would move up the coast and lay off near San Clemente or Coronado Islands.

Aconcagua would run out to meet them, load, drop at predestinated locations, and return to dock, preparing for the next run. This part of the operation ran smoothly. The entire enterprise was clipping along, bringing in loads of bottled and pure canned alcohol on a regular basis. As what happened in any operation, an unforeseen event raised its ugly head.

Late in 1928, Fred lost his boat, the 1365. The West Coast was experiencing unusually rough seas and wind. In spite of the weather, the boats captain and doryman took the 1365 out despite of the weather. They left for Rosarita Beach at 1:00 p.m. Fred liked to bring the boats in just before dark. This particular day, the weather made it difficult to see any distance along the coast. Fred liked the hour because most people are sitting down to dinner, and traffic was usually scarce. Fred checked the conditions that afternoon and determined a dory could not be landed without the waves and riptide pulling it back out to sea. Gus left for Rosarita Beach that morning to tell them not to load the alcohol and to lay over in a protected cove and load the next day. They got to Rosarita around five thirty tired and angry from fighting the conditions all the way down.

Gus met the boat and told them Fred didn't want it loaded and to wait till tomorrow.

"We battled this ocean all the way down, and we can get the load back!" said the captain. "Tell the boss to be on the beach. We'll get it there!"

Fred went to the beach with the crew and waited past the time they should have been arriving. Gus and Fred sent the trucks back and sat on the beach all night. Still no sign of 1365. In the morning, they return to the plant. Later that day, the radio reported that a rum boat with a dead crew of two was found floating one hundred yards off the beach at the Del Coronado Hotel. A lifeguard had spotted the boat at eight that morning. He swam out and climbed aboard. It seemed abandoned until he looked below deck, finding two dead men. The engines had died, and in trying to get them going, they had suffocated on the fumes. Fred lost his first boat and two crew members.

Fred immediately contacted the men's families and gave them each $50,000.

It was a costly loss. The Coast Guard confiscated the boat. Fred had reported it stolen that same morning after the radio report.

The money was so good that Fred commissioned another boat. He abandoned can alcohol following the loss of the 1365 and continued importing the bottled goods until he could replace the boat.

The business continued to thrive. Prohibition continued to drive more to the bottle, and Fred would be there to fill the demand. He began selling bottled liquor to "speakeasy" owners who came to depend on the quality goods Fred brought in from Canada. He continued opening up plants in residential areas. He rented houses and would fill the detached garages at the rear alleys that serviced them. Loading was easier and out of general sight. His latest rental was at 501 North Serrano, a house owned by the biggest bookmaker in Los Angeles, Zeke Caress. Again, the money was hidden at the bottom of a laundry hamper out in plain sight.

Fred installed one of his many employees at each of these plants so the house wasn't looking abandoned. Fred only hired married men. The family was spread thin throughout the various smuggling activities, and outsiders had to be drawn in. Family men were more reliable because of their dependents. Fred and Gus paid them well, and in some ways, they feared potential consequences of disloyalty. The newspapers always had stories about killings involving criminal elements. There were numerous stash houses around the city. As one place started to become hot, it was emptied and moved to a new location. The office remained in Beverly Hills not far from the Ladoux Road residence. Customers would phone in orders or drop them by in person. Fred delivered.

In 1928, Fred opened a "speakeasy" in Hollywood. It had formally been a deli owned by a man caught spiking beer. After the man's arrest, Fred bought the building along with renting additional adjoining space. The place was located on Vine Street between Sunset and Hollywood Boulevards. The place was called the *1551 Club* and was private, access to members only. The clientele was issued gold cards, which had to be shown before entry. Patrons entered through an 8×8 wooden box attached to the rear of the building.

Fred served fine food, and all well drinks were $1.25. Specialty spirits were priced based on their labels. There were no tables, only quality upholstered booths surrounding a large dance floor.

Otherwise, the club was richly carpeted. There were forty bottled brands at the bar and tap Bohemian draft. Bottled beer was available when not consumed by the smuggling crew.

The club's inventory included the best French wines and cordials made by Marie Bazard. He brought in the top French champagnes. At times, to liven things up, Fred dropped balloons with notes, giving away free bottles of the stuff.

The glasses were imprinted with the "1551" logo. The studios' prop warehouses provided much of decor. Since many of the patrons were movie people, it wasn't hard to get them to donate items that were readily available.

Clark Gable and Louis B. Mayer frequented the club regularly. They always stood at the end of the bar, never taking a booth. They drank Johnny Walker Black Label, nothing else. When they arrived, the bartender brought out two glasses, a fresh bottle, soda, and a bucket of ice. They opened and poured their own drinks.

Tom Mix came in to drink and drink. Rex Bell, who later became governor of Nevada, the Talmadge Sisters, Buster Keaton, and Vince Barnett were all regulars. The Muller brothers, Frank and Walter, were there every day. They came in the afternoon and stayed until early evening. The club entertained an assortment of guests. Ace Hutchins and Joe Benjamin, both topnotch fighters, came in for as many rounds as they fought. Vincent Barnett, comic actor, spent evenings at the club and sometimes was part of the entertainment, delivering outrageous comic insults to some of the patrons. Other smugglers also found their way to Fred's gin den. Larry Potter, for instance, who had a place at Washington and Vermont, seemed to prefer drinking at Fred's place.

Joe and Nell Yule were regulars and became close friends. Their son, Mickey, was the same age as Bobbie. They were a big vaudeville act for years and later brought Mickey into the act. The club operated until late 1933 when Fred sold it to S.S. Sugarman. The faithful patrons asked if they could have some of the artifacts from the club, and Fred was happy to oblige. It had been a fun business, and everyone knew about it, including the authorities. They stayed away because most of the customers were members of the Los Angeles and

Hollywood elite. A raid at any time of the day would have netted big names that they did not want to offend. The major studios were all within a mile radius of the *1551 Club*.

The Great Depression, which began in 1929, only intensified the demand for alcohol. Business was brisk and running smoothly. In 1930, Fred was contacted by Kells & Grant, a real estate company. They had a boat that had belonged to one of Pepsodent's executives. The man was going through a divorce, and the boat was tied up in litigation. The boat called the *Can Can* was a beautiful pleasure yacht. The realtors told Fred it had originally cost $142,000 but could be had for $6,000. Fred went down to San Pedro to look it over. He called the realtors back and said, "I'll take it!"

Fred and Gus went to their offices on Western and Sixth with cash in hand. They sat while the call was made to the attorneys. An hour later, the call came in that it was theirs and the paperwork was being brought by messenger. They handed the title and documentation to Fred, and he was beside himself for acquiring such a wonderful boat. The boat was forty-five feet long with a "V" hull. Fred and Gus took it to Ashbridge at the boat works. Ashbridge looked at it as if it were a beautiful woman. He had some thoughts about it being used to haul booze.

"Fred, this is a luxury cruiser," he said. If you plan to use this in your smuggling, you'll have trouble in rough weather. We need to fill in the step in the hull and round it out like the other boats."

"No, you can't be serious!" Fred moaned. "This is a work of art!"

"Granted, Fred!" Ashbridge returned. "This hull will get you arrested!"

Fred conceded, and Ashbridge went right to work. He knew what had happened to the 1365 in bad weather and didn't want a reoccurrence. The boat was admired by Los Angeles society, and a reporter had seen it in Wilmington in dry dock. He ran a story in the newspaper that contained the line, "The next time you see the *Can Can*, it will be wearing a gray coat." The Coast Guard painted their boats gray for the same reason Fred did. It was more difficult to identify at distance and almost disappeared against a cloud-filled horizon.

While the *Can Can* was being reworked, Fred began a project with his partner, Pete Baker. Pete had bought a large home in Beverly Hills. It had a large attached multicar garage. Fred and Pete were tiring of continually moving stash houses ahead of the federal authorities. The feds were starting to take more interest in West Coast violations of the Volstead Act. Gus had come up with a way to create a hidden warehouse in Pete's garage. Fred had tried something similar earlier and had hired an engineer to design it. Fred and Lilly had moved to the hills above Sunset Boulevard into a home on King's Road. The design by the engineers to create a hidden storeroom under the garage was so noisy it had to be abandoned.

Gus's design was simpler and worked without any significant sound. The loaded trucks would pull into the garage. As soon as the door was closed, the truck's weight sunk the floor. The mechanism was locked in position, and the truck unloaded. Once unloaded, the lock was released, and the counterweights would return the truck to grade level. This became the principal warehouse for the remaining term of Prohibition.

The Great Escapes

THE WORK ON THE *Can Can* was completed and ready to be relaunched. The family gathered at the boat works and celebrated with a cracked bottle over the new hull. Fred had changed the boat's name to the *Bobbie* after his daughter. The family began going to Catalina on weekends. Trips to the Avalon and the Isthmus were alternated. The Casino on Sugar Loaf Point had been completed in May of 1929. Its ballroom and theater became a mainstay of the island's entertainment. The theater was the first theater designed and built for talkies. Fred and Lilly loved to dance and would go to the ballroom where bands played on the weekends.

During the week, Fred and Gus would schedule the boats for loads off the Mexican coast and in some cases go along. The Irvine Ranch and the Laguna area were coming under scrutiny by the Coast Guard and feds. Fred began moving north up the coast to different beaches on moonless nights. He began landing along the Newport/Balboa strand after midnight. It was an area that had barely over one hundred residents in 1932. Most of the cottages there were summer second homes. The chances of being discovered were next to nil. The access to Pacific Coast Highway was much easier than driving through Irvine Ranch.

Soon Fred was landing boats as far up as Palos Verde on the Dominguez Rancho. The coves there were secluded but more difficult to use. It was there that Fred lost the *Aconcagoa*. Someone had tipped off the Coast Guard that a smuggler was bringing in a load of liquor. The Coast Guard could not be juiced. They took their mission very seriously and were a smuggler's only major threat. They began patrolling more often with more boats in the 1930s. The Orange County Sheriffs were more cooperative. Many times, they would escort the loads to the county line. The FBI had agents that were on the take during that period, and Fred had cordial relations with many of them.

Fred and Gus were with the beach crew waiting for the *Aconcagoa* that night. The trucks had gotten to the upper edge of the cove above the beach. The dories had been loaded and were just coming ashore when two cutters appeared, firing warning shots at the boat. There was no safe escape for the boat or the crew. The captain turned the *Aconcagoa* and beached it. The crew scattered along the cove, dropping cases of liquor. The dairy trucks, seeing the searchlights and hearing the shots, left the ridge where the beach trail ended. Fred and Gus ran in opposite directions. Police were coming down another trail to the beach and arrested Gus, his brother, George, and the others. Fred found a vertical crevasse on the cliff and began climbing up from the beach. He ran in the dark toward a light, which turned out to be a cottage. He had grabbed two bottles of Canadian from the case he dropped in the surf and had stuck them in his jacket pockets. He knocked on the door, waking its resident. A grizzled old man answered the door. He stood there in his union suit, blinking his eyes.

"I could use some help if you have a phone?" Fred exclaimed.

"Well, sure!" he said rubbing his eyes. "What's your problem?"

"This!" Fred returned, pulling the bottles out of his coat.

"It's right over here on the wall."

It was an old-style wall mount with a crank. Fred got the operator and gave her the number and waited for it to ring back. He noticed the old guy looking at the bottles.

"This is really good stuff! And it's imported," he said, looking at the labels.

The phone rang, and Fred was put through.

"Honey, it's me!" He spoke into the extended mouthpiece. "We've been hit in Palos Verde!"

"Yeah!"

"They got the *Aconcagoa* and everything!"

"Call Morton and tell him they're bringing the crew in to the jail"

"Don't worry about me I'll get home as soon as I can!"

"Love you too!"

Fred replaced the earpiece and turned to the old guy. The man was still looking at the bottles as if in a stupor. Fred didn't think he even heard the phone conversation.

"You got a car?" Fred asked. "Got a truck? Can you give me a lift into Los Angeles?"

"Tonight?"

"Yes, it's an emergency!" Fred pleaded. "I'll pay you!"

"Well, sure, if it's that bad."

"I had an accident down in the cove!" Fred explained. "I need to get to Los Angeles as soon as possible!"

The man grabbed his pants and shoes. He sat down and laced up his shoes and grabbed a coat. Fred headed out the door.

"Hey! You forgot these!" the old guy shouted.

"They're yours!"

The old man smiled and stuffed them under a cushion of one of the chairs.

Fred had expected, at some time, he was going to lose a boat. The enforcement had stepped up over the last year, and he didn't want to lose a boat and have to cut back his operation. He chose to expand his supply as demand increased. A great number of people were drowning their Depression ills in liquor.

Four months prior to losing the *Aconcagoa*, Fred had commissioned Ashbridge to build two more boats. The boats were about ready and had been outfitted in similar fashion as their predecessors. Both were thirty-eight feet long, and Fred named them the *Dixie* and the *Bobbie*.

Fred had hired one of the most knowledgeable boat captains on the coast, Poker Anderson. Pete Baker was upset that Fred was using an exceptional pleasure cruiser for running liquor and decided to leave the partnership. Pete was much older and was not participating in the activities requiring a physical fitness that had long left him.

The business was getting riskier by the day, and he knew it was over for him. Fred bought him out. He took $100,000 and rented his house back to Fred, where the mechanical warehouse was.

This buyout was not anticipated, and Fred decided to start up the pure alcohol traffic again. There was still a demand for mixing and selling the cheaper stuff, thanks to the Depression. After the split up, Fred started using the *Bobbie* for more runs. Poker was the captain on the *Bobbie*. Fred had started using the Irvine Ranch once in a while as it was easy to unload there, and he could get an escort if needed.

Poker called the office, "Fred, the doryman is puking up his guts and can't make today's run."

"I'll be there in an hour and a half."

Fred sent Gus ahead to Tijuana to change the delivery time by two hours. Fred got to Wilmington, and Poker fired up the Liberties. They pulled out of the harbor and headed down the coast to Rosarita Beach. They loaded up and headed out sixteen miles and started back north toward Laguna. They had taken on almost two hundred cans, and the *Bobbie* was riding lower than usual in the water.

They turned eastward and began making their run to the ranch. At fourteen miles of the shore, they ran into another rum boat, the *Zeigiest*. It was heading back out to sea. Fred was getting ready to unload on the Irvine Ranch. He was in the back checking the fifty extra cans on the stern. As he looked up to wave to the *Zeigiest*, he saw a gray boat heading from the south toward them. It was the *Arrow*, the Coast Guard's fastest cutter.

"Poker, the Coast Guard!" Fred yelled.

Poker turned the *Bobbie* seaward and pushed the throttle forward slowly, and the bow began lifting up as their speed increased. The *Zeigiest* turned and started running north. The *Arrow* had to make a choice.

"Hope they don't chase us!" Poker screamed over the engines and bow beating.

Fred watched the *Arrow* coming on to the place the two rum boats separated. He'd had grabbed the binoculars and was standing behind the tied loads on the stern.

"Damn, we're the losers!" Fred yelled. "They've turned toward us on an intercept! Get her moving!"

"Keep an eye on them!" Poker returned. "See if they're gaining!"

Fred watched for a few minutes and said, "Can't tell yet! They're still too far!"

Soon it became obvious that the *Arrow* was gaining. Poker had the throttles wide open, but the load was not letting the bow lift the hull any higher. Fred continued to watch the *Arrow*. Dusk had begun as they encountered the *Zeigiest*, and soon it would be darkening up.

"They're closing on us, and two guys are manning the bow gun!"

"They'll fire a warning shot!" Poker called out, just before a swish over their heads exploded on their port side. "That was to get us to heave to!" Poker screamed. "They would have to be lucky to hit us at this speed!"

"They're catching up, Poker!"

"We're too heavy! We should have pulled away by now!"

Just as soon as Poker had yelled, the *Arrow* began machine gun fire. At first, the rounds were falling short in the wake of the fleeing boat. In the next few minutes, the shots were hitting the crates of alcohol tied to the stern decking. Fred was down low behind the crates peering with the binoculars over the tops. The light was fading fast, and now the tracers were visible.

"Cut half the stern load loose!" Poker commanded. "We've got to lighten the load and lift the boat up!"

Fred cut the ropes and the crates holding twenty-five cans of alcohol each slid off the stern. He could feel the boat start to lift. He looked back, but the *Arrow* was still gaining but slower now. Rounds were still hitting the stern, and the crates were leaking over the deck.

"Cut loose another twenty-five!"

Fred let the rest of the stern load slide off and ran forward now that his shield was gone. The rounds were lobbing on to the stern deck pretty much spent.

"Fred, get the hatch open and start heaving cans over the side!"

Fred popped the cover and stepped down into the shallow hold where 150 cans were packed. He started tossing the cans overboard one by one. After ten, he was heaving for breath. The *Bobbie* continued to pick up speed. The *Arrow*'s lights were starting to dim as the gap began to widen between boats. The cutter had stopped shooting.

Fred looked back, but the binoculars were of little use. He could see the spotlight and figures moving around the deck. In the next thirty seconds, it looked as if the *Bobbie* was fleeing at an impossible rate.

Fred turned, "Poker, they've stopped!"

"No way?"

Fred turned to point, and there were no lights to be seen. The high-speed chase had lasted for almost forty minutes but seemed an eternity to both men. They were now somewhere south of Catalina heading northwest, probably through the gap between Catalina and San Nicholas Islands. Poker slowed the boat and turned it north, looking back to see if the *Arrow* was anywhere in sight or running dark like they were. There was nothing.

Suddenly, a light pierced the dark in our rear. It was as if it was bobbing like a buoy, waving back and forth. Poker started laughing so hard he had to sit down. He tried to speak, but more laughing was all he could do. Finally, he blurted out, "They sank!"

"What?" Fred asked.

"The reason that light is all over the place is they want us to pick them up!"

"No way in hell!" Fred returned. "We have enough holes in our ass end and rails that we're probably taking on water!"

Poker popped the hatch, and everything looked good. Fred wondered what Gus was thinking now that they hadn't landed the alcohol.

"Radio Ashbridge and tell him to call Lil at home and that we'll come in at Newport in three hours," Fred told Poker.

They unloaded in Newport and hightailed it to Wilmington and the boat works. Ashbridge put it immediately into dry dock. The *Bobbie* was riddled with bullet holes and chips where the slugs grazed the rails and hull. The boat was restored on a 24-7 basis. Fred and Poker knew the Coast Guard would come looking.

The next afternoon, the loss of the *Arrow* made the papers. It had completely vanished, and it was feared the crew had been lost. In the meantime, Fred bought two more Liberty engines and replaced the old ones. The search for the *Arrow* went on for two days, and it was given up as lost with entire crew. Fred and Poker were the only ones who knew where they had sunk. They considered calling the authorities but decided against it. After all, they were sure there were plenty of half-submerged crates of alcohol around them.

Five days later, the rescue story broke. A fishing boat came across them on its way in. While on the boat, the Coast Guard commander found a case of whiskey the fishermen had stashed for medicinal purposes. Upon reaching the fishing boat dock, they arrested the captain and the crew for having a banned substance, six bottles of hooch. This demonstrated to Fred that the Coast Guard couldn't be bought even if you saved their lives.

It was on the sixth day after the encounter that the Coast Guard showed up at the boat works. Fred and Poker happened to be checking on the boat to determine when they would put it back in service. They could tell these officers and federal agents were prepared to seize the *Bobbie*. They called Poker over, and one could tell that they weren't happy about losing their best cutter.

The lead officer was most likely the commander of the *Arrow*. He pointed to the boat while addressing the federal agents and said, "This is the boat we were chasing that night off Laguna!" He continued, "Poker, we know it was you! This is the boat that sank the *Arrow*!"

"Excuse me, gentlemen, but how did your boat sink?" Fred asked, pretending ignorance of the whole event.

"We hit the contraband that this boat's crew was throwing off the stern!" he said. "Poker, you're the only one with a boat that could outrun the *Arrow*."

"It couldn't have been me!" Poker claimed, looking at them with a straight face. "If I could outrun you, then why would I throw my cargo overboard?"

Fred could see the anger welling up in the man's face. He was trying not to embarrass the uniform and his position of command.

"We've got you dead to rights, Poker!" the officer shouted. "We peppered your ass end with enough lead to sink you. The damage to your boat is all the evidence we need!"

"There's the boat, gentleman!" Poker pointed. "Please, let's go aboard and see what you're talking about."

They walked over to the dry dock and across the gangplank onto the *Bobbie*. They immediately went to the stern and peered over to look at the back end. Members of the crew were running their hands along the rails, looking for any signs of splintering. Ashbridge had freshly repainted the entire boat and varnished all the rails. The lady looked as fresh as she was when first launched.

"As you can plainly see, there are no bullet holes or otherwise on this boat," he said, opening up his arms. "You're welcome to climb down and inspect the hull."

"We brought the boat in to replace her engines and clean her up!" Fred offered.

"Poker brings this boat here in regularly for service," claimed Ashbridge. "There are the empty crates from the new engines."

"This may look like similar to the rum boats," chimed Fred, "but I assure you that I use it for taking my family to Catalina on the weekends. Ask anyone at the docks in Avalon or the Isthmus!"

They looked hard and long trying to prove their claim. The federal agents finally turned to the Coast Guardsmen, saying they obviously made a mistake. Having found nothing, they left in disgust.

After the *Arrow* incident, the Coast Guard began paying special attention to the *Bobbie*. Poker, Fred, and Gus were conscious of the attention and began taking the family to Catalina on a more frequent schedule. They would go from Catalina up the coast to the other Channel Islands and pull into Santa Barbara now and then. The Coast Guard spent a lot of time shadowing the *Bobbie*. During this time, Fred had Ashbridge build two more boats, the *Jackie* and the *Winifred*.

While the Coast Guard tied up boats following the *Bobbie*, Fred's other boats were making the runs off Ensenada. Fred began the "importing" of Chicken Cock, an American-Canadian whiskey and one of the finest made at that time. The boats could carry five hundred cases each. The two new boats would leave a full hour behind one another. Poker hired a second captain and a doryman and commanded the *Jackie*. He would load off the Mexican coast where the big tender ships parked. First the *Jackie*, and an hour later, the *Winifred* would load. Poker would cruise slowly waiting for the trailing boat to catch up.

They would sail behind San Clemente, north to a position closer to Catalina, and lay off until dusk. Poker would make his run to Laguna while the other boat would run to Newport. Gus would run the pickup crew at Laguna and George ran the Newport group. George usually got a police escort out of Newport and would meet Gus along the Pacific Coast Highway. The AI trucks would then caravan into Los Angeles from Orange County.

The twin Liberty engines in these thirty-eight boats allowed them to outrun any and all cutters that might stumble upon them. Going in behind each other gave one the opportunity to warn another if an interception was attempted. A flare would be used to warn of potential trouble. Still, on occasion, the two boats would go to Red Top for straight alcohol runs, each carrying 780 cans of the pure stuff. Fred continued to make his own label for whiskey for the 1551 Club and selling the rest as affordable substitute for drinkers on a budget. The cosmetic companies bought the excess as it was cheaper and less red tape than the legal sources.

Fred had Poker and the other captain sign the registrations with the port authorities. Business continued to be good, but the Coast Guard was increasing pressure on smugglers. It wasn't long before Fred decided to put the *Bobbie* back in action. He and Gus were old hands by this time running the boats. They made a decision to run three at a time and increase their warehousing inventory. This time, they would land the loads at three locations instead of the usual two. Fred would land his load at the Vanderlip Estate at Portuguese Bend, which Fred had gained access through their caretaker, Ness.

The *Jackie* and *Winifred* made successful landings at their sites well south of the *Bobbie*. The Coast Guard was still dealing with wounded pride after the sinking of the *Arrow*. It was a moonless night. The *Bobbie* was coming in to what was known as Smuggler's Cove, just north of Portuguese Bend. She was approaching from the southwest. Fred and Gus were running dark looking for a signal light from the shore. The pickup crew flashed their headlights three times.

Fred steered toward them, centered in the cove. Unknown to them was the fact that the *Diatone*, the Coast Guard's largest ship, was lying to the north in Abalone Cove along with a number of smaller faster boats. As the *Bobbie* cleared the two points forming the cove, all hell broke loose.

"Fred! There are boats everywhere!" cried Gus as gunfire erupted.

A round grazed Gus's calve as he ran toward the wheelhouse. Fred turned the boat toward the beach and gunned the two Liberty engines. The deck loads shielded them from most of the gunfire. Tracers lit up the night. Fred and Gus leaped from the bow onto the beach and ran for the closest truck and hightailed it away from the shore. Ranging through the sixteen-thousand-acre estate, they made their way out while Ness delayed the authorities at the Old Ranch Cottage.

"We lost the *Bobbie*!" Gus moaned. "The damned assholes got what they wanted!"

"We also lost a hell of a load of whiskey!" Fred sighed. "Someone tipped them off!"

There were people associated with the CG that would give Fred tips on where the boats were patrolling and safer landing areas. Fred used these tips many times and successfully made runs with the boats. Gus felt this last tip was a setup. Fred agreed and went back to the office to lick his wounds. The loss of boats and loads over the years plus the amount of rolling stock he owned was narrowing his margins. He decided to sell the *1551 Club* in September of 1933. Pete Baker had been bought out of their partnership in '32 and reimbursed Fred for 50 percent of the *Dixie* as he wanted to use the boat personally. The business had provided a great living for Fred and the extended family, but costs were rising, and everyone seemed to have their hands out. The loss of the *Bobbie* caused him to rethink the entire proposition.

"Gus, let's go into Hollywood and see Les Brunaman!" Fred suggested.

"The bookie?" Gus asked.

"Yea, that's the one."

Brunaman was one of the biggest bookmakers in Los Angeles. His partner, Eddie Neals, and he operated in a place right on Hollywood Boulevard, just east of Highland Avenue. They were brazen about it. They operated on a wide-open basis, posting their daily booking sheets in the windows of the place. No one bothered them.

Fred and Gus walked in and went right to the back where Les kept his office.

Les and Eddie were regulars at the 1551 Club and entertained there on many occasions.

"Fred, Gus!" Les greeted them. "What brings you down here?"

Fred outlined his proposition. At first, Les didn't want any part of it. He and Eddie believed smuggling was too dangerous a line of work because it involved federal penalties. Fred explained the money end of it.

"Look, all I'm asking is for you to finance some loads for us. We'll take the major risks of getting the stuff ashore. You put up the funds for the distillers, and we'll do the rest. You'll make twenty percent on your money!"

"What kind of scratch are we talking about here?" Les asked.

"Fifteen thousand a load," Fred offered. "We run to boats at a time, so thirty thousand dollars!"

Les agreed and had Eddie get the cash. They stayed in the deal for five months. The event that gave them cold feet occurred the day Fred made his last run to Red Top at Rosarita Beach. Another boat was loading at the same time. It was the *Dixie*. Both boats headed out to sea. They were in one hundred yards of each other when they reached US waters. Just north of San Diego the *Diatone* intercepted them. The CG decided to go after the *Dixie*. It was their best chance at interdiction. They recognized both boats, but the *Dixie* appeared over loaded. Poker Anderson made a dash to the northwest out to sea. The *Dixie* tried to turn south but lost momentum coming about, which gave the *Diatone* a chance to close on her. She never made the border and was boarded.

Poker kept moving at full speed to the area behind San Clemente, heading north to Catalina. Poker thought that Baker had gone into the smuggling business with the *Dixie*. The next day, the papers reported the capture, but as coincidence would have it, the captain's last name was Anderson. The family was in shock, thinking it was the *Jackie*. Gus called the port authorities, asking the name of the boat. Discovering the confusion, he grabbed the crew and left for Newport. That night, Poker and Fred flashed a light, and Gus on shore answered it.

"It's Fred and Poker!" Gus yelled. "They made it!"

Les and Eddie read the same story and didn't want any more action. They had done quite well over the last few months but decided they were backing something they knew nothing about. Fred gave them their last payment and tried to persuade them to stay in to no avail. They said it was too dangerous, and they had a safe bet being bookmakers. Fred and Gus were alone again. Les Brunaman was shot to death a few months later at the Roost Cocktail Bar on Temple Street.

"Did you read about Brunaman?" Fred asked Gus.

"Yes!" Gus answered. "And he thought our business was dangerous!"

Prohibition was coming to a close as Christmas 1933 was at hand. It was going to take a while for the US distillers to come back on line. Alcohol was scarce. Consolidated, Riffles, and Brothmans said they would keep the tender boats as long as the *Malahat* could keep them supplied. Fred contacted the local agents but was continually put off with one excuse after another. He couldn't wait any longer. He had too many people depending on him. Fred went looking for another backer. He ran into an acquaintance, Fred Irwin, whose real last name was Billingsly. His brother was involved with the *Stork Club* in New York.

Irwin put up the money, and for a time, they were getting ahead. Just when it looked like business would start taking care of itself, the roof caved in. The *Jackie* was vandalized and burnt done to the water's edge. The last warehouse on Third and La Brea with fourteen hundred cans of alcohol was emptied, and the $14,000 in the office safe was gone. Irwin was gone along with everything. Fred sold the remaining boat, *Winifred*, and began unloading all the assets associated with the business. By 1936, the house on King's Road was sold.

Fred and family temporarily moved into their apartment building on Alvarado. Vincent Barnett was still hanging out at the *1551 Club*, Fred's former speakeasy. Fred greeted him at the bar. After the usual pleasantries, Fred explained his situation.

"Fred! I've got neighbors down the street from me who are looking to rent their house while they go to Europe!" Vince offered.

"Where are you at?" Fred asked.

"Just above the pass into the San Fernando Valley. Behind the *HOLLYWOODLAND* sign." Vince said. "Up in the Lake Hollywood area."

"When can I meet them?"

"Here's my address. Come by Saturday at noon and we'll go talk to them."

Vince introduced Fred to the older English couple that wanted to return to Britain. Fred brought the family over to meet them on Sunday. The house was in the hills above Cahuenga Pass at 3300 Knoll Drive. They decided to forgo a lease and told Fred he could occupy the house and just take care of it while they were away for the next two years. The home was lavishly furnished. Fred, Lilly, and Bobbie moved in the following week. The day after the couple left, Fred moved in what was left of his inventory. He was dealing in malts for making Scotch. He brought in Fern Tosh, Sheriff, and Grandella malts, storing them with his whiskeys, cordials, and champagnes.

Fred bought a new La Salle from the Cadillac agency in Riverside and had it delivered. He kept one delivery truck and his Cadillac. Business continued as usual. He and Gus worked out of the Knoll house for about four months. His plants had become of interest to the various authorities. This one was no different. Usually, he had gotten a tip-off before impending raids, and this time was no different. As a contingency, he had rented another house on Princess Drive in Highland Park near South Pasadena. This was a four-story home that stepped down a hillside.

One of Fred's customers, working in the Hollywood Division Station, called to inform him of a raid on the Knoll location. Fred,

Gus, and George quickly moved the illegal goods to the Princess Drive location. They had just finished and drove back to the Knoll house. It was swarming with feds and police as they drove by. Fred went a little further and turned around in Vince Barnett's driveway. As he drove by the house, he saw Lilly and Bobbie leaving with packed bags and their fur coats. Further down Knoll Drive, he passed a taxi that was headed up to get the ladies. He stopped the cab and gave the driver $50.

"You're going to 3300 Knoll, right?" he asked.

"Yes, how do you know?" he answered.

"You're picking up my wife and daughter!" Fred told him. "Take them to this address on Alvarado Street. Tell them I'll see them there."

"You got it, buddy!"

The driver smiled at the $50 in his hand and headed up the drive. Fred and his brothers-in-law went down to Barham Boulevard and waited, making sure that the cab wasn't being tailed.

They followed the cab back to the Alvarado apartment house. They went into the lower unit that Fred kept purposely vacant and put together a plan. Fred would go to the Princess Drive house and make sure it was safe and then return for the girls. Gus and George would keep an eye on the general area, making sure that the apartments were still a safe location. Fred left in his Caddy and headed to Highland Park, a short drive away. Playing it safe, he proceeded with prudent caution.

Fred parked the car two blocks away on another street and walked to the Princess Drive house. It was dark, and everything looked normal. He decided to enter from a lower level and descended the exterior steps along one side of the building. He entered the laundry room door and turned on the light. He left the laundry room and went to the staircase heading up to the living room level, two floors above. As he started up the servants' staircase, the hall lights went on, and a bevy of federal agents stood at the top of the stairs.

"Are you Fred Whalen?" one of them asked.

"Yes, I am!" Fred replied casually. "What seems to be the problem?"

The men motioned for Fred to come up the stairs. As Fred reached the landing at the intermediate level, he bolted into that portion of the house and ran down the main stairs into the bedroom area and out onto the slope. He reached the rear wall and vaulted it, continuing downhill. He heard a warning shot and orders to halt. He kept on until he reached a lower street where he turned and continued down the slope. He eventually made it to a phone booth and called to be picked up. Two days later, Gus dropped him at his Cadillac and followed him back to Alvarado.

Lilly's brand new La Salle was gone, confiscated by the authorities, along with everything in both the Knoll Drive house and the repositioned liquor and malt in the Princess place. Fred had a few thousand in cash and thought the best thing was to drive east. Gus parked the Caddy behind the apartment building and drove Fred and the family to a car dealer Fred knew on Figueroa Street in the downtown area.

"I need a new car," Fred told his friend. "I want to trade in my Cadillac. Gus will bring it down tomorrow as a trade-in. I'm heading up to San Francisco with the family."

"How about this late model Packard?" he offered. "It's about an even trade for that Cadillac of yours."

The deal was made, and Fred slid in behind the wheel. Gus completed the paperwork, and the ladies jumped in.

"We're going to San Francisco?" Bobbie asked as they drove off.

"Hell no!" Fred returned. "We're going to Chicago! I told the salesman that in case he was asked where we were going!"

On the way out of town, he picked up Charlie Fagan. He had the chauffeur's uniform. Gus would take care of things along with his brother, George, and watch over Jack at Black-Foxe. Just like old times, the family and friend were back on the road, hustling their way east.

Busted

THE TIME IN CHICAGO was spent returning to old haunts, playing pool, and missing life back in California. Fred did well playing big money games. The weekdays were spent working the "rich California boss" routine. Bobbie had begun modeling at department stores and at nineteen was a hit in the fashion circles. Lilly worked part time as a cashier at a local drugstore and was asked by a cosmetic company to do hand modeling for various products.

After three months, Bobbie became homesick for her friends in Los Angeles. During one of her fashion stints, a producer from Los Angeles offered her a position as a showgirl in a stage production that was opening in the early summer. He had seen her dancing at an after-show party and felt she could be in the chorus line and possibly more. Fred and Lilly put her on the train to Los Angeles with instructions to see how things stood. Fred had been getting regular letters from his mother as was Lilly. Both parents begged them to return, but not knowing if things had really cooled down, Fred was hesitant to leave Chicago.

While away, a former employee of Fred's started running homemade whiskey and gin. Jim Woods was arrested, and rather than admit he was his own boss, he told the authorities he was working for Fred. He had agreed to a suspended sentence for his future cooperation should Fred return to Southern California. Soon letters from Bobbie and Gus suggested that all was fine and that there had been no hint of legal action involving any members of the family.

They left Chicago in early August and again hustled their way across the country. All concerned were eager to get home. Fred wondered what he would do to earn a living. Bootleg was slowly fading as more and more smugglers and mixologist were being arrested or just plain getting out of the trade. He knew his cue could keep him above water, but it was not going to make him financially stable. Jack was fifteen and had two more years to graduate from Black-Foxe. Fred had been able to keep him in the academy but barely. Jack was the class-commanding cadet every year since he finished the eighth grade. He was an all-around athlete, playing football, basketball, baseball, and the polo team. Jack found he was especially good at training horses.

Once Fred returned, Jim Woods contacted the FBI. Fred received a phone call from Woods stating that a gentleman was interested in backing Fred in a startup of a new liquor operation. Knowing that the old business was coming to a halt made Fred wary and suspicious of the offer. Woods said he would meet him at corner of Sixth and Western not far from his former drive-up operation. Fred parked around the corner and walked to the meeting point.

When he reached the corner, not seeing anyone, he crossed to the drugstore and walked in buying a pack of gum. As he left and turned up Western, he heard someone call his name.

"Freddie!" someone called out behind him.

Fred continued walking, ignoring the repeated calls of his name. Finally, after three attempts to get his attention, the person called out again, "Whalen!"

At that moment, Fred felt a hand on his shoulder, turning him around. The men showed Fred their credentials.

"Look, Fred, it's all over!"

They loaded Fred into their car and took him down to the jail. Lilly posted bail, and he was released the following morning. Fred retained Russell Graham, a former federal attorney.

"Fred, you'll most likely receive probation and nothing more!"

Fred appeared before Judge Yankowitz in late September in federal court.

The judge sat reading through the indictment and putting it down asked Fred to stand and face the bench.

"Mr. Whalen, you have brought a great deal of alcohol into the country that wasn't taxed, and I am not going to let you off."

Graham was standing with Fred in front of the judge.

"I'm going to send you to jail!" Yankowitz declared.

Fred kept poking Graham with his elbow, wanting him to say something.

The judge noticing Fred's repeated attempts to get Graham's attention brought his hammer down.

"Sit still, Fred!" Graham whispered out of the side of his mouth.

"I'm giving you 120 days at Terminal Island!"

"Your Honor!" Graham appealed. "Can my client have ten days to get his affairs in order?"

"Granted!"

Fred and Graham turned to leave, but the judge wasn't finished. "Just come back here! Both of you!" Yankowitz ordered. "I'm not finished with you, Mr. Whalen!"

Fred returned with his lawyer to the bench. The judge looked down.

"I'm giving you five years' probation on top of your 120 days at Terminal Island. You will report to the bailiff's office in ten days. You're dismissed!"

Ten days later, Fred turned himself in and was taken to Terminal Island. The facility was brand-new, and Fred was one of its first inmates. His time there was not bad. He worked outside getting the lawn and landscape areas ready for plantings. When not outside, he spent the remainder in the kitchen helping out there. Everything taken into consideration, it wasn't going to be a bad 120 days. He reminisced later in his life that it could have been worse, Alcatraz worse!

Fred was down to his last three weeks. He was working in the landscaping department when he was suddenly surrounded by a group of men brandishing guns. He had been indicted once again. He was taken to the warden's office where he was told that the federals had seized a boat, the *Cleveland*, in San Pedro with 1,500 cans of alcohol. They knew Fred's connection with Red Top Distillery but couldn't prove it came from Rosarita Beach. The *Cleveland* was a large fishing vessel, much larger than those Fred ran. It was Fred's shipment. Gus and George were running things at their end while he was incarcerated. No one could know the connection except Jim Woods.

Fred was taken back to Los Angeles federal court and appeared before Judge McCormick. Jim Woods came in and was brought before the bench and stood by Fred, shaking. The judge ordered the trial set for February 1937.

Fred was granted bail and was bonded out the following day. He knew Jim Woods had made a deal to testify against him. Fred wasn't going to standby and be resentenced without confronting Jim. He drove to Jim's home and knocked on the door. He knocked on the door forcibly. Jim answered the door. He stood there in disbelief, blood draining from his face.

"You dirty son of a bitch!" Fred screamed. "You ratted me out for your own smuggling while I was in Chicago!"

Jim tried to speak. His mouth dropped open, and he began breathing with much difficulty. His knees buckled, and he fell backward into the entry hall of his house, reaching out for Fred's arm. Fred stepped in and bent over him, slapping his face with authority.

"Dora! Get down here, Jim's collapsed!" Fred yelled into the house.

Jim's wife ran from upstairs and knelt at his side. Neither one could get any response from the man. Dora called the police to send an ambulance and returned to Jim's side.

"I'm so sorry, Fred!" Dora pleaded. "He shouldn't have done any of this to you. You were very good to us. He knew if he went to jail, we would lose the house. I guess you were his easy out!"

The ambulance arrived and took Jim to Los Angeles County Hospital. Fred drove Dora down following the ambulance. Jim was pronounced dead on arrival. He had a massive heart attack. Dora was more dazed than alert. She sat down hard in the lobby, staring at the floor. Fred sat down beside her and offered her his handkerchief.

"I'll help you make arrangements," Fred offered.

"Don't worry, Fred, I want to help you out of the mess Jim's made for you!"

Jim was buried, and Dora went with Fred to his lawyer, confessing to what Jim had done. Russell Graham told Fred that the feds wouldn't believe her at this point and that their best hope lies with the judge.

"McCormick is a reasonable man and may accept Dora's testimony," Russell cautioned.

Fred's appearance before Judge McCormick went well for Fred. The judge was inclined to accept Dora's statement as a dying declaration.

"Mr. Whalen, it seems to this court you've been persecuted enough. Your record at Terminal Island was exemplary, and there is nothing to suggest you were connected to the subject boat and its contents. I believe time served is sufficient, and I will sentence you to five years' probation, running concurrently with Judge Yankowitz's sentence. This court is adjourned!"

The 1938 World Championship

THE PROBATION PERIOD WAS terminated after a couple of months. Prohibition was now in the rearview mirror. There wasn't a chance in hell that part of Fred's life would ever return. Pool playing and hustling was all that was left. He never liked the dry-cleaning business. The last location he sold ended up becoming a chain.

Later in 1938, Fred played Ralph Greenleaf for the World's Championship at Busy Bee Billiard Room in Hollywood. Fred lost to Ralph but not by much. He felt there was no shame in losing to the best pool player that ever lived. The newspapers announced the match. The game would be for $500 and the championship, but it wasn't altogether accurate. The match was actually for $2,500. This was a side deal made between Fred and Ralph. The bet was that Fred would not exceed eight hundred balls to Ralph's one thousand. Harold Lloyd put up the money for Greenleaf, and George Hart sponsored Fred for $1,500. It was a four-day match. Eight games were to be played in two sessions per day, one in the afternoon and one in the evening. Each session was 125 balls of 14.1 straight pool.

Ralph won seventeen World titles, the first in 1919. He and Fred were the same age. He played in the Midwest and East Coast for most of his career. He married a beautiful Eurasian girl, half English and half Chinese. She was known as the "Chinese Nightingale" and performed on a circuit of vaudevillian performers that included Ralph making fabulous trick shots, which were displayed by an arrangement of large mirrors. She was billed as Princess Nai. They were part of the Orpheum circuit, which traveled throughout the States. They were performing in Los Angeles, and Ralph was playing locally. Fred was the local favorite. Ralph was a superb player. In many ways, he and Fred had similar physical traits, lean and fluid.

Both men had great concentration. The difference was that Fred was a money player and Ralph wasn't. The biggest difference was Ralph's unquenchable thirst for whiskey. Although Fred ran liquor for years, he never had more than one drink in any one day, even socially. He'd seen alcoholism first hand growing up, helping his childhood friends square up their fathers. Ralph could outdrink most men. He held the stuff well. During previous trips to the west, Ralph would ask Fred to play exhibitions with him. There were times when Ralph was not able to run great strings of balls without missing. Fred would pick up the count and run a large number then miss on purpose, giving Ralph a chance to start a multi-ball run. The paying customers came to see long runs of balls. Nai learned quickly that she had to put Ralph in quarantine days before a big match or exhibition play and then monitor him closely during the performances.

The opening afternoon match on the first day was a crowd pleaser. Ralph broke, and Fred ran nine balls and missed. Ralph approached the table and slowly analyzed his first shot, moving his cue through his figures. He ran 125 balls and out. That evening, the same story was repeated. Fred had only shot twice and was behind 250 to 24. Fred was getting his ass kicked and wasn't happy with his performance.

It was common knowledge among the better players that Ralph's weakness for alcohol could be used against him to offset his remarkable concentration and skill. Most players hid a bottle in the men's room and let Ralph do the rest. Nai had gotten wise to this ploy over the last year. Entering the men's rooms didn't put her off. Ralph would ask for the whiskey. His body demanded it at this point, and his opponents were all eager to help him out. This time was no different.

"Fred! Can you get me a pint?" Ralph asked. "Nai has cut me off since we got here."

"Ralph, I don't want to make that fireball you married pissed at me!"

"You've got to help me out!" Ralph begged. "If I don't get a little shot or two, I'll start shaking, and my hands will embarrass us both."

This was an important event for Fred, and he didn't want to mess it up. He grabbed Gus before the third match and told him to get a pint of *10 High*. He asked him to put it in the ladies' room in toilet tank and lock the men's room.

Just before the start of the third match, Fred and Ralph were standing together looking at the crowd that was gathering to watch.

"It's in the ladies' room!" Fred whispered. "Gus will be in the men's room with the door locked. You'll have to use the ladies."

Fred signaled Gus who went to the men's and locked the door. Fred and Ralph shook hands. Fred passed him a breath candy. Nai was no one's fool. She walked with Ralph to the men's room and finding it occupied sent Ralph into the women's. She stood outside waiting. Ralph emerged after rinsing his mouth out, and they returned to the table. Ralph nodded his appreciation to Fred, and the introductions were made, stating the current score. Fred hoped the pint helped them both. Ralph was looking at a pretty girl in the crowd when Fred came over a stood beside him.

"How do I look, Fred?" he asked. "Do I look bad?"

"You're playing extremely well!" Fred returned. "The score says you're doing fine!"

"No! I mean, how's my face look?"

"Since your visit to the men's room, your color is coming back."

Ralph told Fred he finished the whole pint and would probably need more before the evening match. Fred assured him that he would take care of it.

Fred broke the balls, and Ralph ran 125 balls and out again. Now he was down 375 to 24. This was not what Fred expected. Again, he wasn't able to get back on the table after the break.

"We might have saved the cost of the pint and just given him milk!" Fred said to Gus.

"Maybe we should get him more before the evening match," Gus returned.

That evening, Fred could see the liquor was taking effect. Somehow, Ralph had purloined more whiskey between matches. Gus brought the children over to watch, Jack and Bobbie along with their Aunt Bernice, who was only two years older than Fred's eldest. They wore jackets with pints in each pocket.

Ralph could not hit the end rail on the lag. He had the honors of breaking. Fred got on and ran ninety-one balls before missing. Ralph got up and ran three balls before he missed. Fred took his turn and ran off with another fifty-one before missing. The evening match ended with an overall score, 378 to 149. There were two more days left in the competition, and Nai wasn't going to let Ralph out of her sight.

The third afternoon, Fred got his stroke back and was making runs of seventy and eighty balls and passed Ralph to take the lead. Nai was on hand and was keeping her man straight. The final day ended with Ralph finishing with 1,000 to Fred's 878. Fred lost but won the money as he exceeded eight hundred balls.

Horses on a String

FRED WENT BACK TO shooting pool and hustling all over California. He continued to keep himself open to new moneymaking ventures along the way. His *1551 Club* had been converted to a pool hall, and all the best players were frequenting the room. It had Brunswick tables and bowling alleys. While playing one afternoon, Willie Masconi approached Fred. He had just made the trip west and was broke. Willie was twenty-five while Ralph and Fred were both forty. He asked Fred to book him some exhibitions. Fred obliged and contacted Ralph, who was still touring with Nai on the Orpheum circuit. The match would be hailed as the young blood challenging the aging champion. Fred took the duo on a tour around Southern California promoting the match up. The money was good for all concerned.

Fred as The Masked Marvel 1938

Masconi got better with every meeting, but Ralph was still the grand master of the game. Ralph eventually sank deeper into his alcoholic tendencies, soon attracting the attention of the police. Nai was fighting an uphill battle to keep Ralph straight and losing ground every day.

Through 1939, Fred would often play with Bill Robinson, Beau Jingles as he was called around the movie studios during the thirties. He taught Shirley Temple how to dance in Paramount's *Little Miss Marker*. He was an outstanding dancer but was quite a pool player and gambler. He liked to play the best and always for money. Bill, Willie, and Fred played many times together. Bill beat Willie constantly. Fred beat Bill afterward.

The difference between Bill and Willie was that Robinson was a money player. Willie was stiff when money was on the line. Like Ralph, they were pool perfectionist, not accustomed to the hustler's life. Championships meant more than the money. This was the edge Fred and Bill had over many of the best players.

"They can't play when the cabbage is down!" Fred would say.

In 1940, Ponzi was World Champion. Willie went east to meet him in a match, but Ponzi remained champion. Willie eventually won in 1941 and racked up the title fifteen times. Fred had told Masconi that he needed to look the part and start dressing better. Fred liked Willie and would play exhibitions and help him through the years, but like Greenleaf, the booze became his best friend. Like Fred, his father had not liked him playing pool. Both men were proof of the adage; forbidden fruit always makes it sweeter.

About that time, a man named Dave Walsh came out west. He fancied himself a player but was not a good one. While playing Fred, he mentioned a moneymaking scheme involving horse racing. Its principal goal was beating bookmakers. Beating them so badly that they didn't know what happened. Dave was sitting down while he talked. As Fred moved around the table shooting, he noticed Dave's shoes were worn and had holes in the soles. Fred thought that if this deal was so profitable, why wasn't he wearing decent shoes at the least.

Fred put him off several times. Finally, to put a stop to the constant pestering, he told Dave that he'd introduce him to a friend that knew about betting horses. Carl Jameson was a small-time bookmaker, an acquaintance of Fred's from the rum-running business. Fred asked Carl to give Dave a chance at the scheme and see what happens. Dave went to Carl and told him he was working at Paramount Studios and that he would see him the next day. After two days, Carl called Fred.

"Freddie! We need to meet!" Carl said excitedly. "It's got to be right away!"

"What's the rush?" Fred asked.

"We need to talk privately about your friend, Dave!" Carl gasped, catching his breath.

"I'll be at your place in an hour," Fred assured him.

Fred grabbed a sandwich and drove to Carl's home. Carl met Fred at the door and asked him to sit down. He had barely sat down when Fred got the news.

"He beat me, Fred!" Carl burst out. "Beat me bad!"

"Who beat you?"

"That guy you sent me!"

"Dave Walsh?"

"Yes, that's the man!" Carl gasped. "Beat me madly!"

"How?" Fred asked, scooting forward in his chair.

"I don't know! I was watching him that closely. I can't imagine how he did it!"

"I'll get hold of him, and let's see if he can do this every time!" Fred said with a puzzled look.

Fred was perplexed and was finding this hard to swallow. Carl was not a newcomer to bookmaking. If this guy was on the level and could beat bookmakers, Fred wondered why he was attired so shabbily. He would have to look into this a bit more. He didn't have to wait long. The next morning, Dave found Fred at the poolroom practicing.

"Fred, look here!" Dave said, holding a sheet of paper in front of Fred. "I've won a bunch of money, but I can't read your friend's writing, it's like mush to me!"

Fred took Dave to his car and told him to get in. They drove to Carl's house. On the way, Fred explained to Dave that the plan was to test Dave's claims in real time. He and Carl didn't think it could be done, definitely not on a big scale.

"Can you do this all the time?" Carl asked Dave. "Can you beat anyone?"

"Yes, I can!" Dave exclaimed.

"Show us how, and I will get you every book in the city!" Carl told him.

Dave Walsh slowly explained how he did it. Fred and Carl looked at each other in disbelief. *This is too good to be true*, they thought. Fred was skeptical and still stinging from the betrayal that sent him to Terminal Island.

Both Dave and Carl wanted Fred to come in with them, but he declined. Carl steered Dave to every bookie in town. They beat them all, winning lots of money. It was a great con. Fred knew that some of these bookmakers were connected to organized crime groups that he didn't want any part of.

During the next few months, Fred would check in with Carl and Dave, mainly to see if they were still alive. Beating bookies was dangerous business, Les Brunaman being the perfect example. Fred started to see them more often, and it seemed to be working for them. At least he thought Dave was dressing better. On occasion, Fred would go along and watch from a distance. They even explained by acting out the process. Fred became thoroughly familiar with the action and even added improvements to the finished schemes.

Carl and Dave would travel to a new city, say Fresno. They would get the biggest book in town to steer them to the bookie's competition. Without telling the steering bookie how it was done, they would be introduced as more action than the bookie could lay off. The steering bookie was cut in at one-third of the take.

The story was that these bets were coming out of the local hospital and were about $1,400 in small bets made by individual hospital staff that liked the ponies. He continued further by saying that an intern had been handling the action but had left to go to a residency at another hospital. A doctor had taken his place and now was looking for an outlet. The doctor wanted 25 percent of the bookie's take for the bets brought to him. The best part, and most convincing, was that the doctor couldn't risk being associated with illegal dealings for fear of losing his license. Due to this, the doctor would meet the bookie at a neutral site of his choosing and give him the day's bets. He would meet the bookie before the first races started. Bookmakers loved this kind of action. It was regular and profitable. The steering bookie would take the mark to the hospital to meet the doctor, leaving them to fill in the blanks.

Dave and Carl went to a uniform shop and purchased doctor outfits with their alias names embroidered on them. Stethoscopes completed their outfits, along with white shoes. In Oakland, they would work out of Highland Hospital. Large hospitals were the best as they handled a lot of staff and out-of-the-area doctors visiting their patients. At first, the setup would involve the steering bookie, bringing the mark to the hospital and introduce him to either Carl or Dave in the lobby. The steering bookie would then leave. The mark and Carl would talk. Carl would be polite and professional, directing the mark to a less busy area of the lobby.

"I think we should go to your car and discuss an arrangement for you to receive the wagers," Carl would suggest. "There is always a chance I may be called on the intercom system."

They would adjourn to the mark's car, and the conversation would continue.

"You can understand that I cannot risk being associated with anything illegal and that I want to protect my license and reputation." Carl would continue, "I'm replacing a staff member that used to collect the wagers from the employees here that like to bet on races."

"I really don't want to know your name," the mark would say. "I'll call you Dr. Kildare, and you can call me Bob."

"First thing, Bob. If you're looking for big bets this is not for you," Carl warned. "The people here make $2–$20 bets. We play a lot of Daily Doubles and Parlays. We have won a lot of money in the past at times."

The mark was always happy to take the action. He would ask the doctor what he would take for doing the business. The doctor would say he needed 5 percent of the money bet or 50 percent of the net winnings.

"I'd prefer 50 percent of net winnings."

This was what the mark wanted to hear as it was the best deal for him. This touch went a long way in seducing the bookie into believing the doctor was on the level. The doctor would then suggest they meet the next day at a motel/hotel. The doctor would then bring the written wagers on 3×5 cards and let the mark copy the bets. That way both the doctor and the mark had records of the bets. Usually, it would take about three days for the bookie to drop the business.

"What if the bookie became suspicious?" Fred asked.

"The very first thing we do is go to the hospital reception or switchboard with a box of candy," Carl said. "This is what we say, 'Good morning. I'm Doctor Moore. I'm visiting a patient here, and she gave me this box of candy. I really don't want it and thought you might enjoy it. I'm going to be here a while. I'm expecting a call from my office later. Would you be so kind a to page me?'"

Carl would then tell the mark to just call the hospital and ask to speak to Dr. Moore. "They'll page me."

When the mark called, he could hear the page go out for Dr. Moore. This put the bookie at ease. He then believed the entire story.

Fred decided to participate and got his doctor outfit. He thought of an even better method to make the target bookies even more comfortable. He suggested that two doctors where better than one. This would preclude any suspicion on the bookie's part. When the introduction was made in the hospital lobby, the second doctor would interrupt the meeting by asking to consult with the other while the bookie waited. The steering bookie would leave the hospital, and as the mark and Carl were talking, Fred would insert himself for the consult by asking Carl to speak with him a moment.

This con worked for years. Between 1940 and 1959, Fred, Carl, and others would participate. The scheme would eventually involve Fred's daughter, Bobbie, as a nurse asking for treatment orders for imaginary patients. The marked bookies took the bait every time. In some instances, Bobbie would meet the bookie, as the doctor's nurse, and pick up the winnings. Hospitals weren't the only set up, manufacturing plant and parking lots worked too.

The scam was a basic past post-operation. The trick was to meet on neutral ground away from the hospital or plant. The doctor would set the transfer of wager information at a hotel room with an adjoining room connected by a closed door. The betting cards were filled out the night before using the racing form, which covered the racetracks across the nation. These cards contained random picks with small $2 bets. In most cases some of these random selections won, all the better.

The hotel room would be staged to allow the hidden transfer of the winning cards. A table was set next to the door that separated the two rooms. The mark would sit opposite the doctor who read off the random and past post-winning cards. A paper clip held the winning cards to the string, which would be pulled from one room to the other under the table to the doctor's knee. The string made into a continuous loop would travel from carrying the ringer card to be inserted by the doctor into the random bet stack.

The doctor would read the information from the cards to the mark who would be writing the bets down on his own sheet. That way, when the mark was busy concentrating on writing the bets, the doctor would insert the bogus card containing winners. Tracks, due to time zone differences, had multiple races being run at the same time. This way there was a steady uninterrupted flow of cards for a few hours. Fred improved the system by adding an eye hook under the table by the doctor's knee. The card would stop at the hook, and the accomplice in the adjoining room could tell when the card reached its destination. The tug as the card was pulled told the man in the adjoining room to return the clip for the next card.

Fred and the boys became so good at this that there were no miscues. The hand is faster than the eye, especially when the eyes that should be watching are occupied by making written copies of the bets. Sometimes, the doctors would let the bookie win a little one day if they felt the mark was going to play longer than a couple of days. It was never long before the mark was so beaten that they made their last payment of losses and called it quits.

They would travel the country working this scam. Fred would hustle pool along the way. They would take in cash anywhere from $2,500 to over $10,000 each day of the play. Usually, a three-day period would rake in $10,000 to $15,000. They purposely stayed away from large cities where the families controlled the bookies. Chicago, Detroit, New York, and the like were skipped. The men would be gone three to five weeks, depending on how far east or north they traveled. All those years, Fred would return home with the Caddy's trunk filled with boxes of cash.

PART 4

Jack Frederick Whalen

JACK WAS BORN ON May 11, 1921, in St. Louis. He was a huge baby. Lilly had a hard labor, and the family thought he weighed sixteen pounds. His birth weight was never recorded but he grew into a six-foot tall, extremely handsome man. He had the blackest hair and the best combination of the Whalen/Wunderlich traits, which also included a temper inherited from both sides. He was his mother's joy, and she doted on him. Fred wanted Jack to have the things he never had, one being a complete education. His father thought he needed discipline that he wouldn't get from a father that was always moving from one venture to another. Fred and Lilly decided that Black-Foxe was the best alternative to a life that ran on the edge of social norms.

Jack's years at Black-Foxe were filled with activities that formed the person he became. He was naturally athletic and participated in most sports. Even polo and boxing were included with the more common sports. He excelled in everything. He was his class commander and demonstrated a leadership quality that he maintained throughout his years at the academy. He missed his mother and kept her perfumed letters under his pillow for a while. Other cadets made the mistake of teasing him about it and paid the price. When altercations arose, the commandant would have them settled in the ring. The outcome was the always the same, even upperclassmen discovered this.

Jack and Fred at Black Fox
Father/Sons Charity Baseball Game 1932

Jack and Sister Bobbie 1934

Fred would visit the school and play exhibitions for the boys. He would attend all the games and events that involved his son. He also supplied Major Black with the best whiskey during Prohibition. When Jack was still an adolescent, his father took him flying with his uncle Gus. Even though Fred had had only one flying lesson, Lilly allowed her son to go up on Fred's first solo flight. Lilly always believed in Fred's ability to survive any adverse situation.

Taking off was the second easiest part of flying. Flying the plane was the first. Landing was a different story. Somewhere in his only lesson, Fred didn't get the altimeter part. As they flew through Cahuenga Pass into the San Fernando Valley, everything was going off without a hitch. At the new airport in Van Nuys, the landing part raised its head. Fred brought the *Jenny* around and lined up with the runway. He descended, reading the altimeter, which had not been corrected for the Van Nuys airport. Since the landing airport was higher than the takeoff location, the plane came down hard and bounced back into the air. This got Gus concerned, especially after the second attempt produced the same effect. Little Jackie loved the jolt and bounces and wanted more.

"Fred! Next time we get close to the ground, I'm jumping with Jackie!" Gus screamed.

The next attempt was successful as Fred just let the plane settle. Little Jack remembered his first plane ride and wanted more. He would always ask his father to take him up again, but Fred decided owning a plane wasn't for him and sold it.

At eighteen years old, Jack was caught up, as was the nation, with Joe Louis, the Heavyweight Boxing Champion. He had enjoyed boxing at Black-Foxe and had decided that boxing competitively might just be for him. He begged his father to arrange for a trainer. Fred thought that boxing was a dirty and corrupt sport even though he would attend fights with his cronies.

Fred decided to put an end to this fantasy of Jack's. He knew a boxer, Jack Roper. He arranged for Jackie to spar with Roper during the boxer's training camp as he prepared to meet Joe Louis for the title in Los Angeles. Fred asked Roper to play around with Jack for a round and then knock him out in the second. In the second round, Roper unloaded on Jack, knocking him down but not out. Jack got up and knocked Roper down and out for ten minutes. Jack ripped off his gloves and threw them back into the ring.

"Fred! You gotta let me train your son," pleaded Roper's trainer. "I could make him the next heavyweight champ!"

"You were right, Pop!" Jack exclaimed. "This is a dirty sport!"

"Buddy, that's your answer!" replied Fred.

Jack continued to play polo with various clubs and worked with horses all along the way. The war had begun and Jack yet twenty-one. He flirted with the idea of getting into movies. He liked westerns and believed he was just the type. Along the way, with the help of his father's many celebrity connections, he met Katherine Sabichi and her sister, Barbara. The Sabichi family were members of the Old Californios, original Spanish settlers in California. Kay was a few years older than Jack but decided that this handsome "Gringo" was the man for her. Jack had never gotten over flying, and the war effort needed pilots. He enlisted in the Army Air Corp and was accepted for flight training, based on his education and military training provided while at Black-Foxe.

He was being sent to Caldwell, Idaho, for flight training but first had to do a minimal stint at the College of Idaho. After basic flight in Class 44-D-I Flight, Jack was sent to advanced pilot training in Pecos, Texas. He completed his multiple engine training and was commissioned a second lieutenant. His call sign, given to him by his classmates, was Errol Jr. for obvious reasons. Like a lot of men going overseas to fight, he proposed to Kay, and they were married in 1943. Kay's mother adored Jack, and he returned the affection. In fact, when Katherine's father passed away, Jack took care of his mother-in-law until she died. Katherine and her mother were never close, and Jack would complain about her neglect of her mother. Unfortunately, this same trait was passed to their daughter, Karen.

J. F. Whalen, Jr.
"Errol Jr."
St. Louis, Missouri

Jack Army Air Corp Training

The Sabichi trust, which cared for the sisters' mother, was passed on to Barbara and Katherine, affording them an income for life. Barbara was a sweet, kind woman who lived alone in Pacific Palisades until her death, at which time the entire trust passed to Kay. Jack would bring his children to visit Barbara even though Kay disapproved. Many times, he would include his sister's children on the weekend visits. Through the greater part of the 1950s, Jack and Bobbie would schedule picnics in Griffith Park with the entire clan, trailering his horses to the picnic site so that the children could ride.

Jack would complete his pilot training on B-25s, B-17s, and B-29s. He requested combat duty but was told that he was too valuable as a training pilot. The war ended, and Jack was stationed at Waco, Texas, where he continued to instruct. He was promoted to captain and soon after resigned his commission. Before leaving the Air Corp, he flew his family and all their belongings to Los Angeles in a B-29 that he ferried to the West Coast on its way to Hawaii. Jack bought a five-acre ranch along Woodman Avenue. He began training horses and dogs. Clayton Moore lived just up the street, and he would ride down to Jack's with Jay Silverheels, in costume, and thrill the children at their birthday parties. Leo Corrillo and Duncan Renaldo would do the same.

Fred's grandchildren grew up calling Carrillo Uncle Leo. Jack would ride with Leo in the Rose Parade on his palomino, Sundown. Carrillo's equestrian group all rode palominos sporting silver saddles made by Edward Bohlin. These celebrities frequented Fred's *1551 Club* during Prohibition.

Jack worked for Denver-Chicago Trucks Lines during this time. He was able to procure substantial shipping contracts facilitated by Fred's Hollywood connections that were investors in major manufacturing companies. Jack owned a twin-engine Beechcraft and would fly charter for various businesses and their executives. In all, his attempts to have a normal family life would be shorted by circumstances that spilled over from his father's activities.

Jack Frederick Whalen 1954

Las Vegas was coming into its own in the early fifties. Guy McAfee, a former Los Angeles policeman, had been on the payoff rolls of Jack's father, along with other rumrunners and bookmakers in Southern California. Guy opened the Golden Nugget Casino just ahead of the Flamingo. Jack would sometimes go to Vegas with a pocketful and play craps. Sometimes, he won big. He set a limit and if he lost, he'd head home. It was on one occasion after winning a small fortune that the trouble began. Jack had stopped at an all-night café early one morning. An off-duty plain-clothes policeman was walking by and saw Jack standing in front of the cashier, taking a large quantity of bills from the cash register. Seeing this hulk of a man and the cashier almost emptying the register, he assumed a robbery was in progress. Without identifying himself, he reached for his concealed gun. Jack, seeing this action from the corner of his eye, felt that this man was going to rob both himself and the café. Turning quickly, he punched the officer in the stomach area, sending him to the ground, dislodging the half-drawn pistol onto the floor.

Jack later found out that the blow had ruptured the man's stomach, and internal bleeding had almost killed him. The waitress called the police and an ambulance. The answering officers attempted to arrest Jack, but the cashier explained what took place, and Jack was released. In retaliation for almost killing a fellow officer, they went to Denver-Chicago Trucking and threatened to stop all their trucks from entering Los Angeles unless Jack was fired.

Jack was let go the next week. The general manager related the strong-arm threat to Jack.

"If this is the way they want to play, then I'll give them something to really fret about!" Jake told the family at one of the picnics.

So Jack began making book with a partner, Al Levit, a Jewish boy who had been taking bets for a while. Having Jack around gave him more confidence in growing the business. Al had muscle now, and gaming debts would be collected. Bets were collected at various bars and businesses.

During this time, Jack's sister, Bobbie, began helping out. She had played the nurse, Beverly, for years with her father, adding more credibility to the scam. Carl Jameson continued making the plays with Fred. Bobbie and her husband, the colonel owned the White House in Los Feliz, and Jack had plans for using it as a base of operations. Col. Eric Manfred von Hurst, Bobbie's husband, was one of MacArthur's staff officers during the later part of the Pacific Campaign. He commanded Northern Japan during the occupation. He had been an artillery officer prior to WWII, horse artillery. He was the Army Eventing Champion and patrolled the southern border with Mexico when war was declared.

Lillian Virginia Whalen-Von Hurst (Bobbie)

Bobbie had no interest in relocating to Japan and stayed in Los Angeles with her family, living in the same apartment complex as her mother and father. They lived on Lodi Place, two blocks east of Vine Street, not far from where Fred's *1551 Club* had been, across from *The Hollywood Studio Club*.

In March 1947, Bobbie's first child was born, John Frederick von Hurst. He was named after his great-grandfather and Fred. Carl Jameson also lived at the same complex. This was convenient in many ways. Lilly was close to help with little Johnny, and Carl was close, working with Fred. Fred was comforted by the thought that Lilly was close to Bobbie. This made leaving on road trips, beating bookies, much easier. Having the *Studio Club* across the street provided instant babysitters. Bobbie would take Johnny out in a stroller up and down Lodi Place. Young starlets and hopefuls would stop and admire the child's shock of blond curly hair. They'd asked to hold him and even volunteered to watch him. From 1947 to 1951, many actress crossed the street to watch the big curly-haired child, including Marilyn.

In 1948, Fred was walking his grandson, from his parents' apartment, on their way to the Hollywood Farmer's Market, two blocks away. Before they reached the street, two men left a running car at the curb on Lodi and ran toward Fred and the child, pistol-whipping Fred across the mouth, knocking out his front teeth. They muscled him into the waiting car, leaving Johnny walking toward the car with his arms out for his grandfather. The car sped away with Fred in the back seat between two men. Luckily, John's father had heard the squeal of tires and looked out the window, watching his boy head for the street. Eric got to his son just before he tried to step off the curb. It was a close call as no one would have seen him between parked cars. Two of the girls were just leaving the Studio Club when the car pulled away, allowing them to see the toddler heading for the street.

The kidnappers called later, threatening to throw Fred out of a plane over the valley if Lilly didn't hock here diamonds and furs and pay the ransom. Jack got wind of who these guys were and where they were holed up. He and his uncles drove to the location where Fred was being held. They hired a taxi, and George got into the chauffeur's uniform and carried a Western Union telegram envelope. The door opened, and he handed the envelope to the man inside, saying he was to wait for a reply. The man left the doorway and called to someone in the back.

"Hey, are we expecting a telegram?" he yelled.

Jack and Gus leaped from the cab and rushed the door. George had started inside when another man reached from a hallway for the telegram. By then, the three rescuers were in the house grabbing the kidnappers as they left the back room where Fred was tied to a chair. A gun was laying on the bed in the room, but none of the men thought to grab it in their haste to get to the front of the house. George tackled the man who answered the door, and Gus grabbed the first guy out the hallway. Jack met the third man as he left the bedroom with a solid punch to his face, feeling the man's nose and cheek collapse. Seeing the gun, he threw it through the window, turned, and went to assist his uncles. Gus had his man against the wall.

"Gus, go get dad!" Jack yelled as he began working the second man over.

Gus stepped over the unconscious man crumpled in the bedroom doorway. He got to Fred who had dried blood down the front of his suit and pants. Untying him, he helped Fred stand. He'd been tied up for over twenty-four hours and was pretty stiff. Jack was taking care of George's charge when Fred entered the front room. Fred turned over the guy in the hallway.

"This is the son of a bitch that knocked my teeth out!" Fred declared.

Seeing a crescent wrench lying on the kitchen table, he reached for it and proceeded to knock every tooth out in the front of the guy's mouth.

"How's that for payback you motherfucking bastard!" Fred screamed, standing over the man.

"He ain't gonna feel good when he comes to!" Gus observed, grabbing him by the hair to assess the new dental work, teeth spilling like Chiclets on the man's chest.

"Let's get out of here, the cab's waiting!" Jack said, taking his father's arm.

"Hey, I think he must have swallowed some!" George said, counting the white specs on the man's chest.

As they got Fred into the back seat, the cabbie took a deep breath and asked, "Is he alright?"

Jack jumped in alongside the driver, slamming his door. "Get the hell out of here!" Jack ordered.

"Hey! I don't want any trouble!" The cabbie begged.

"There won't be!" Jack assured the driver, stuffing a $50 bill into his shirt pocket. "You never took this fare! Got it?"

The driver nodded and said, "Where to?'

The county sheriffs found the three men after receiving an anonymous tip. A passerby noticed the open front door and heard someone moaning inside. It was all in the papers.

They took Fred home, and Lilly cleaned him up. Bobbie called the family doctor, James Faganey. He arrived at the apartment and checked Fred out.

Other than the missing teeth and a black-and-blue face with lacerations, he was fine. Faganey recommended a dentist and stayed for drinks. A month later, Fred and Carl were back on the road clipping bookies and playing the chauffeur gig.

Jack and Al's enterprise was paying off. In 1952, it expanded, much to the discomfort of the Cohen Outfit. The little fat Jew the families had sent west brough real organized crime to Los Angeles. Mickey Cohen was involved in many aspects of criminal activity, and he was brazen about it. He'd lay off bets through intermediaries and renege if he lost. If he won and wasn't paid, he became very aggressive in collections. He made the mistake of not paying Jack Whalen.

Jack's habit of going to Las Vegas and playing over the weekends put him in constant contact with friends of his father, such as Benny Binion. Jack would get a complimentary room and drinks during his stay. He began checking out newer casinos, such as the *Flamingo* and later the *Sands*. It was at the Sands one night after a late show that he was sitting in the cocktail lounge and noticed Frank Sinatra and his entourage sitting at a table on the opposite side of the room. A cigarette waitress was making the rounds of the seated patrons when she accidentally knocked a drink into Ol' Blue Eyes' lap. Frank jumped up and slapped her. Jack stood up and crossed the room.

"Don't let that guy near me!" Frank told his bodyguard, a former heavyweight boxer.

As Jack approached Frank's table, the man reached out, putting his hand his hand on Jack's chest. "That's far enough, fella! Go sit down before there's trouble," he said, putting pressure on Jack's chest.

Jack slapped his arm away with his left forearm and unloaded an uppercut with his right, breaking the man's jaw. The guy collapsed between tables, and Frank stood up trying to get out of the way. Jack picked up Sinatra by his sport coat jacket and pushed him up the wall.

"I ever see you slap another woman, you'll be singing a new tune!" Jack told him, letting Frank slide down into his seat. Giving the girl $20, he walked out of the Sands. Sinatra was a weasel that mistreated wait staff and smaller individuals in public places. His favorite stage for these antics was the *Polo Lounge* in the Beverly Hills Hotel although he did it in other venues.

Frank would frequent nightclubs along the Sunset Strip and invariably ran into Mickey Cohen on occasion. He was smart enough not to bet the ponies with Cohen. Most of Sinatra's gambling was done in Vegas or the tracks around Southern California. He and his pack would have a box in the *Club Houses* at Santa Anita and Hollywood Park. Fred shared a box at these same tracks with Mickey Rooney and Mick's mother, Nell Panky, and stepfather, Fred.

Mickey liked the horses, maybe too much. His mother and Fred were big drinkers and enjoyed the ponies. Nell had overseen her son's career from his childhood and had put most of his early earnings in an irrevocable trust, which proved a godsend when he faced tax evasion charges later in life. His many marriages and other issues forced him to work harder than most in the film business. Bobbie and Mickey were good friends, and the Whalen family often partied with the Pankys at their home in Sherman Oaks. Jack took care of some of Mickey's run-ins.

In October of 1956, Fred was playing the doctor in New York. He and Carl inadvertently beat a couple of the family's bookmakers. They were strong-armed at their hotel and threatened. Fred immediately called home. Jack was taken to the Los Angeles airport and put on a TWA nonstop to the city. Arriving early the next morning, Jack went to the hotel. There he waited for the two wise guys to return. When they arrived, Carl opened the door, and they shoved their way in. Carl stumbled backward as Jack walked out of the adjoining room.

"Who the fuck's this? Another doctor?"

Jack crossed the room and took both men down before they could utter another word. He pulled them to their feet, one in each hand, and threw them on the couch. Still dazed, the men slumped into each other. Jack removed their hardware, handing the rods to his father and Carl. As the men came to clarity, Jack helped them reach it sooner by cross slapping their faces.

"Listen you fucking pricks!" Jack shouted. "You go tell your boss that if he ever threatens my father again, I'll stuff you in barrels and roll you down Broadway! Get out of here you dago pieces of shit!"

"We'll take care of your pieces!" Fred added.

Jack pulled both men to their feet and shoved them out the door.

"I'm staying here!" Jack told his father. "Have a roll-up bed sent up."

They waited to hear from the outfit. They were called at 9:00 a.m. They were prepared for the worst. After all, now they were armed.

The phone rang. The boss was downstairs and was going to come up, but Jack thought better of it and told him they'd come down to the lobby. Better in public for health reasons. Carl and Fred each had one of the guns taken from the two thugs the night before.

As they left the elevator, Jack noticed two men standing on each side of a chair in a less active portion of the Park Sheridan lobby. The man in the chair turned out to be Joe Profaci, smoking a cigar. He wore glasses. He wasn't a big man and seemed impressed by Jack's physicality. He stood up and met Jack a few steps in front of his chair.

"Look!" Profaci said. "I don't want to have you people disturbing our gambling operations in New York. I want to offer a proposition. My boys will steer our bookmaking competitors to you. For that, the families want 60 percent of the action."

"We'll break your opposition, but we'll take the it all!" Jack returned. "Otherwise, we will leave town with what we've got. That's the play. Take it or not!"

Profaci looked down for a second and then turned to his men. "Carlo, get the gentlemen a list of bookmakers we want done!" Joe ordered. "I want it delivered to these men today!"

Looking back at Jack, he offered, "You know, I could find a place for a man like you here in New York. If you ever want to come into the family, I'll see you're taken care off."

"I'm sure you would!" Jack replied. "I like the weather in California."

Profaci waved his men to leave. One led the way to the door while the other walked behind him. Jack and Fred walked a few steps behind the trio. They noticed a big Cadillac waiting out front.

"He's got good taste in cars!" Fred said. "Big and black! I'll bet the whole damn outfit has black Cadillacs. I like white. They don't show the dust as much."

"Watch these guys!" Jack cautioned. "I'm flying back to Los Angeles."

Fred and Carl returned home with over $20,000.

Welcome to the White House

IN THE SPRING OF 1952, Bobbie and her husband purchased a home in the Los Feliz area. Just east of Hollywood, the house set above Franklin Avenue with a view of downtown Los Angeles. The house was a smaller version of the White House. From that day on, it became the main gathering place for the Whalen/Wunderlich clan. Most holidays were spent there. The Saturday before Christmas, the home hosted the city's political figures from 11:00 a.m. to 2:00 p.m. and the notorious from eight till after midnight. Most New Year's Eves were at Jack's ranch in the valley. For the better part of thirty-four years, this was the scene of happy and sad times.

Fred helped his daughter and son-in-law make the down payment and later moved into the house in 1956. The three floors included six bedrooms, three and a half baths, a tea house, three-car garage, and a bar-room. The basement sported a Brunswick 5×10 pool table

5137 Franklin Avenue LA CA

and mirrored the main floor. Fred maintained his billiard skills and played serious money games on occasion. The house had a private drive that ran behind the house from North Normandie Avenue. Above the house, a slope rose over sixty feet and was lined with other homes, one being Cecil B. DeMille's. Built in 1913, the house was one of a kind. Under the long front porch was a 10×80 wine cellar, which was vented to the outside and remained cool in the summers. The half circle portico, with columns, centered the house. It was all white with shutters on the windows and French doors that opened unto the front porch. Two houses east was a Lloyd Wright House that was involved in the Black Dahlia Murder Mystery.

It sat empty for years following the investigation.

Jack spent a great deal of time at the home and often spent the night rather than driving back into the valley. It was some time in 1953 when he decided the basement would be an ideal location for a centralized book. Jack and Al installed desks and blackboards in the central room below the grand entrance hall. This included three reel-to-reel tape recorders. These recorders each had their own dedicated phone line installed by Pacific Bell confidants. These phones rang at three separate, empty apartments located around the city. The betting public had their individual coded accounts. Tracks were given a letter designation. Using the race number first, the postposition second, and the bet, followed with a one, two, or three finish. In cases of the Daily Double, DD proceeded the bet. Parlays were treated similarly.

Two men manned the betting center daily. Runners would pick up wagers from various bars and gas stations. Newsstand operators, on a percentage, handled bets. Bobbie would pick up her children at three o'clock from Immaculate Heart of Mary and proceed on a route that took her to a variety of locations, one of which was the El Dorado Cocktail Lounge near Santa Monica. Jack opened the bar in Bobbie's name. Eventually, Bobbie would drop off payouts and pick up receivables. These were done with paper lunch bags. Her son, John, began dropping and collecting at gas stations and newsstands where she could keep him in sight. The 1948 kidnapping of her father still haunted her. There were never issues about picking up. The losers knew what the alternatives were.

The recordings were kept until all bets were settled and then erased by using a large electromagnet. The house continued in this venue until 1958. Just before Christmas 1957, a shot was fired through the stained-glass window one night when John passed the window going down the stairs. Bobbie decided it was time to join the colonel in Tennessee. In February 1958, the von Hurst's left the White House and drove to Springfield, Tennessee, pets and all.

Fred and Lilly had moved into the home in 1956 and would reside there until 1986. Fred continued his doctor scam with Carl until December 1959. Bobbie and Eric didn't return to the house until August of 1960 when John was enrolled at Loyola High School. Eric had left the Army and had been hired by Northrup Corporation in Hawthorne. In later years, Eric would install missile systems for Northrup in Huntsville, Alabama, and consult at the Pentagon. During the years after the war, Eric had been assigned to the OS as it transitioned into the CIA.

The parties resumed during Christmas and Easter. The guest list had changed somewhat. Fred's friends who had retired from the various law enforcement agencies would still come early, but the later crowd was restricted to family. As all the grandchildren became older, they could invite their dates and much later their families.

Jack's death, at the hands of Mickey Cohen, in December 1959 changed the Whalen/Wunderlich clan in many ways. Fred, who had been only a social drinker during Prohibition and special events, started drinking heavily. Lilly was never as happy as in the past and became short-tempered and reclusive. The family picnics disappeared altogether. The only remaining tradition was Christmas. It grew smaller.

Jack "The Enforcer" Whalen

PRIOR TO HIS DEATH, the term "Enforcer" was not associated with Jack. He was tough and had all the confidence needed to believe he was invincible. He was the definition of a man's man. His father had tried to keep him away from the family business; sending him to a military school was Fred's solution. Bobbie was daddy's girl, and Jack was his mother's little man. Lilly was not in favor of sending him away but preferred the stability that Black-Foxe would provide.

He was a standout at the school in every way. His participation was an application of intense effort to achieve the ultimate result. He learned from his family that loyalty to one's kin was the most important aspect of a man's character. Fred had taken on the care and well-being of every member of his and Lilly's families, sharing the bounty of his activities, legal or otherwise. Jack was dedicated to the same pursuit, no matter the cost or risk to himself.

He could be strict as the toughest drill sergeant, yet when playing with the family's children, he was just a big kid. He loved his family, his animals, and those he called friend. He expected the same loyalty from all. He taught his children, nephews, nieces, and cousins about horses and dogs. On many occasions, he gifted dogs to family and friends. He trained them to protect those he gifted. There was, in most cases, a reason for the dogs.

Jack and Bobbie were very close. They played and partied together throughout Jack's shortened life. Kay was, for her part, jealous of the siblings' relationship. Jack and Kay had heated disagreements over extended family issues. How a dark Irishman and an equally dark Spaniard ever got together was an obvious contradiction in human nature. There were times that the heated words got the best of both. Jack would typically retreat to his sister's. In 1950, Bobbie had sent her children to spend the night with Fred and Lilly at their Hollywood apartment. Jack had come to Bobbie's new home in Culver City after a blowup at the ranch with Kay. They both decided that a night out on the Strip was in order. The colonel was away being a soldier, and Mom and Dad were willing babysitters.

After partying through the night, Jack took Bobbie home. It was after 2:00 a.m., and for some reason, Jack felt something was not right. As they walked to the front door, Jack unlocked it and asked Bobbie to wait while he checked the house. As he went from room to room, Bobbie stood in the doorway waiting. Jack went into the master and opened the closet. Standing there was a naked man. The intruder's first reaction was to grab his crotch. Jack's first reaction was to grab the would-be rapist's throat, pulling him from the closet and beating the living crap out of him.

He dragged the unconscious man by the legs into the living room. Bobbie heard the scuffle and gasped as she viewed the result.

"Sis, you're getting a dog!" Jack declared, dragging the limp man unto the porch, his head bouncing off the concrete steps onto the walk.

Jack opened the Cadillac's trunk and threw the man inside, slamming it shut. He waved to Bobbie, standing in mild shock, and drove away. He took the man to the Hollywood Fire Station. It was around 3:45 a.m. He pulled up to the apron in front of the truck doors and unloaded his battered cargo. Jack drove to the phone booth at the Hollywood Ranch Market and called the Hollywood Police Station, next door to the firehouse, and reported seeing a naked man in front of the fire station. He drove back to Cole Avenue and parked across the street and watched the fun.

Two days later, Jack brought over a Doberman pinscher he was training at the ranch. John and his sister, Terri, were thrilled. The dog was their first pet. Later, he brought over a Great Dane puppy, and the children named it Carla. Jack continued bringing dogs to his sister's children. After his death, his German shepherd, Pages, was given to John upon the family's return from Tennessee. Kay said the dog was morose, and John was the only person he responded to.

Jack was an extremely handsome man. Women would fawn over him, even in front of his wife. Kay was very territorial about Jack and would not hesitate letting women know it. She was a tall lady and big-boned. Smaller women, especially, did everything to get his attention. They had drinks brought to his table, and it didn't matter whom he was with. There were times he and Katherine would separate. One of those times he had gone to Vegas and met a showgirl there. He was like a kid bringing home a stray dog. Naturally, he brought her to the big house.

"Sis, can I keep her?" Jack asked, making the lady blush.

"You sure as hell can't take her home!" Bobbie declared, looking her over. "I'll put Ricky in with John tonight."

Her name was Kathy, and Jack lived there for two weeks until he got her an apartment below the Sunset Strip. She got a job as a hostess at one of the nightclubs on the avenue. Eventually, the girl wore off, but for years, she would stop by hoping to see Jack at the Franklin Avenue house.

The bookmaking continued in the basement, and Jack added another bar as a front. This was the Sultan Room on Hollywood Boulevard, not far from the big White House. Bobbie had the El Dorado, and both places did a big betting patronage. She continued picking up the children from school and made the rounds, picking up and dropping money. On one occasion, John opened his paper bag lunch and found $600 instead of peanut butter and jelly.

The house was a hive of activity. The children played outside, sliding on cardboard sheets down the terraced slope to the street. A casual passerby wouldn't suspect anything. It was just another family home like those around it. Fred was still playing doctor and would park the Cadillac and give John the keys.

"Palley, bring the boxes in my trunk to the dining room," he asked.

John would go out and bring in cardboard boxes filled with money. Fred would spread it out on the table and put it in piles. He'd give $5 to each of the kids, telling them to put it in their pockets. Fred counted out the bills and wrapped them with rubber bands. He would grab one pile and hand it to John. It was like rote.

"Palley, take this up to your grandmother," Fred requested, handing him thick stack of one hundred bills.

He'd give a stack to Bobbie and put the rest back in the boxes. When John came back, they would take the boxes down and lock them in the wine cellar.

"Grandpa! Shouldn't we put the money in a bank?" John asked.

"No, Palley! Banks ask too many questions," he said, roughing up John's hair.

Every three to five weeks, the routine never varied. John knew never to talk about family matters. He learned that the hard way one night while staying at the ranch with his cousins. Jack and Aunt Kay loaded their second car, a Ford, with the children and drove into the night. They were already in their pajamas, and John thought they were going to the drive-in movies. Jack parked on a street that wasn't very well lit. He turned the lights and motor off.

"We're going to wait here for a while," he said, looking over his shoulder to the back seat.

"Are we going to the drive-in?" Karen asked.

"No, honey. We're meeting someone here," Kay said.

The children sat quietly in the dark, waiting. It wasn't long before another car pulled to the curb and a man got out and walked to the Ford. Jack rolled down the window.

"O'Hara?" he asked.

"I'm O'Hara," Jack answered.

The man turned and walked to his vehicle's trunk and opened it. He reached in and pulled out a satchel. While he was doing this, John said the wrong thing.

"Uncle Jack, I thought our name was Whalen!" John whispered.

Jack turned and slapped John on the cheek. "Never mention the family name when we're out with people you don't know!" Jack said. "Do you know that man?"

"No, sir!" John replied, trying not to cry. "I don't know him!"

It was the only time his uncle ever struck him. The man walked back to the Ford, handing the small bag through the window. Jack set it down on the seat between him and Kay.

"It's all there!" the man said. "Should I wait while you check it?'

"No! If it's short, I'll be visiting you," Jack answered. "It won't be a social call!"

The man turned and left in his car. Jack waited a few minutes and then started the Ford. He backed out and turned on the lights, driving away.

"Are we going to the drive-in now, Daddy?" Karen asked.

"No, we're going home," replied her father. "And you're all going to bed."

A year later, Jack became concerned that the White House was not the best place for running the book. He had found twenty-six acres in Hidden Valley, and its remoteness appealed to him. The home was even larger than the Franklin house and put him in the county where only the sheriff's office had jurisdiction. The Los Angeles Police Department was now concerned with keeping organized crime, backed by the East Coast families, out of Los Angeles. He had become close with one of Los Angeles's detectives. The groups of undercover detectives were putting pressure on Mickey Cohen and his activities. Even though Jack felt a heads-up from his contact would preclude any action toward his operation, he wanted the family outside the city limits. He wanted more room for the horses and children.

He convinced Bobbie that together they could sell their current homes and pool their assets to purchase the larger property. The families got together on a Saturday and took a drive out to the prospective ranch. It was gated and fenced back in a small ravine. Buried in the trees, it had eight bedrooms and six baths and was three-story high. Each family would have its own floor, with room for their parents, Fred and Lilly. A barn and stables rounded out the estate, and the children went crazy exploring. They spent the entire day.

The house had been empty for a year and was ready to move into. Everything was set to proceed when Kay had one of her jealous tantrums, citing the closeness of Jack and Bobbie. She felt she would become irrelevant. The children begged their parents to make it work. They had been reared together, and the five were sadly disappointed when the arrangement went south. This move would have put everyone closer to Uncle Gus's ranch in Reseda and their cousin Dirk.

In time, the incident was put behind them, and life continued between the Woodman Ranch and the Franklin house. Jack was becoming more entangled with the police and the antics of the Cohen outfit. Fred warned his son that getting too close to the police in their efforts to bust Cohen that lines would become blurred. Fred's good friend, Lt. Harry Fremont, would come by the house and keep him informed if necessary. Harry was the only policeman that attended the evening portion of the Christmas party.

By 1958/59, Jack was slowly removing himself from bookmaking and starting to become more involved in the movie industry. The family connections through the years with Hollywood personalities offered an inside tract to be cast in certain roles. He had provided stunt horses for the westerns in the early part of the decade, and some of his wranglers became stuntmen and bit players. In 1958, he performed a small role in *The Restless Gun*. This had gotten the attention of the producers of the upcoming series, *Bonanza*. His thirteen-year-old daughter, Karen, would help him with his lines, and he was asked to audition for a role in *Bonanza*. Fred would later appear in the series, hands only, making pool shots with Dan Blocker.

Portfolio Shot The Restless Gun

Jack at the ranch

New Years 1958, the usual party was held for the family and friends at Jack's new residence in Encino. That next morning, Jack came into his daughter's bedroom and woke up John who had spent the night.

"Hey, buddy, how would you like to go to the Rose Bowl game?" Jack asked his nephew.

"Sure, Uncle Jack! That would be great!" John whispered, not wanting to wake his cousin, who could sleep till noon if allowed.

"Get your clothes on. We have to stop along Ventura and pick up the tickets."

"Is it just we guys?" John asked.

"No. I'm getting three tickets. Dad is coming too."

John got dressed and met Jack in the kitchen. They walked out the back door, and John petted Pages, the huge German shepherd. Jack opened the gate at the side of the house, and they got into

Jack's Cadillac. They drove south on Ventura into Sherman Oaks and parked in front of a bar. It was nine o'clock, and there was little street traffic.

"You wait in the car. I won't be long," Jack said.

Jack got out and walked into the building. John had rolled down the passenger window and was looking out watching where his uncle had gone. A minute later, another car parked on the corner a way behind the Cadillac.

Two men got out and walked to the front door and stood on either side but didn't go in. John thought that strange and wondered if he should leave the car and go inside with his uncle. He didn't like the looks of these two guys.

Just as he was about to open the car door, Jack came out. One man grabbed his shoulder as he exited. The other man, that was blocked by the door opening, started to come from behind as Jack faced the first one. Jack blocked the man's arm on his shoulder and came around with a right to the left side of the man's head. The guy's knees buckled as Jack turned, blocking a punch from the man behind him. Jack slid his left hand behind the man's head and brought it down as he lifted his knee into the man's face. Lifting the man back up by his hair, Jack punched him in the face.

John heard something pop as the punch landed, and blood flew as the man's head snapped backward. He crumpled to the sidewalk. Jack dragged him to the curb and pushed his head into it. Jack walked to the driver's seat and got in.

"Let's go get dad!" Jack said, turning to John.

He smiled, started the car, and they pulled away from the curb. They picked up Fred at the house and drove to Pasadena. Oregon was playing Ohio State that day. John thought the Webfoots (Ducks) were small compared to the Buckeyes. The Ducks lost by three points in the last forty-seven seconds. Although John watched USC as a child, he decided to go to Oregon for architecture.

There have been many accounts of Jack's death that night in December 1959. The most recent was the book by Paul Lieberman, *The Gangster Squad*. Fred was back east, and Lilly was at the house in

Hollywood. Jack would spend a great deal of his time there when his father was gone. That was the case on December 2, 1959.

Jack and his associate, Rocky, were there until evening when a call came to Lilly. It was Kay asking for Jack. She had gotten a call from Joey Bishop informing her that Mickey Cohen wanted to settle the debt that evening at Rondelli's Italian Restaurant in Sherman Oaks. Jack was going to collect a gambling debt that was owed his former partner, Al Levitt.

"Mom, I'll be back later and spend the night," Jack told her as he hung up the phone.

"You be careful, Jack!" Lilly said as Jack kissed her cheek.

"That fat-ass Jew owes Al nine hundred dollars, and I'm going to get it!"

The newspapers, in their usual fashion, sensationalized the story. In the last fifteen years, Los Angeles had some high-profile gangland style shootings, none of which involved Jack. It was the newspapers that coined the name "Enforcer." It sold papers and was splattered all over the local television stations. Even the murder trial was sensationalized for public consumption.

John came home on Thursday afternoon to find his mother, Bobbie, crying while she ironed some clothes. She gathered her three children to give them the news. Their father, Eric, was taking Bobbie to Nashville to fly back to California. The funeral procession was said to have over five hundred cars following the white hearse. Jack was interned at Forest Lawn in Burbank on the grounds where he had played polo as a boy.

To his family, he was the big kid that entertained his children, their cousins, and neighbors, taking them all to Disneyland the week it opened. He was loved by many and feared by some. His death ended a family era and, in many ways, helped the Los Angeles police put away Mickey Cohen.

The Later Years

FRED'S GRANDSON, JOHN, TURNED fourteen in March 1961. His baby brother, Jack Manfred von Hurst, was born earlier that month. He was named after his late uncle. Since his son's murder, Fred had begun drinking. John had grown three inches in the fall of 1960. He was six feet two, soon to be six feet five and 218 pounds by his senior year at Loyola. Fred had been taking John with him since the boy was four. He would sit the child down at bars and poolrooms throughout Los Angeles. Fred gave the boy money for the bartenders to keep the Shirley Temples coming while he hustled. He taught John to drive, and from his fourteenth birthday on, John drove Fred everywhere.

Fred Whalen 1970

"Grandpa! I'm only fourteen! What if we get pulled over?"

"You're so big they won't pull us over unless you make a mistake!"

John drove Fred every weekend. They went to the horse races, to bars, and poolrooms until John married. If John was home from college, he drove his grandfather. From the time he turned eight, Fred gave him money to make side bets, just as he'd done with John's uncles. There were other nuances to the hustle. Like his uncle Jack, John and his siblings had been in the movies. Mickey Rooney had signed their early cards, and they appeared in TV series, feature films, and even commercials. John had worked three days on *The Defiant Ones* at Columbia's soundstage where they shot *Gunsmoke*.

So becoming a featured player in grandfather's hustle was no problem.

Fred had been the Pacific Coast Champion for fifteen years. Many serious pool players knew him, but in the average bar or neighborhood poolroom, he was just and older gent waiting to be fleeced. This was especially true in Black and Latino portions of Los Angeles.

When John was younger, Fred would seat him at the bar and order an Old Taylor for himself and a Shirley Temple for John. He'd give John four $5 bills and put a $20 on the bar.

"This is for our drinks," Fred told the bartender. "Keep my son's glass filled while I play some pool. Palley! If anyone asks who I am, tell him I'm your grandpa. Nothing else!" Fred told him. "If they ask if I'm any good, you know what to say?"

"Yes, I do. I'll bet he can beat anybody in here!"

John would take $5 out of his shirt pocket and put it on the bar. If the person matched it, John would say, "Bartender, would you hold this bet?"

Most times, the person would go to Fred and ask, "Do you let your son bet?"

"That's up to him," Fred would answer. "It's his allowance!"

Bartenders and owners became familiar with Fred and his grandson so much so they would call the house if they thought a customer was worth clipping. In some cases, the bar wanted to get rid of a player that was cleaning out their patrons.

By the time John was sixteen, the hustle added a new wrinkle. When they'd hit a bar, Fred would take a mouthful of whiskey and rinse his mouth, spitting it out in the street. Going in, they would go directly to the bar and order. John was drinking cokes while Fred ordered a 7 and 7, tall. The two would sit there and watch the game being played on the 4×8 table.

"Come on, Grandpa!" John would say. "We got to get home! Grandma is going to be pissed!"

"No, no, Palley! Just one more!" Fred would slur.

"You said that three places ago!" John would exclaim in a loud voice so everyone would notice.

"Bartender, give my boy anything he wants!" Fred called out, putting a ten on the bar as he walked over and put a quarter on the pool table for the next game.

Usually, the payer, taking everyone's money, was hitting his victims up for $20 per game of eight ball. As soon as the game was over, Fred would grab a cue stick, fumbling it around in his hands in a sloppy manner. He'd chalk the cue and drop the chalk on the floor or table and misstep while trying to retrieve it. John would leave the bar as if to grab him.

"That's enough, Grandpa!" John would caution. "You can't play this way!"

"I'm fine, Palley!" Fred slurred. "I can beat this gentleman!"

"Okay, one game and we go home!" John relented.

It all looked like luck. Fred would play the way he had perfected since running with Mr. Brown back in St. Louis. It was a thing to behold. Balls blocking pockets, limiting the mark's shots. Cue balls doing the same thing. The appearance of luck and easy shots even a drunk could make. On one occasion, Fred cleaned a man out for two thousand. The guy kept double or nothing Fred until he was broke.

"I'm flat out of cash!"

"Well, let me give you ten dollars at least so you can get home!" Fred offered. "My grandson wants to leave anyway, and my wife's going to have my hide!"

"No, I'm parked outside, and I've got plenty of cash at my hotel!" the man said. "You just wait here and have another drink. I won't be fifteen minutes!"

"Okay, if you insist!" Fred returned, swaying into the table. "I've never been so lucky!" *BURP!*

The man ran out the door. Fred walked over to John and said, "Go see where he goes!"

John walked outside and looked up the street. The man got in a car and drove off. John came back to the bar.

"He drove off, Grandpa!"

"And so are we, Palley!" Fred returned as he laid a $20 on the bar. "Let's get home! The guy's not going for more money! He's going to get a gun!"

Other times, the duo would park ways from the bar and walk a half block. Fred didn't want to leave the El Dorado in a parking lot or directly in front of the place. It would stand out among those the bar's clientele came in. These places were in neighborhoods' most sane people would avoid at dark.

They were the places where young egos could be encouraged to clean out an old drunken man. The show was the same, but the finale was always different depending on the temperament of the victims.

After an hour or two, Fred and John would have a feel for the atmosphere, hostile or mild. Fred gauged the mark while John watched the crowd. Anyone paying too much attention was always suspect. This included friends of the loser. If the crowd and player looked suspicious, Fred would lose the last two games and say, "I better stop before I fall down or make a fool of myself!"

He would miscue or completely miss the object ball. Sometimes, for excitement, he'd jump the ball off the table, apologizing profusely. John would approach the table and call the game.

"I'm taking you home!" John demand. "You've had way too much to drink, and Grandma is going to be mad as hell!"

There were times, late at night, when Fred would be out alone, playing and seriously drinking. The bartenders who knew him had the house phone numbers. John would give them a card with the information. Once in a while, these bars were known places where

Fred and his son, Jack, had frequented. After Jack's murder, some people were downright insulting and cruel to Fred over the loss of his son. These were men who were basically lowlifes who wouldn't have dared to insult Fred while Jack was alive.

On many occasions, a call would come asking for John. Lilly would answer and go get her grandson, sometimes in bed. John would find out which bar he was at. To the credit of these bartenders, they warned the perpetrators that they shouldn't bother Fred.

"Who cares," they'd say. "Jack's dead. The old man is a drunk!"

"You're right! But his grandson will be here in a few minutes, and he's bigger than Jack was!"

"Yea! Right!" one would usually reply.

John, at sixteen, was around 215 pounds and five inches taller than Jack. He had a long fuse, but if someone was bothering a smaller friend or family, it blew. John would have to ask his father to come along if in town. Sometimes, his mother, Bobbie, would drive him to the bar so John could drive the Cadillac home. When John would walk in, he'd more than likely find one guy harassing his grandfather, sometimes two.

Upon seeing John, the bartender would come up to Fred and his antagonist(s) and mentioned that his ride had arrived. Most turned and walked away, saying nice things to Fred as they departed his side; others got very still and lifted their drink(s). Fred would back off the bar and giggle as he turned to leave with John. If the person or persons had been especially nasty, Fred would punch one. Then the scene turned ugly. The bartender would come from behind the bar as John began throwing people around. John rarely smacked anyone, but tossing them seemed more fun than hurting his hands.

Fred had connections at the two Los Angeles racetracks. Every so often, he'd get a call from the track people. They'd let him know there was going to be a "boat race." These were sure things arranged by the jockeys or results from morning workouts that made it almost impossible for any other horse in the field to win. These informers were not allowed to bet, so they touted inside information on various races during any one day. On these days, Fred would have John go to the track with him.

Just before the first race of the day, the informant would meet Fred at a predetermined spot and give him a list of the horses that were a sure bet to win. Depending on which race it was, you could wheel the predicted winner with every horse in the Daily Double. If the sure thing were in the first, you'd wheel it with the entire field in the second or vice versa. You checked the odds to see how big the potential payout would be and bought tickets that kept the proceeds from each winning ticket under $600, not making it too spectacular a win. This worked in parlaying also. In the thirty-two trips John made with Fred, all but one race didn't work out. The touted horses lead the whole way until the final stretch; the jockey pulled him up when the animal blew a nosebleed.

These were big moneymaking events. John would get friends to go and meet him there, and they would copycat all the bets. The first few times, his friends would hold back, testing the waters. Once the first two tips ran in the money, the gang was all in. This went on for years. Not an everyday thing, only when the call came in. A jockey might be riding a claimer that the owner/trainer wants to move out. The other jocks would give him the win by keeping the race close. Usually, the odds on the horse were exceptional, and Fred and company would bet it. The crew would go to dinner afterward and spread the wealth around. The Tam O'Shanter in Atwater was the favorite post-track destination.

When John was away in college, Fred had his younger brother, Ricky, chauffer him around. The entire family knew the drill. Fred knew the kids were the most believable when playing the pool hustle. As John got older, his grandfather would call him about the racetrack betting. Sometimes, John would fly in from wherever he was or just have his mother fund his bets.

Fred taught John the ins and outs of the crap table. The 5×10 Brunswick in the basement would act as a table. The family had a full-size crap felt they'd roll out and rails that narrowed the field. The family would make excursions to Las Vegas about four times a year, mostly to see performers, like Elvis. They would always attend the late shows. It was after 1:00 a.m. that the high rollers usually came out. These were serious players. Fred always said that a table got hot when the energy flowed around the dice.

It was true. John got so hot with the dice at the Hilton after an Elvis show that he made thirteen passes and held the dice for twenty minutes, rolling everything but a seven. Rickey got the cubes and ran for over ten minutes. It got so crazy that people were lined up three deep around the table. The pit bosses were bringing $10,000 trays in. As family members won, they sent relatives to the cashier to convert chips. Gambling was part of family life, in the genes, so to speak.

Lillian Emma Whalen passed at age eighty-six at home in the White House from complications due to surgery. She had seven great-grandchildren, not near as many as most of her Wunderlich siblings. She never got over Jack's murder and the great split in the family it caused. Jack's children dropped away, and only Karen showed up for her grandparents' seventieth anniversary. She was buried near her son at Forest Lawn. The house was sold in 1986, and Bobbie and Eric moved to Sisters, Oregon, to be near John. Terri and her husband kept a house at Black Butte, and in 1992, Jack von Hurst moved to Bend, Oregon.

Fred continued doing what he did best, hustling. He continued doing exhibitions at the Elks and various other venues. His hands appeared in many pool movies, including *The Hustler*. He was asked to get Paul Newman up to speed with some basic lessons, but Paul declined while they were flying to New York. *The Cat from Outer Space* was the only movie Fred appeared in as a character. He sponsored four World Championships in Los Angeles. Along the way, a former acquaintance, a Denver Madam, snagged him, and they spent almost six years keeping each other company.

Bobbie moved her father to Oregon with the rest of the family, but he'd take off back to Los Angeles and Marianne. Between 1986 and 1991, he spent most of his time with John on his ranch outside of Sisters. They'd go to local taverns and play pool. He would consistently win eight- and nine-ball tournaments for as long as the establishments would allow. They eventually banned him as no one would enter if he was playing. At times, someone would recognize him and interrupt a tournament and ask him to do a mini exhibition. At ninety-three years old, he was still as accurate as he ever was. In his mind, he was still, Young Tennessee Brown, boy pocket billiard wonder.

Afterword

FRED LLOYD WHALEN WAS a child prodigy in pool history. As an adult, he exhibited unflagging confidence and gumption. He never lacked the courage to try something new even if it was illegal. His dedication to his family and friends were traits admired by all who knew him. His passions in life were Lillian, billiards, and automobiles. At ninety-three, he was still a healthy, alert individual. When confronted with the loss of Lilly, coupled with being banned from pool games, and finally not being able to pass Oregon's driver's test, he called the game. His said good night to his daughter, Bobbie, and died in his sleep from a broken heart. His life was lived on his terms.

August John Wunderlich passed away in Nevada in 1985. His son, Dirk, kept his father's ashes, and they were spread with Fred's over the Catalina Channel where they spent their youth as rumrunners. Only two members of the family remain in California, both, by choice, estranged from their family.

Jack Manfred von Hurst and his wife, Teresa, lived on a ranch in Central Oregon. They have five children. Jack left the Los Angeles Sheriff's Department and the DEA in 1992 and started a very successful contract installation company.

Terri Whalen Simon, John's sister, lived in San Francisco and was president of the Art Commission for a number of years. She continued riding her horses, bred, and exhibited Arab horses in California and Arizona. She passed in 2007 at fifty-eight.

A. John Wunderlich, Dirk, was a well-known artist with Walt Disney and Thomas Kinkade. He toured the country at various art exhibitions, and his work was highly prized by collectors. He spent six weeks a year in Florida at Disney World and EPCOT displaying his art to his many fans and collectors. His wife, Patricia, was with the Miss America Pageant during her career and was now retired, helping Dirk.

Mary Florence Wunderlich Navarre, Lilly's younger sister, was a character in her own right. She was a private nurse who cared for a number of clients. She was Nell Panky's caregiver for many years. Mickey Rooney's mother was an especially fun person who was warm and entertaining. A talented lady, Nell kept Flossie in stitches. The Wunderlich women were adventurous and always ready to step into the breech. Her daughter, June, lived with Fred and Lilly, attending Fairfax High School with her cousin, Bobbie. She was one of the family members that kept the gatherings at the White House memorable.

About the Author

JOHN FREDERICK VON HURST is a cattle and hay rancher in Central Oregon. He graduated from the school of architecture at the University of Oregon. He was born into a family whose roots hailed from New Orleans, north along the Mississippi River to St. Louis. His people were plantation owners and dirt farmers. In the early part of the twentieth century, they migrated to Southern California. The story, which he presents, details that journey and the events that led up to and followed.

He is the grandson of Frederick Lloyd Whalen and the nephew of Jack Frederick Whalen, the former being one of the greatest pool hustlers and salesman of the previous century who played and defeated many of the well-known champions of that era. John's uncle Jack was an Army Air Corp bomber pilot during WWII who attended Black-Foxe Military Academy in Los Angeles. He later became a notorious bookmaker and part-time actor while training horses for motion picture stunts.

As a child, John participated in the many activities and lives of his infamous family. This biographical novel is that story. John aided his grandfather in the hustle from the age of five until 1991. Fred Whalen never lost his extraordinary abilities in billiards or the con. Between the ages of seven and ten, he dropped and picked up money after school for his uncle Jack. It was the 1950s and it was the middle of transition in Southern California, a time that will never be seen again.

Printed in the USA
CPSIA information can be obtained
at www.ICGtesting.com
LVHW012354180724
785740LV00002B/165